THE WRITINGS OF
MARCEL DUCHAMP

THE WRITINGS OF
MARCEL DUCHAMP

Edited by Michel Sanouillet
and Elmer Peterson

A DA CAPO PAPERBACK

Library of Congress Cataloging in Publication Data

Duchamp, Marcel, 1887-1968.
[Marchand du sel. English]
The writings of Marcel Duchamp / edited by Michel Sanouillet and Elmer Peterson.
p. cm. — (A Da Capo paperback)
Reprint. Originally published: Salt seller. New York: Oxford University Press, 1973.
Bibliography: p.
ISBN 0-306-80341-0
1. Duchamp, Marcel, 1887-1968 — Philosophy. 2. Art — Philosophy. I. Sanouillet, Michel. II. Peterson, Elmer, 1930- . III. Title.
[N6853.D8A3 1989]
759.4 — dc19 88-32416
CIP

Permission to use copyright materials is hereby gratefully acknowledged:

To George Heard Hamilton for his translation of *The Green Box* and to Richard Hamilton for his chart of *The Large Glass*, from *The Bride Stripped Bare by Her Bachelors, Even* (London: Percy Lund, Humphries & Co., n.d.), copyright (c) Marcel Duchamp, George Heard Hamilton, Richard Hamilton.

To the Associates in Fine Arts, Yale University, for the Duchamp texts from *The Catalogue of the Société Anonyme*, copyright (c) 1950 by the Associates in Fine Arts at Yale University. To Arne H. Ekstrom for *A l'Infinitif (The White Box)*, copyright (c) 1966 by Cordier & Ekstrom, Inc.

To *ARTnews* for "The Creative Act."

To The Art Institute of Chicago for "The Mary Reynolds Collection," copyright (c) 1956 by The Art Institute of Chicago.

To the Museum of Modern Art, New York, for "A Tribute to the Artist," from *Charles Demuth by* Andrew Carnduff Ritchie, copyright 1950 by The Museum of Modern Art, New York; and for "The Great Trouble with Art in This Country," first published in "Eleven Europeans in America," *The Museum of Modern Art Bulletin*, copyright 1946 by The Museum of Modern Art, New York.

This Da Capo Press paperback edition of *The Writings of Marcel Duchamp* is an unabridged republication of the edition entitled *Salt Seller: The Writings of Marcel Duchamp* published in New York in 1973. It is reprinted by arrangement with Oxford University Press.

Published by Da Capo Press, Inc.
A Subsidiary of Plenum Publishing Corporation
233 Spring Street, New York, N.Y. 10013

Manufactured in the United States of America

Preface

DUCHAMP'S WRITINGS

It may come as a surprise to some that there is such a thing as "The Writings of Marcel Duchamp." The tendency is to think of him either as a major force in modern art or as a picturesque character who abandoned art for a lifelong game of chess. His writings constitute a relatively unknown side of his creative work.

When *The Bride Stripped Bare by Her Bachelors, Even (The Green Box)* was published in 1934, André Breton immediately recognized its importance, calling it a major intellectual event. However it was not until 1958, in Michel Sanouillet's *Marchand du Sel* (Paris: Le Terrain Vague), that an attempt was made to collect and publish all of Duchamp's written work.

It has been fifteen years since the publication of *MDS;* Duchamp lived and continued writing for ten of those years, and during that time some of his earlier writing was published, including an important collection of notes, *A l'Infinitif (The White Box;* New York: Cordier and Ekstrom, 1966). The editors' intent in *Salt Seller,* as we have chosen to translate the Marcel Duchamp/ Marchand du Sel joke, is to make the original *MDS* material available in English (a revised and updated French *MDS* will be published this year in Paris by Eric Losfeld), as well as to include the rest of Duchamp's signed and published work.

THE BRIDE'S VEIL

Notes relating to his major work, *The Bride Stripped Bare by Her Bachelors, Even (The Large Glass),* make up a significant part of Duchamp's writings. From the summer of 1912 until 1923, the year he left his *Large Glass* "definitively uncompleted," Duchamp worked slowly and deliberately on these notes, which lift the veil of his elusive bride. Calvin Tomkins has written:

> *The Large Glass* stands in relation to painting as *Finnegans Wake* does to literature, isolated and inimitable; it has been called everything from a masterpiece to a tremendous hoax, and to this day there are no standards by which it can be judged. Duchamp invented a new physics to explain its "laws," a new mathematics to fix the units of measurement of the new physics, and a condensed, poetic language to formulate its ideas, which he jotted down on scraps of paper as they occurred to him and stored away in a green cardboard box for future reference.[1]

1. *The Bride and the Bachelors: Five Masters of the Avant-Garde* (New York: The Viking Press, 1965), p. 28.

Duchamp actually "published" his first collection of sixteen notes and a single drawing in 1914; and the three copies of that "edition," now commonly called *The 1914 Box,* were mounted on matboards and put in a standard box for Kodak photographic plates.

In 1934 he published a second box of notes, *The Bride Stripped Bare by Her Bachelors, Even* (Paris: Editions Rrose Sélavy). The color of its binding was green and it is usually referred to as *The Green Box* to avoid confusion with the long title of *The Large Glass.* The preparation of this box was described by its author in an interview with Michel Sanouillet:

> Twelve years after finishing, or rather putting aside my *Glass,* I came across my working notes, scribbled at random on some hundred scraps of paper. I wanted to reproduce them as exactly as possible. So I had all of these thoughts lithographed in the same ink which had been used for the originals. In order to find paper that was exactly the same, I had to scour the most unlikely nooks and crannies of Paris Then we had to cut out three hundred copies of each lithograph with the help of zinc patterns that I had made to fit exactly the outlines of the original papers. . . . Some ideas require a graphic language if they are not to be violated: such is my *Glass* But the notes may be useful, like the captions that accompany the photographs in a Galéries Lafayette catalog. This is the *raison d'être* of my Box.[2]

In February 1948 the painter Matta, a friend of Duchamp, published a facsimile of a previously unpublished note, *"Cast Shadows,"* in his magazine *Instead.* Ten years later, Pierre André Benoit published a Duchamp note entitled "Possible" (PAB: Alés, France). Finally, seventy-nine previously unpublished notes were published in New York in 1966 by Cordier and Ekstrom under the title *A l'Infinitif.* That title was chosen because many of the notes are indeed in the infinitive. This is also referred to as *The White Box,* again because of the color of the cover. The present volume includes English translations of all of Duchamp's published working notes for *The Large Glass.*

RROSE SELAVY & CO.

Three characteristics stand out in *Rrose Sélavy,* Duchamp's short book of puns and word games (Paris: GLM, 1939): surprise, frequent complexity, and gaminess. The surprise comes from a use of words which has nothing to do with ordinary logic. A letter disappears or is displaced and everything goes haywire, suggesting one or several new meanings. The wordplay is often complex and shows Duchamp's kinship with the playwright Raymond Roussel who invented such intricate double entendres as: "Les vers (The lines of poetry) de la doublure (of the under-study) dans la pièce (in the play) du Forban Talon

2. "Dans l'atelier de Marcel Duchamp," *Les Nouvelles Littéraires* (Paris), No. 1424, December 16, 1954, p. 5.

Rouge" (of Red-Heel the Pirate), which could also be read as "Les vers (The worms) de la doublure (of the lining) dans la pièce (in the patch) du fort pantalon rouge" (of the heavy red trousers).

Duchamp once called some of his sayings "morceaux moisis" or "wrotten writtens," and there is a certain amount of gaminess in many of his short sayings. The surrealists had proclaimed in the twenties that words were no longer playing around but had started making love. This description seems to fit the sayings of *Rrose Sélavy* and other collected puns and wordgames, where we find some of the most joyous and ingenious couplings and uncouplings in modern literature. It must be admitted, however, that along with the "howlers" there are some "groaners," for Duchamp was not above popular–and sometimes lame–schoolboy humor.

Finally for those who wish the comfort of a grammatical rule in deciphering Rrose Sélavy and Co. (the Co. referring to related "wrotten writtens" not published in *Rrose Sélavy),* their author offers the following:

> If you want a grammatical rule: the verb agrees with the subject in consonance: For example the negro-ego, the negress-egress or regress.[3] (Trans E.P.)

MARCEL DUCHAMP, CRITICAVIT

In 1959 Duchamp signed a short autograph note for a Mina Loy exhibition "Marcel Duchamp, Admiravit." Duchamp was intimately involved in the artistic life of two continents for more than a half century and during this time he authored important texts on art and other artists, ranging from an address on "The Creative Act" given at the annual convention of the American Federation of Arts to short punning notes which appeared in exhibition catalogs. He also prepared, from 1943 to 1949, thirty-two critical notes on modern artists for the catalog of the Société Anonyme, a collection of more than six hundred works of art now in the possession of Yale University, which was created by Katherine S. Dreier and by Duchamp who for a long period of time was its secretary and administrator. The notes written by Duchamp for this important catalog are included in *Marcel Duchamp, Criticavit.*

TEXTICLES

BALLS, a cabled refusal to participate in a data manifestation, is one of Duchamp's shortest texts. Other short statements which fit none of the preceding catagories make up this last chapter.

3. *Le Pilhaou-Thibaou,* 6 (Paris, 1921). Reprinted in *View,* March 1945, p. 36, and in a reedition of *391* (Paris: Le Terrain Vague, 1960), p. 102. The saying was followed by the following play on editor Francis Picabia's name: "mâcheur Fran[cfort sau] cisse Pisqu[e quand elles] habilla." This was signed Marcel Duchamp, (RROSE SELAVY).

A DISCLAIMER

The Arts Council of Great Britain held a major exhibition in the summer of 1966 and called it "The Almost Complete Works of Marcel Duchamp." A similar title would seem appropriate for his written work, since items keep surfacing to suggest that there is still more to come. It seems prudent to state that, while this volume hopes to include all of Duchamp's writing which he published, caused to be published, or whose publication he approved, as well as the material from the original *Marchand du Sel* which was approved and proofread by the author, it *does not* include unpublished texts, i.e. notes relating to *The Large Glass* which were discarded by Duchamp and are now held by various friends and collectors; all the interviews, published or unpublished, that Duchamp gave; collective writings (manifestoes, collective letters, etc.) signed or endorsed by Duchamp, who hardly ever took part in their actual writing; all the statements attributed to Duchamp and quoted in various books and periodicals; correspondence which is spread among innumerable recipients—some of whom are categorically opposed to the publication of documents which concern their private lives; the assembly writings for *Given: 1. The Waterfall / 2. The Illuminating Gas,* Duchamp's last great work, which will not be available for publication for several years; and finally, the writings on chess, which are too technical for most readers.

THE TRANSLATIONS AND ARRANGEMENT

The sixteen notes of *The 1914 Box,* the notes from *The Green Box,* "Possible," "Cast Shadows," and many of the notes from *The White Box* have been translated into English by Arturo Schwarz in his facsimile edition *Notes and Projects for the Large Glass* (New York: Harry N. Abrams, 1969). The standard and authorized translation of *The Green Box* is by George Heard Hamilton in *The Bride Stripped Bare by Her Bachelors, Even* (London: Percy Lund, Humphries & Co., 1960). The authorized translation of *The White Box* is by Cleve Gray in *A l'Infinitif* (New York: Cordier and Ekstrom, 1966).

The present book includes Arturo Schwarz's translation of "Possible" and "Cast Shadows;" George Heard Hamilton's translation of *The Green Box;* Cleve Gray's translation of *The White Box;* and some translations in the Rrose Sélavy chapter by David Ball, Ron Padgett, Roger Shattuck, and Trevor Winkfield. All other translations are by Elmer Peterson.

It should be noted that Duchamp "authorized" two orderings of the notes from *The Green Box:* one for George Heard Hamilton's translation in Richard Hamilton's brilliant typographical rendering (*The Bride Stripped Bare by Her Bachelors, Even* referred to above); and the other for *Marchand du Sel,* which we use here.

ACKNOWLEDGMENTS

The editors are deeply grateful to the translators and publishers just mentioned who have generously allowed their excellent work to be used in this book.

We would also like to thank Mr. James Johnson Sweeney, whose two perceptive interviews with Duchamp form such an important part of this book; the Museum of Modern Art, which published the first; and the National Broadcasting Company, which broadcast the second.

We would like to thank the following for permission to include text material in their possession: The Associates in Fine Arts at Yale University *(The Catalogue of the Société Anonyme); ARTnews* ("The Creative Act"); The Art Institute of Chicago ("Mary Reynolds"); Simon Watson-Taylor ("Apropos of 'Readymades' "); The Museum of Modern Art, New York ("A Tribute to the Artist," "Si la scie . . .," and "A Propos of 'Readymades' "); Matta ("Cast Shadows"); Pierre André Benoit ("Possible"); Enrico Donati; Sidney Janis; and Arturo Schwarz.

We would like to thank Richard Hamilton for permission to use his excellent typographical chart of *The Large Glass.*

We would like to thank the Philadelphia Museum of Art for permission to reproduce the following in their possession: *Virgin* No. 1 (A. E. Gallatin Collection); *The Bride Stripped Bare by Her Bachelors, Even* (Katherine S. Dreier Bequest); *To Have the Apprentice in the Sun, Nude Descending a Staircase* No. 2, *Chocolate Grinder* No. 2, *Why not Sneeze Rose Sélavy?, Comb, With Hidden Noise, Apolinère Enameled, Bride* 1912, *Glider Containing a Water Mill in Neighboring Metals, Oculist Witnesses* (all from the Louise and Walter Arensberg Collection).

We wish to thank the Museum of Modern Art, New York, for permission to reproduce the following in their possession: *3 Standard Stoppages* (Katherine S. Dreier Bequest); *Fresh Widow* (Katherine S. Dreier Bequest); *The Passage from the Virgin to the Bride; Rotary Demisphere (Precision Optics)* (Gift of Mrs. William Sisler and Purchase); *Monte Carlo Bond* (Gift of the artist); *The Box in a Valise* (James Thrall Soby Fund); and *Fountain.*

We would also like to thank the following for their permission to reproduce works in their collection: the Bibliothèque Nationale, Paris ("Chamber Music" and "Walking Doll"), and Pierre André Benoit (photograph of Duchamp by Man Ray).

The following very kindly furnished us with photographs: the Philadelphia Museum of Art (of "Walking Doll," "Chamber Music," and all works in their collection except *The Box in a Valise);* the Museum of Modern Art, New York (of all works in their collection); Arturo Schwarz (the Bacci Attilo photograph of *Beautiful Breath, Veil Water);* Nathan Rabin *(The Box in a Valise);* and Mrs. Duchamp (the photograph of Duchamp on the jacket).

Our thanks go also to Yves Poupard-Lieussou and Craig Adcock who gave us invaluable advice.

We would also like to express our deep gratitude to Anne d'Harnoncourt of the Philadelphia Museum of Art and to Kynaston McShine of the Museum of Modern Art, New York, who gave most generously of their time and counsel.

And finally no one has been kinder than Mrs. Alexina Duchamp, to whom we express our profound gratitude.

To all of you,
Nos salutations très Mistinguett,

Michel Sanouillet
Elmer Peterson

September 1973

Contents

THE WRITINGS OF
MARCEL DUCHAMP

Rrose Sélavy est le marchand du sel.

ROBERT DESNOS

Introduction

It is obvious that the bulk or popularity of an artist's work is a poor measure of its actual importance. Best sellers and "with-it" paintings give rise to popular and necessarily superficial ideas about what is artistically significant, and once the initial publicity surrounding such popular successes has subsided, all too often we are left with a sense of emptiness. We feel somehow that both less than this and much more is needed to affect our personal behavior or our aesthetic judgment—in short, to put us in tune with ourselves and with our times. An idea, a word, a clashing of colors can be powerful enough to work changes in us, but a kind of foreknowledge is needed in the artist to start the process, and several generations are required to finish it.

The *important* artist is perhaps like an alchemist whose work, incommunicable to the general public, can nevertheless bring about that process of transmutation in certain especially receptive painters, poets, and musicians. These act as middlemen, popularizing in their own works one or two borrowed seminal ideals, and thereby help to form the artistic taste of a period. For the average viewer or reader, sensitive only to the passing value of the daily event, the painter in vogue or the popular novelist appears important because his work seems to express the sensibility of the time. The fact is that this is simply the mark of a successful man: his work, at best an imitation, at worst a watering down and explanation, is always a product destined for general consumption, which reaches an immense public. But if one is willing to consider the actual source of the product's success, one will recognize fairly readily the extreme importance of those artists whose work has in fact brought about the really significant change.

Duchamp is a remarkable illustration of this neglected lesson of history. In his subterranean meanderings and mysterious arcana he has known how to undermine the very foundations of our art, literature, and dogmas so that even our daily existence shows the effects of his secret assaults. The Duchampian termites have been on the move since the first Ready-made, even if few of our contemporaries have noticed the implacable progression of their ever-growing army. Crumblings and gaping cracks in the facades of our academies have had to show up before the evidence could no longer be denied by even the most nearsighted. The world we are now entering bears an odd resemblance to the one Marcel Duchamp has been shaping for almost a half century.

In 1923 Duchamp put the finishing touches on his *Large Glass*—or rather the next-to-last touches, for he was never to finish it—and then proceeded to hold his tongue. This act was not so much malice aforethought as a gradual discovery of the value of silence. His silence, like Rimbaud's exile in Harrar, has weighed heavily on contemporary letters. Its echoes are heard very clearly from far off; contemporary authors and commercially successful painters are made so ill at ease that they feel constrained to justify themselves publicly for having dared to write or paint. On the very pages that they darken they are confronted with the question asked by the surrealists in 1919: "Why do you write?"—a question which bordered on a formal summons. In point of fact, Duchamp's existence will have been nothing but a long silence broken by such short and revealing statements as are reproduced here, when the inner pressures became too much of a burden or when some friend, by a kind of clever blackmail, brought him temporarily out of his reserve.

Except for suicide, silence is the most extreme form of revolt. In Duchamp's case, the revolt has consisted of a patient and laborious attempt to forge a world for himself which would conform to his personal concepts, a world sufficiently remade so that it would owe nothing or very little to human reality—as in *The Large Glass*. He attempts to conquer time and space in his roto-reliefs and optical machines, to vanquish chance in chess and roulette; in short, to create a new world confronting the reality of things whose implacable immensity forces him to be quiet—to be quiet but not to accept. This tends to be forgotten because of the illusion created by Duchamp's legendary calm and his reassuring smile. However, to a close friend whose wife had just died, he wired: "SAD AUTUMNAL COUNTERPOINT OF UNACCEPTABLE COWARDLINESS CONFIRMING ONCE AGAIN IMBECILIC INANITY OF ANY RATIONAL JUSTIFICATION." The same day he stated in a letter: "We all play a miserable game, and generalities and generalizations are the inventions of amateur magicians." No, Duchamp's silence is neither indifference, nor abandon, nor emptiness, but a taut and menacing spring. Perhaps this helps to explain how, starting from a very specifically rational attitude which expresses a coherent philosophical conception of existence, Duchamp should consciously wish to achieve a position whose motive escapes definition and haloes itself with mystery. In his life as in his art and writing, he has never accepted any preordained principle or any intangible explanations. The short speech on the creative act which he gave in Houston explains how he opposes all canons of taste—even of bad taste. The sophistry in which he willfully shuts himself ("I force myself," he has said, "to contradict myself so as to avoid conforming to my own taste.") illustrates his constant concern not to be a dupe and implies the acceptance of a rigorous personal discipline—any individual, even the most superior, being at the mercy of the obvious and not so obvious temptations offered by popular success. It is not far-fetched to see a form of humanism in his attitude. After all, is not what distinguishes man from the machine the option granted to man not to repeat himself?

The following pages should be read in this context. They do not represent literary works in the usual sense of the term, but rather milestones of a long mental process and reluctantly made concessions—like the brief and eloquent grunts made by a man doing heavy labor. Despite their terseness they give us an idea of what Duchamp would have liked to do with this world were the limits of possibility extended. André Breton, in his *Anthology of Black Humor,* remarked that

> the question of reality in its connection with possibility, the question which remains a great source of anguish, is resolved [in Duchamp's work] "by slightly straining the laws of physics and chemistry." There can be no doubt that an effort will be made in the future to rediscover the rigorous chronological order of the discoveries in the realm of plastic expression to which that method was to lead Marcel Duchamp. Future generations can do no less than make a systematic effort to go back up the stream of Duchamp's thought and carefully describe its meanderings in search of the hidden treasure which was his mind, and through that mind what is rarer still and even more precious, the very spirit of his period. What is at stake here is a profound initiation into the most modern way of feeling, where humor presents itself as the implicit condition of the work.[1]

Hopefully the present volume will shed light on that research and help facilitate that initiation.

From 1913 on, Duchamp's subversive fervor has been directed against language. We will see how he intends to re-form (not reform) our most common means of expression. Unlike Tzara, Hausmann, or Schwitters, he does not undertake to return to the very sources of language—to elemental phonemes—but rather, following a very Rimbaudian process, he wishes to give to each word and each letter an arbitrary semantic value. This is something like the experiments attempted by Paul Eluard in his little magazine *Proverbe*. What is involved is exhausting the meaning of words; of playing with them to the

1. *Anthologie de l'humour noir,* p. 221.

point of savaging their most secret attributes; finally of pronouncing the total divorce between the expression and the expressive content which we customarily attribute to it. Once words are thus emptied and freed through the sudden visible strangeness of their internal structure or through a new association with other words, they will yield unsuspected treasures of images or ideas. The adventure of language thus unfolds differently from the striving for style, which pursues freshness and visual and auditory sensations. The principle is that a word too much in view, like a landscape, loses its savor, wears itself out, and becomes a commonplace. The interest which its semantic content gives rise to is reduced to the vanishing point. It is only and precisely at the point where the stylist in search of the picturesque gives up that Duchamp intervenes. Once the container is stripped of its content, the word as assemblage-of-letters assumes a new identity, physical and tangible, as a surprising interpreter of a new reality. Duchamp thus investigates how a vocabulary could be totally renewed by "recharging" all the abstract words in the dictionary with a new content in order to end up, as on the threshold of human history, with "prime words," divisible only by themselves and by unity. It is quite possible that some humor emerges in the course of these games and manipulations, much as heat appears in the course of a chemical reaction, but this is not inevitable and is at any rate of secondary importance. This comes out rather clearly in the phrases where, as Breton again notes, Duchamp has been able "to make pleasure intervene even in the formulation of a law to which reality must answer. ('A straight horizontal thread one meter long falls from a height of one meter onto a horizontal plane distorting itself *as it pleases* and creates a new shape of the measure of length. . . .) This is what Duchamp called 'affirmative irony,' as opposed to 'negative irony.' "[2]

Perhaps no one was less dogmatically dadaist, yet more spiritually dada, than Marcel Duchamp. While the dada-surrealist explosion was for many the catalytic agent of a discovery—for example, for the prime movers of the review *Littérature*—and was for so many others a break which gave them a literary life rather cheaply, it is evident that, through dada and surrealism, Duchamp has remained himself. His interior evolution, begun even before cubism, bears the mark of no known influence. In Duchamp are joined the essential elements of the dada revolt: a total absence of principles or prejudices, a freedom to construct or to destroy with the most total impartiality, all things moreover being equal and permitted. "There is no solution," says Duchamp, "because there isn't any problem." This sense of "umor" is dada, as well as the affection for puns and spoonerisms which are so perfectly suited to transcending the comic. "My irony," says Duchamp, "is that of indifference: meta-irony." To these quintessential characteristics of the modern rebel he

2. *Ibid.*

brings the solid and responsible, though rare, qualities of simplicity and rectitude, which owe nothing to morality, although there is much of the moralist in Duchamp—this "Frenchman of the late eighteenth century who engages himself in dissecting sensations and sentiments, just as Crébillon fils or Laclos operate in the domain of the [French eighteenth-century] novel, reducing them and mercilessly translating them into mechanics."[3]

There is no hiding the fact that the written as well as the plastic work of Marcel Duchamp is open to all kinds of accusations. It is not surprising that he is the target of the kind of criticism that no avant-garde artist escapes: gratuitous hermeticism, cold and dry intellectualism, even plagiarism, fraud, flagrant bluffing, and colossal mystification. Moreover Duchamp's success in America provokes French chauvinists to say: "Just look at those Americans. How credulous can they be?" But even the Anglo-Saxon press has not always spared Duchamp, as witness this opinion voiced in the London *Times Literary Supplement* in an article on the dada movement:

> . . . in 1915 Marcel Duchamp, another Cubist *raté,* crossed the Atlantic with the intention of shocking America with studio stunts that had not attracted much attention in France. Duchamp must have succeeded beyond his wildest dreams, for to this day American art historians vie with one another in paying tribute to him. "Perhaps the most inventive mind in twentieth century art. Since Leonardo no artist has been so consumed with philosophical and technological experiment," one has written. Another says of this man who gave up art for chess at a comparatively early age, that "few artists have exercised so profound an influence on their times." Unfortunately, the truth is that art has never favoured Duchamp.[4]

There is no doubt that a good dose of mystification is present in Duchamp's work. His friend H. P. Roché once said: "I watch Normans like Duchamp carefully. . . . I know that I can be had by him."[5] Yet we must not lose sight of the goal and the meaning of that mystification, which is never gratuitous and which is part of an aesthetic position. We should consider the remarks made by André Breton, who surely does not wish to be duped either. "Our friend Duchamp is assuredly the most intelligent and (for many) the most troublesome man of this first part of the twentieth century."[6] Consider also the words of Guillaume Apollinaire, which, remarkably enough, were written in 1913 at the very beginning of Duchamp's post-cubist evolution:

> Just as Cimabue's paintings were paraded through the streets, our century has seen the airplane of Blériot, laden with the efforts humanity has made for the past thousand years, escorted in glory to the [Academy of]

3. Charles Estienne, "Surréalisme et peinture," in *Combat,* July 15, 1954.
4. October 23, 1953, p. 2.
5. *Souvenirs sur Marcel Duchamp,* in *La Nouvelle N.R.F.,* pp. 1133–36, 1954.
6. Breton, *loc. cit.*

> Arts and Sciences. Perhaps it will be the task of an artist as detached from aesthetic preoccupations and as intent on the energetic as Marcel Duchamp to reconcile art and the people.[7]

It is important that we not be over-surprised by the last affirmation of this prophetic French poet. Duchamp certainly incarnates the methods and preoccupations of a sensitivity so modern that many contemporaries have not yet become conscious of its existence. But talking to people from all walks of life shows one how much Duchamp's work, which bowled over the art world more than a half century ago, continues to influence a style of life through certain publicity methods, a new way of looking at things, and a sense of absurd and incongruous humor. His work has passed into the fabric of life.

Duchamp's attempt to rethink the world rests on two supports: the *machine,* the image and incarnation of our epoch, and *chance,* which for our contemporaries has de facto replaced divinity. Toward 1910 he was in contact with futurist experiments and conceived the vision of a society where the automatic and the artificial would regulate all our relationships. It was to better affirm his humanity that he integrated himself into this new world. He was going even beyond our own time, which still persists in wishing to adapt the machine to man. Duchamp was trying to imagine a state of affairs where man would humanize the machine to such an extent that the latter would truly come to life. And from that point certain questions, depicted by his *Large Glass* and described in his "boxes," were raised. What if the machine, stripped of all anthropomorphic attributes, were to evolve in a world made in its image with no reference to the criteria governing man, its creator? What if, like Kafka's monkey, it servilely imitated all human grimaces and gestures with the exclusive goal of freeing itself of its chains and of "leaving"? Then, if the machine were to love, desire, and marry, what would be its mental processes? Our good authors of science fiction, at least those with a certain sense of humor, will see that Duchamp's *Bride* leads us far beyond their wildest creations where piteous robots can never express themselves except in human terms and where all the research into the fantastic never results in anything but a poor animalization of Martians or Moonmen. Even the most stubborn reader, if he reads the notes for the *Bride* and is honest with himself, will recognize the steadfastness, the audacious lucidity, and the resolute calm of Duchamp's thought. According to Duchamp, the machine is a supremely intelligent creature which evolves in a world completely divorced from our own: it thinks, organizes this thought in coherent sentences, and, following the technique described above, uses words whose meaning is familiar to us. However these words conspire to mystify us.

7. *Méditations esthétiques, Les Peintres cubistes.* Paris, Eugène Figuière, 1913, p. 76.

The thought which we follow step by step ends at an impasse, in a dark laugh, and in a new questioning. For Duchamp's machine a "sieve" isn't necessarily a sieve.

On the other hand, what would happen if the machine admitted the possibility of accident, or non-repetition, exclusive attribute of man? Better yet, if, having gotten ahead of us, it learned to use chance for utilitarian or aesthetic ends? I concede that we find ourselves here at a point where serious minds will be tempted to let us venture alone. But finally, are we so far from the poetic "science" which Baudelaire dreamed of?[8] And don't we see that the latitude left to matter, as if each atom was endowed with conscience, consciousness, and sentiments, limits the domain of the relative at the same time as it infinitely multiplies the opportunities left to chance?

Those "dust-breedings" and "standard stoppages" open the door for us to the astonishing poetry of nothingness, to the sense of the senseless, and to the world hidden in the microcosm of every object. We can imagine what the Bride's novel as written by Duchamp might be. . . . But the practical exploitation of his discoveries is of no interest to him. He has been contented with entering them on scratch pads as if in a ship's log. His good-natured contempt for "painters intoxicated with turpentine" as well as his disdain for the majority of "literary people" is legendary. For Duchamp lives a pure adventure of the mind. For some fifty years he has found the keenest physical pleasure in the abstract contact with chance involved in chess. He spent a whole season at Monte Carlo in front of the roulete table in order to study its whimsical accidents, without experiencing any sensation that we can associate with the trivial passion of gambling. When his system proved unproductive he was surprised, but quietly so, and with a naive freshness which helps to explain the originality of the creations which spring up in his mind. Ideas as new as those contained in the *Box in a Valise* could only be brought to life by a mind that was marvelously alert and open.

If we are only willing to lend a minimum of attention to the most insignificant detail in the world which surrounds us, we find that, as in Alice's Wonderland, the most common thing becomes fantastic. For Duchamp, nothing fits a priori into a fixed context. The order of things is neither established, regulated, certain, nor above all definitive. The elements of this world are not linked together like the letters in handwriting by some subjective and relatively rational scheme but follow each other indifferently, juxtaposed like the kinds of type used in printing presses. It is up to the typesetter to group them in a given order and so much the better, says Duchamp, if the foreman is drunk or inattentive, or if an accident jumbles the type and mixes up the composition.

8. Cf. Charles Baudelaire, *Oeuvres,* La Pléiade, N.R.F., Paris, 1954, p. 1381.

Whatever he may say, Duchamp's hand was made for the brush and not for the pen. He finds writing painful, and the slenderness of his written work is a result of that. But despite this, his mind is turned toward a type of intellectual expression of which writing is the most adequate manifestation. Although he devoted himself from childhood on to painting, it was a false vocation. This is seen in the manner in which Duchamp regards the painter's art, and in the skillful and precise way in which he uses language, like an instrument whose resources he controls perfectly.

Helped by a warm personality, Duchamp has known how to nourish the friendship of painters and writers of very different persuasions who leave no doubts about their mutual antipathies. He sees one group, listens to another, and speaks out with his courteous authority. It is no doubt this ability to become involved without committing himself which has earned him the high esteem of other artists. Secretive in his personal life, he neither displays nor hides himself. False modesty is unknown to him; genuine modesty has made his reputation.

While still alive, he feels himself little by little being petrified in the flux of history. At the Philadelphia Museum of Art he can visit the room dedicated to his work, seeing himself the way our grandchildren will discover him in the year 2,000. He is an impassive and benevolent witness to the crystallization of his most banal actions into legendary exploits; it is hard to tell whether or not he accepts the meaning given to these actions. To get maximum utilization out of the cramped space of his Paris apartment he fashioned a door which shut alternately on two door frames placed at right angles; and the legend arose that his real purpose was to catch the French proverb "A door has to be either open or shut" in flagrant untruth. Because they bear the stamp of his strong and original personality, all his actions contribute a fabulous counterpoint to his other life–that of a normal man. Knowing whether or not Duchamp wished to give a certain interpretation to his gestures is perhaps beside the point. A myth has been built around that existence and that work, and the authenticity of the factors which serve to support the myth is less important than the collective state of mind which gave birth to it. If it were demonstrated to us that *The Bride* was only a gigantic put-on, the myth of an enigmatic and infallible Duchamp would only be more alive, and a real and fertile interpretation would be found for that now forever senseless work. Perhaps this is the ultimate lesson given by Duchamp to a modern and narcissistic world which hungers for idols and for publicity. J.-H. Lévesque explains:

> What is important in what we must call a *work* by Duchamp is not exactly what one has before one's eyes but the stimulus that this sign provokes in the mind of the onlooker. The worth of a work of art does not come so much from what its creator condensed in it through his talent

and experience as from the unexpected resonances and harmonics that it sets loose in the reader or viewer.[9]

The reading of Duchamp's texts requires that openness of mind which is the exclusive attribute of the few who are afflicted neither by snobbism, nor by the fear of public and private censure, nor especially by the crushing lack of wit which is so characteristic of our times. To those who will withold judgment until the book is read, we can promise the "resonances and harmonics" mentioned by Lévesque, as well as astonishing discoveries.[10]

Michel Sanouillet
1958
[Trans. E.P.]

9. "La Leçon de Marcel Duchamp," in *The United States Lines Paris Review,* 1955.

10. The editors wish to point out that this introduction was written in 1958 and that some statements made at that time may appear today somehow outdated, naive or self–evident. The fact is that Duchamp's stature in public opinion has changed considerably in the last decade, especially since his death in 1968. It was felt however that basically this text was still valid and that, in any case, having been checked and approved by Marcel Duchamp, it should be included.

A Literary Chronology

1887 Born July 28 at Blainville (Seine-Maritime), France.

1912 Begins the notes which support the *Large Glass.*

1914 Publishes *The Box of 1914,* a precursor to the *Green Box.*

1917 Publication of *The Blind Man* (2 numbers) and *Rongwrong* (1 number).

1921 Publication with Man Ray of *New York Dada* (1 number).

1932 Publication with V. Halberstadt of *Opposition and Sister Squares are Reconciled.* (Brussels: L'Echiquier).

1934 *The Bride Stripped Bare by Her Bachelors, Even* [*The Green Box*] (Paris: Editions Rrose Sélavy).

1939 Publication of *Rrose Sélavy* (Paris: GLM).

1950 Publication of the catalog *Collection of the Société Anonyme* (New Haven: Yale University Art Gallery).

1957 Lecture on "The Creative Act," Houston.

1961 "A Propos of Ready-mades." Talk delivered at New York Museum of Modern Art.

1967 Publication of *A l'Infinitif* [*The White Box*] (New York: Cordier & Ekstrom, Inc.).

1968 Dies at Neuilly, France, October 1.

The Bride's Veil

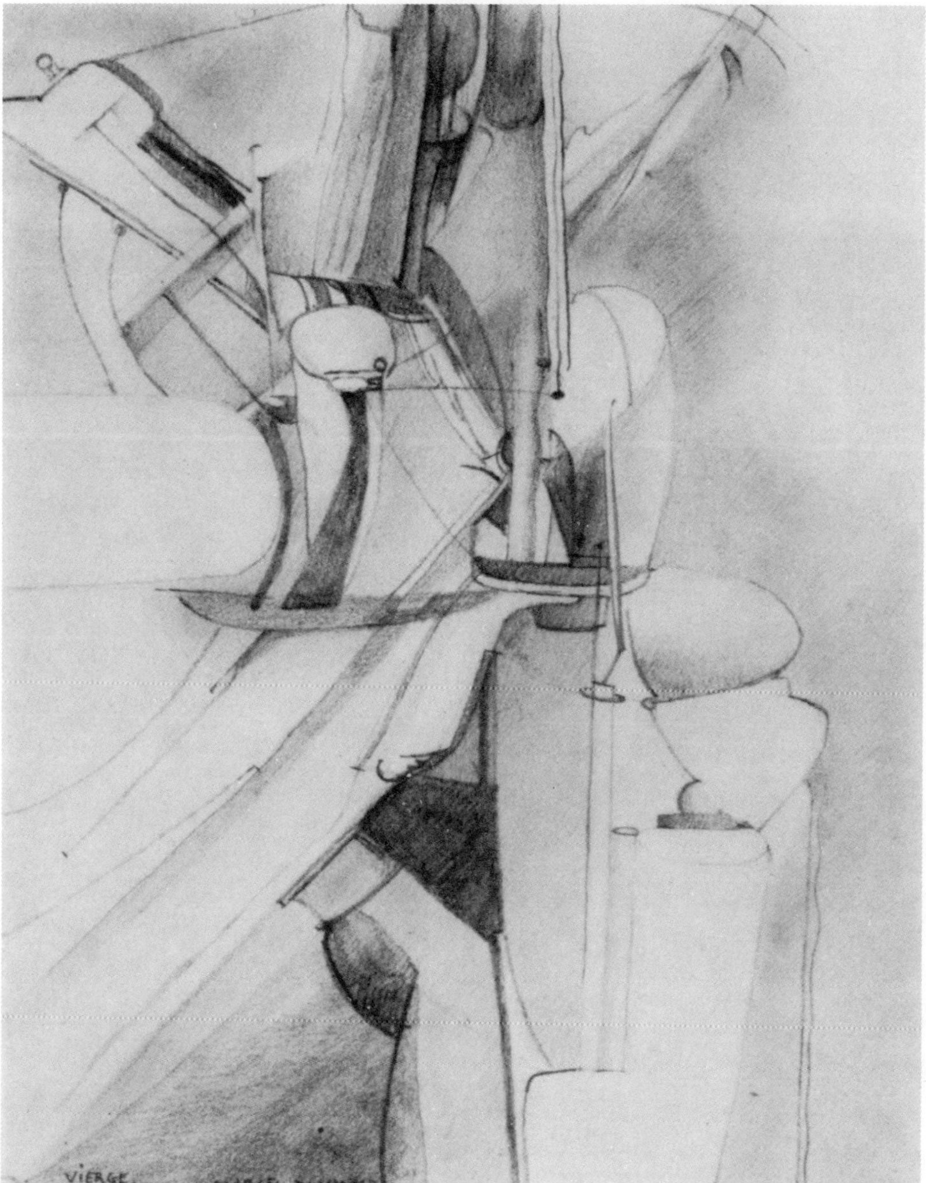

Virgin No. 1, 1912

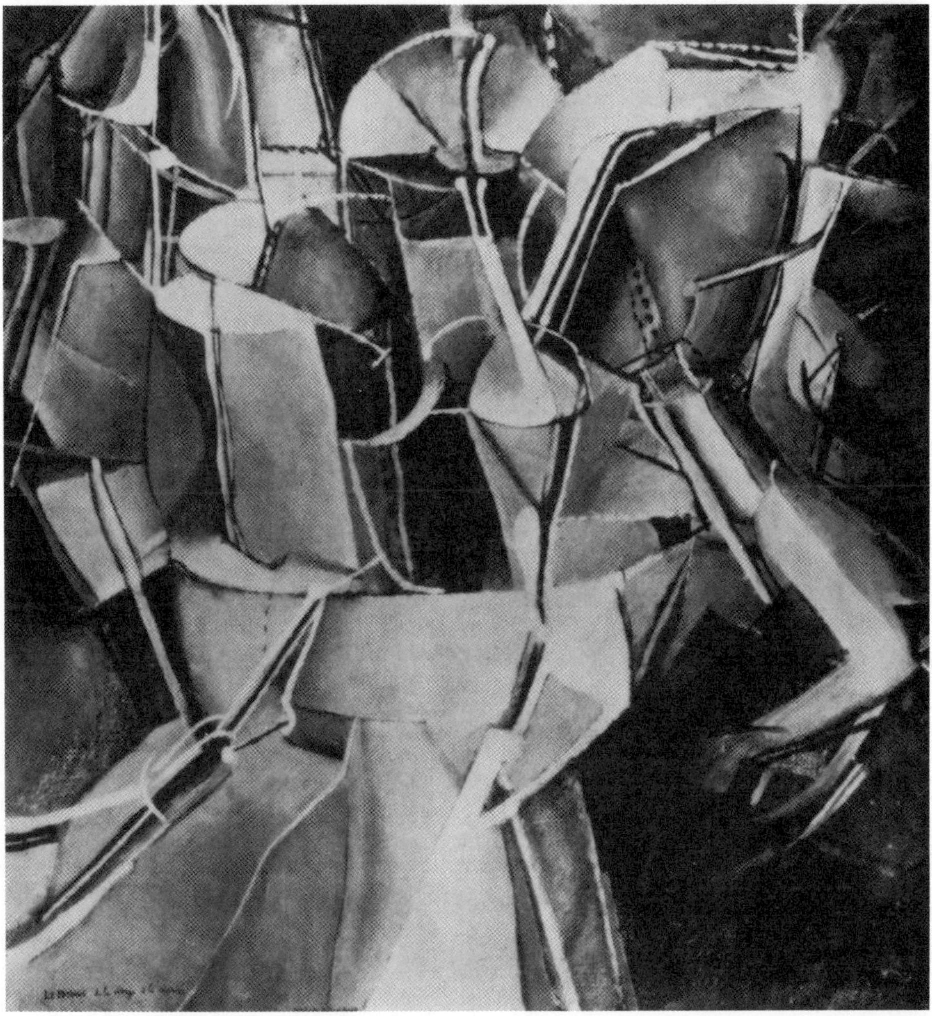

The Passage from the Virgin to the Bride, 1912

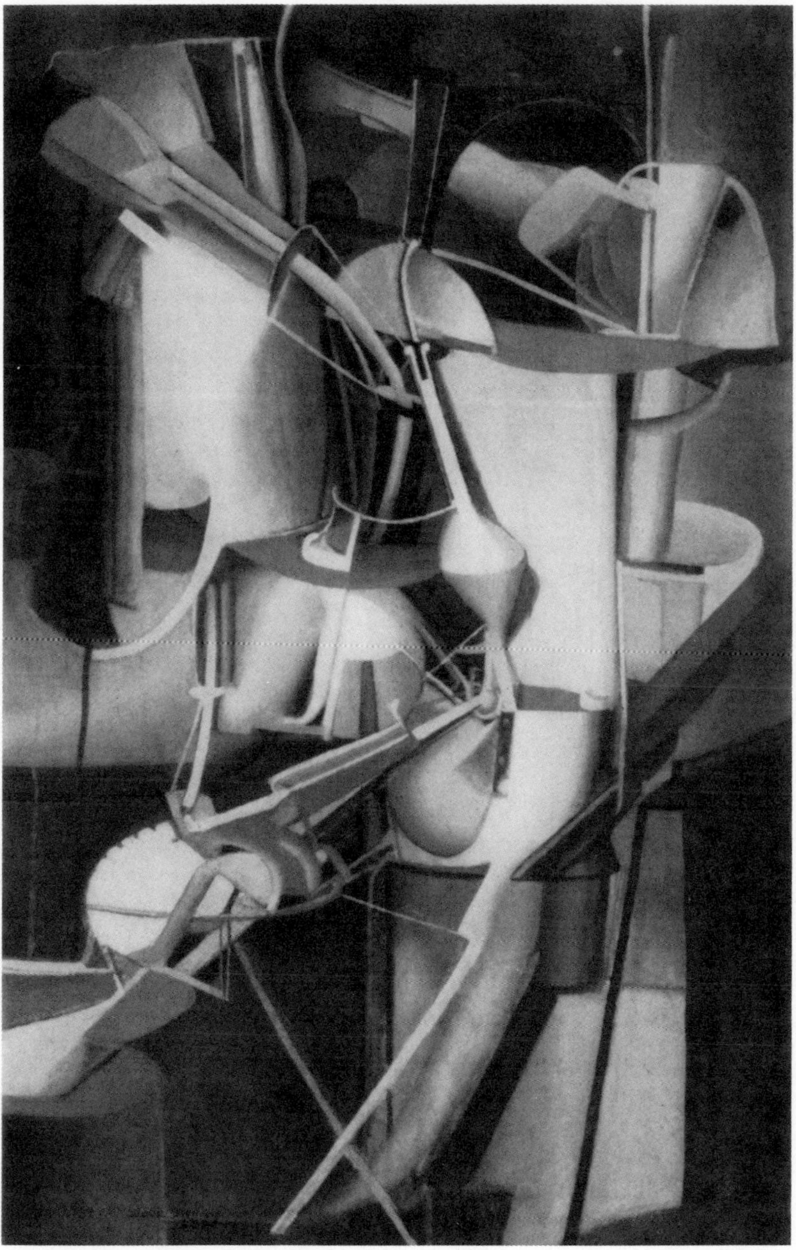

Bride, 1912

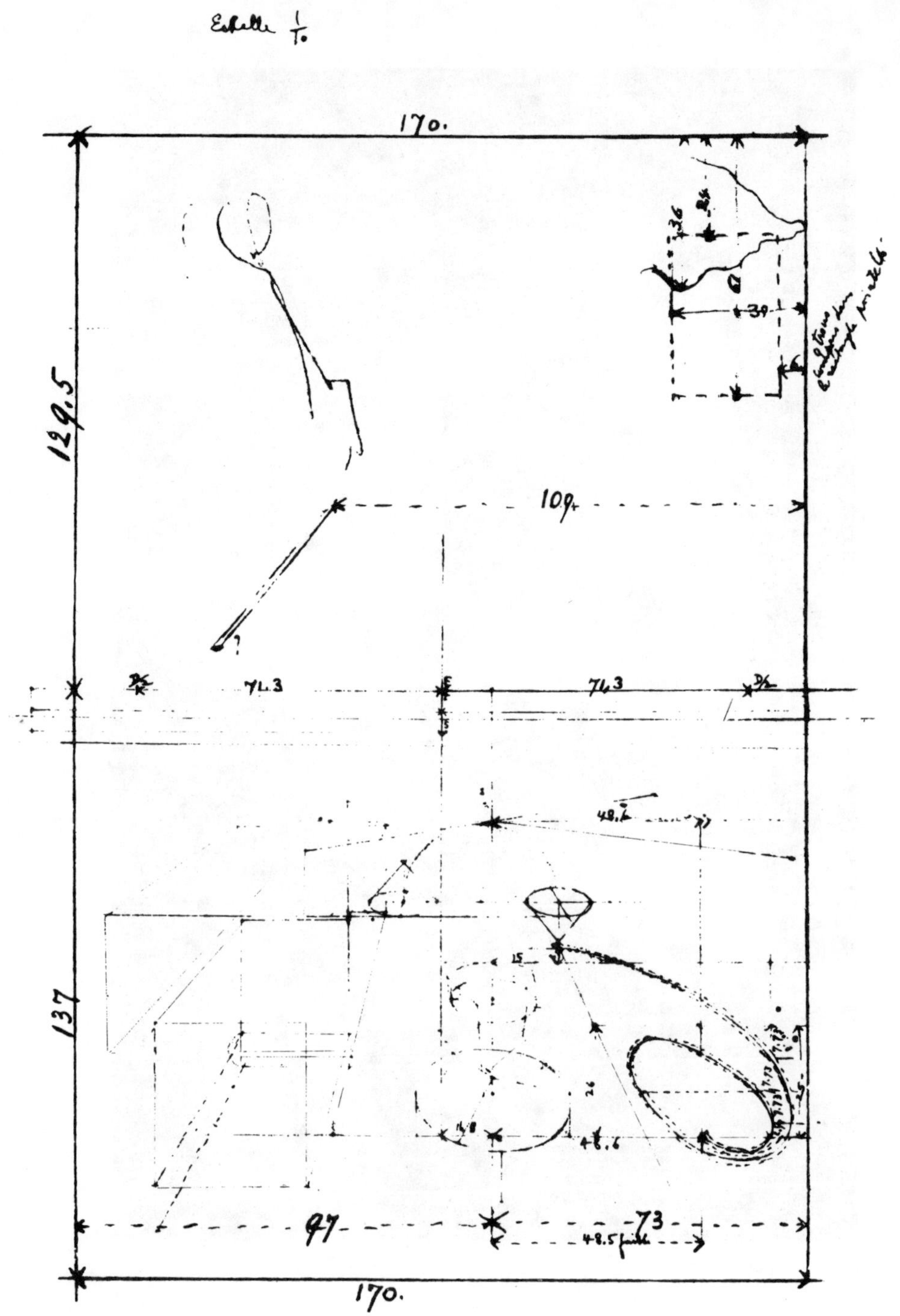

The Bride Stripped Bare by Her Bachelors, Even, 1913 (Sketch)

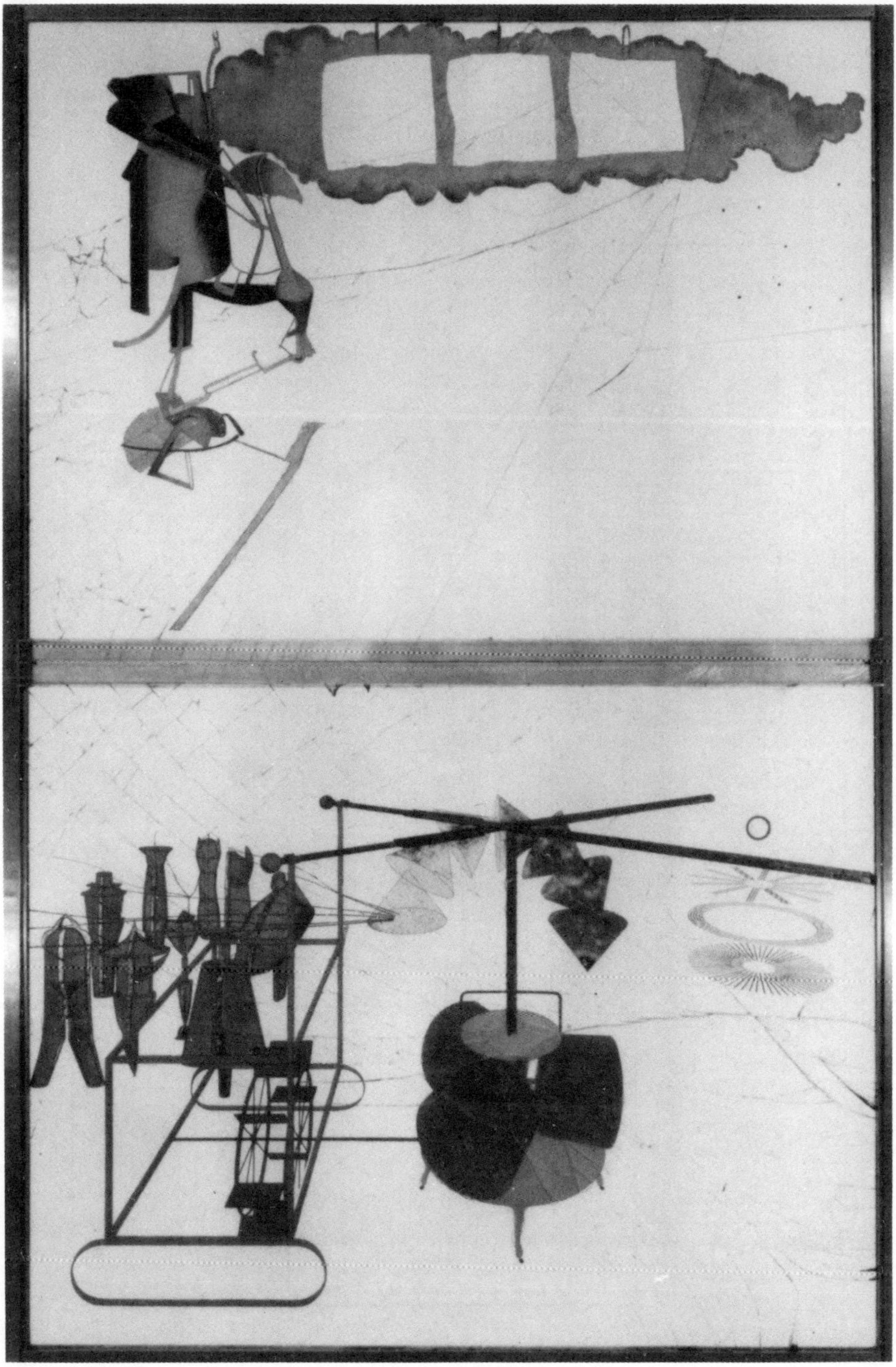

The Bride Stripped Bare by Her Bachelors, Even (The Large Glass), 1915-23

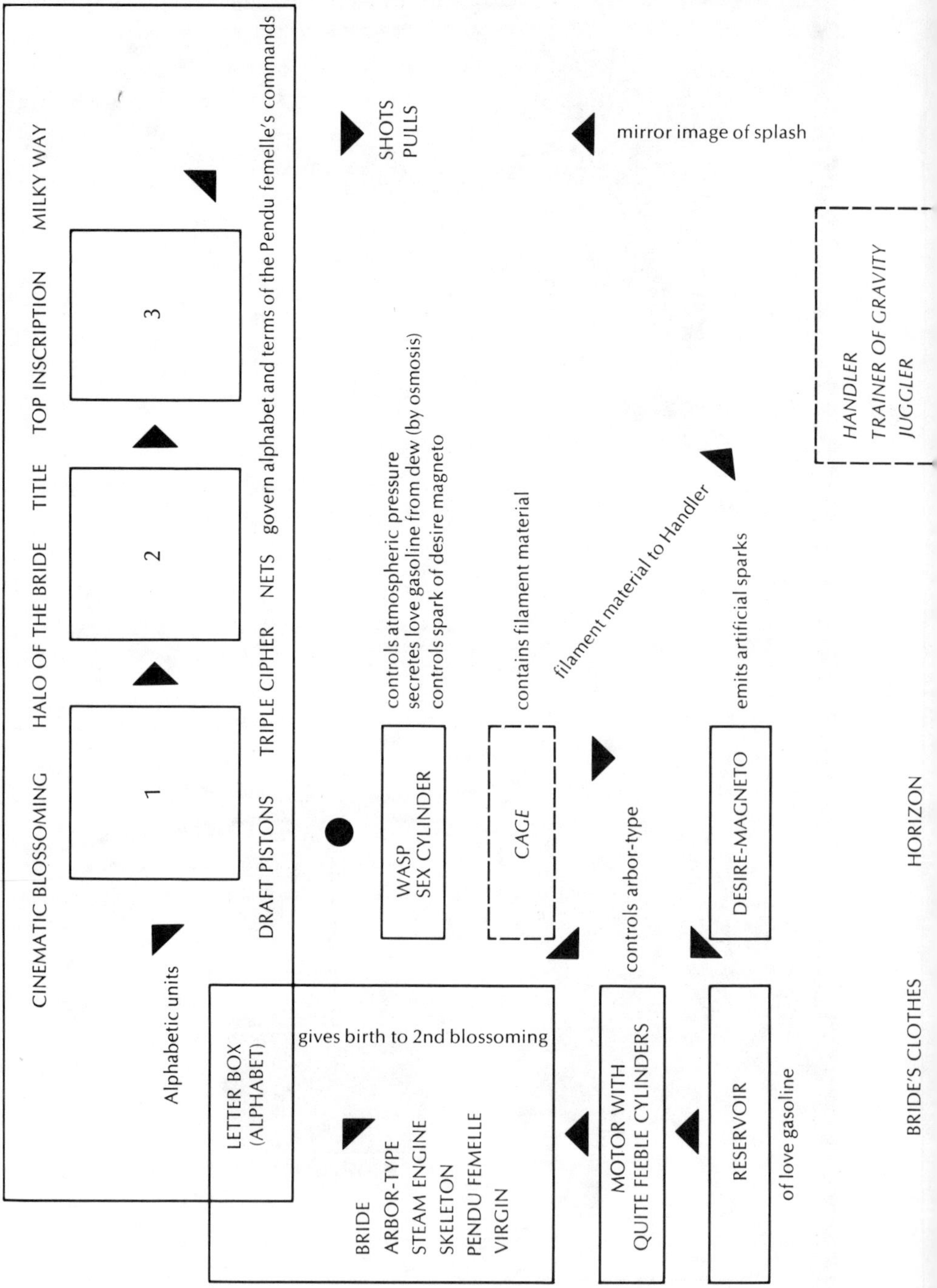

BRIDE MACHINE

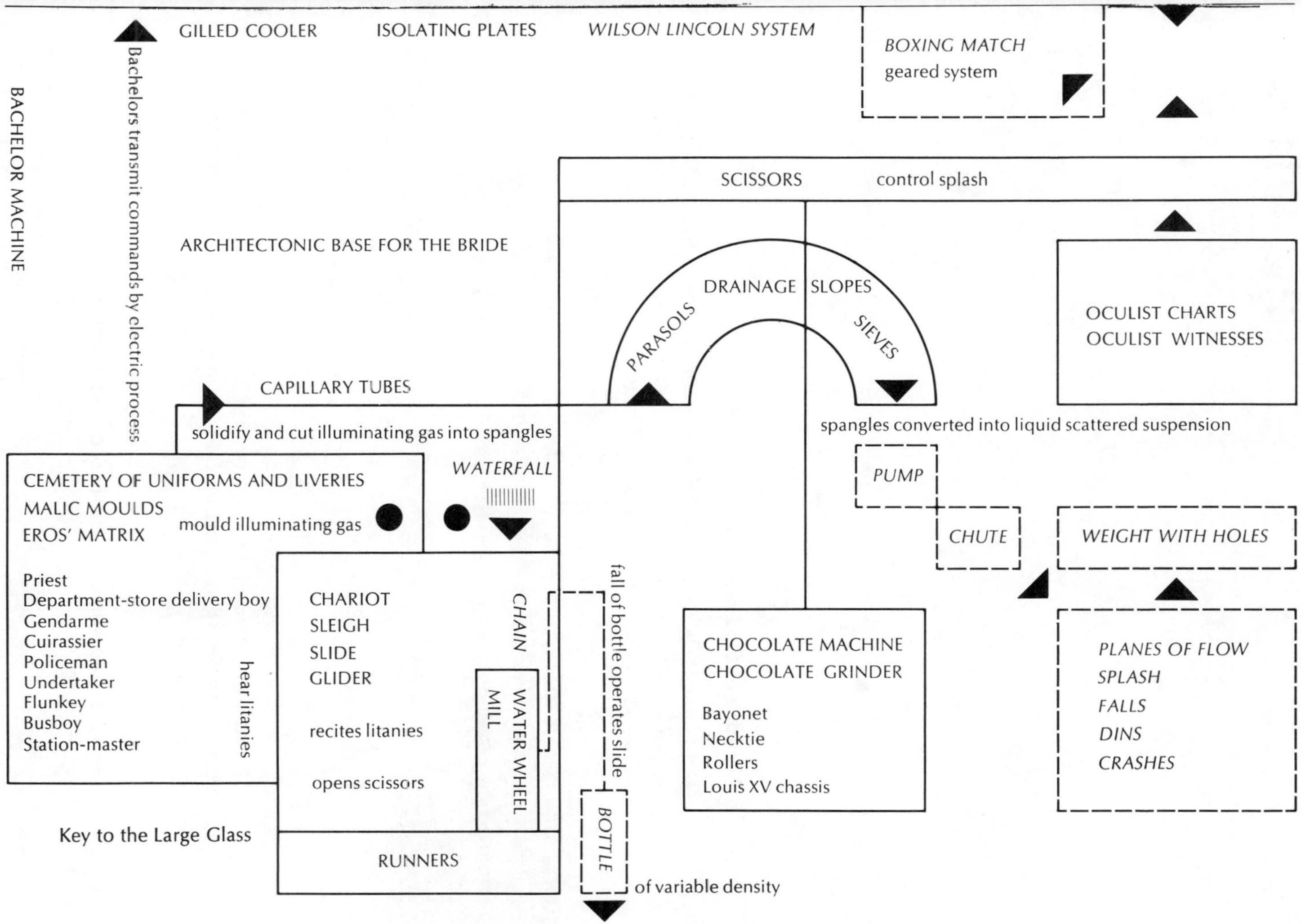

Key to the Large Glass

The 1914 Box

The Idea of the Fabrication

–If a straight horizontal thread one meter long falls from a height of one meter onto a horizontal plane distorting itself *as it pleases* and creates a new shape of the measure of length.–

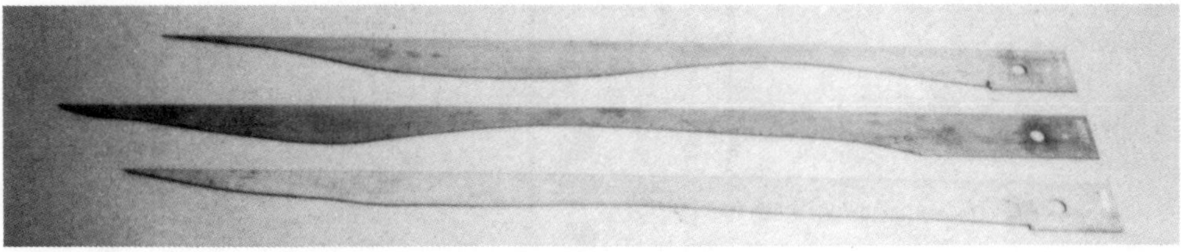

Three Standard Stoppages, 1913-14

–3 patterns obtained in more or less similar conditions: *considered in their relation to one another* they are an *approximate reconstitution* of the measure of length.

The 3 *standard stoppages* are the meter diminished.

Long live! clothes and the racquet-press.

Make a painting: of *happy or unhappy chance* (luck or unluck)

Deferment

Against compulsory military service: a "*deferment*" of each limb, of the heart and the other anatomical parts; each soldier being already unable to put his uniform on again, his heart feeding *telephonically*, a deferred arm, etc.

Then, no more feeding; each "*deferee*" isolating himself. Finally a Regulation of regrets from *one "deferee" to another.*

Electricity Breadthwise

The only possible utilisation of electricity "in the arts."

Given that. . . . ; if I suppose I'm suffering a lot. . . .

[see]
One can look at seeing;
one can't hear hearing.

—one only has: for *female* the public urinal and one *lives* by it.—

A World in Yellow

The bridge of volumes
above or beneath the volumes.
in order to watch the bateau-mouche go by

The barrel game is a very beautiful "*sculpture*" *of skill*:

a photographic record should be made of 3 successive performances; and "all the pieces in the frog's mouth" *should not be preferred* to "all the pieces outside" or (nor) above all to a good score.

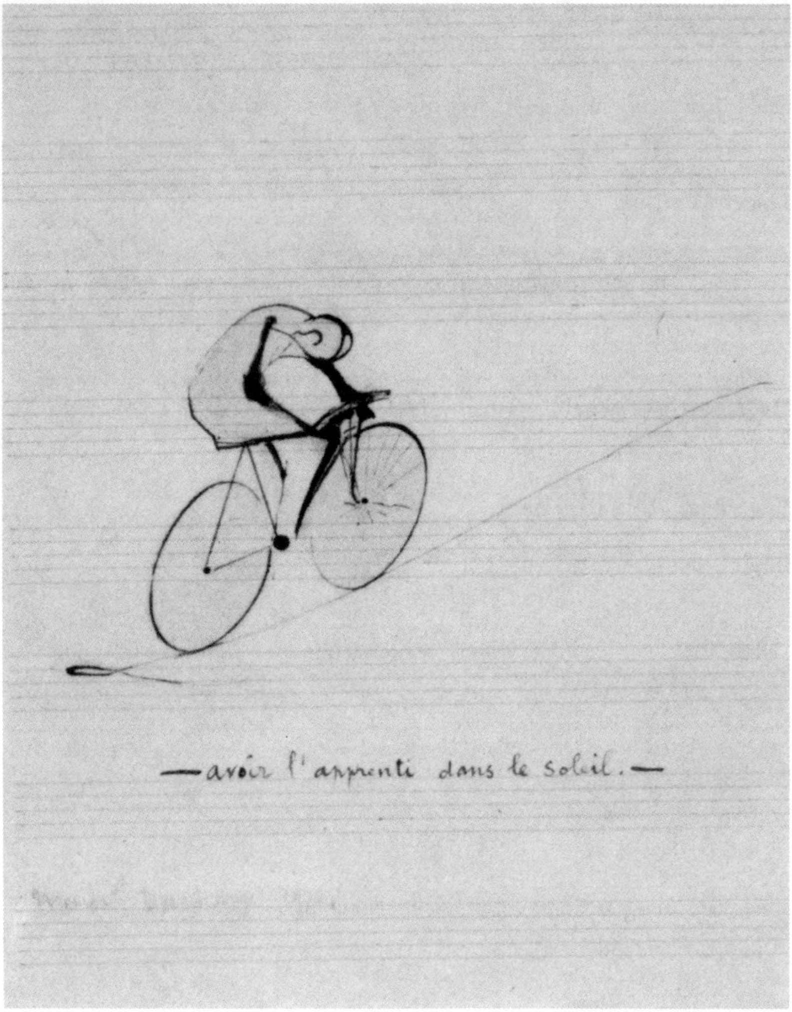

—to have the apprentice in the sun.—

arrhe is to art as
shitte is to shit.

$$\frac{\text{arrhe}}{\text{art}} = \frac{\text{shitte}}{\text{shit}}$$

grammatically:
the arrhe of painting is feminine in gender

Linear perspective is a good means of *representing* equalities *in diverse ways;* i.e. the equivalent, the similar (homothetic) and the equal blend together in perspective symmetry.

Make a mirrored wardrobe.
Make this mirrored wardrobe for the silvering.

Make a painting of *frequency:*

The Green Box

[1. MARGINAL NOTES]

The bride stripped bare by her bachelors even.
to separate the *mass-produced readymade* from the *readyfound*—The separation is an operation.

Kind of Subtitle
Delay in Glass

Use "delay" instead of picture or painting; picture on glass becomes delay in glass—but delay in glass does not mean picture on glass—

It's merely a way of succeeding in no longer thinking that the thing in question is a picture—to make a delay of it in the most general way possible, not so much in the different meanings in which delay can be taken, but rather in their indecisive reunion "delay"—/a delay in glass as you would say a poem in prose or a spittoon in silver

1. *1912*
The machine with 5 hearts, the pure child, of nickel and platinum, must dominate the Jura-Paris road.

On the one hand, the chief of the 5 nudes will be ahead of the 4 other nudes *towards* this Jura-Paris road. On the other hand, the headlight child will be the instrument conquering this Jura-Paris road

This headlight child could, graphically, be a comet, which would have its tail in front, this tail being an appendage of the headlight child appendage which absorbs by crushing (gold dust, graphically) this Jura-Paris road.

The Jura-Paris road, having to be infinite only humanly, will lose none of its character of infinity in finding a termination at one end in the chief of the 5 nudes, at the other in the headlight-child.

The term "indefinite" seems to me more accurate than infinite. The road will begin in the chief of the 5 nudes. and will not end in the headlight child.

Graphically, this road will tend towards the pure geometrical line without thickness (the meeting of 2 planes seems to me the only pictorial means to achieve purity)

But in the beginning (in the chief of the 5 nudes) it will be very finite in width, thickness, etc., in order little by little, to become without topographical form in coming close to this ideal straight line which finds its opening towards the infinite in the headlight child.

The pictorial matter of this Jura-Paris road will be *wood* which seems to me like the affective translation of powdered silex.

Perhaps, see if it is necessary to choose an essence of wood. (The fir tree, or then polished mahogany)

Details of execution.

Dimensions = Plans.

Size of the canvas.

"The Jura–Paris road" refers to a trip taken by Duchamp, Guillaume Apollinaire, and Francis Picabia and his wife Gabrielle Buffet to Mme. Picabia's family home at Etival (Jura). It was during this trip that the decision was made to publish Apollinaire's *The Cubist Painters*.

Perhaps make a *hinge picture*. (folding yardstick, book. . . .) develop the *principle of the hinge* in the displacements 1st in the plane 2nd in space.
Find an *automatic description* of the hinge.
Perhaps introduce it in the Pendu femelle.

Preface

Given 1st the waterfall
2nd the illuminating gas,
we shall determine the conditions for the instantaneous state of Rest (or allegorical appearance) of a *succession* [of a group] of *various facts* seeming to necessitate each other under certain laws, *in order to isolate the sign of the accordance between,* on the one hand, this *state of Rest* (capable of all the *innumerable* eccentricities) and, on the other, a

choice of Possibilities authorized by these laws and also *determining them.*

For the instantaneous state of rest = bring in the term extra rapid

We shall determine the conditions of [the] best exposé of the extra rapid state of Rest [of the extra rapid exposure (= allegorical appearance) of a group. . . . . . etc.

nothing perhaps.

Notice

Given: 1st the waterfall
[*in the dark*]
If, given 2nd the illuminating gas,

consider considerations
in the dark, we shall determine (the conditions for) the extra rapid ex-
allegorical Reproduction [*assaults*]
position (= allegorical apearance) of several collisions seeming strictly
unnecessary
to succeed each other *according to certain laws, in order to* isolate the *Sign of the accordance* between this extra rapid exposition (capable of all the eccentricities) *on the one hand* and the choice of the possibilities authorized by these laws on *the other.*

Given: 1. The Waterfall / 2. The Illuminating Gas was to become the title of Duchamp's last major work which is on permanent display at the Philadelphia Museum of Art.

Algebraic comparison

$\frac{a}{b}$ a being the exposition
b " the possibilities

the ratio $\frac{a}{b}$ is in no way given by a number $c\frac{a}{b} = c$ but by the sign (—)

which separates a and b; as soon as a and b are being "*known*" they become new units and lose their numerical relative value (or in duration); the sign of ratio which separated them remains (*sign of the accordance* or rather *of. . . . . . look for it*)

The right and the left are obtained by letting trail behind you a tinge of *persistence in the situation.* This symmetrical fashioning of the *situation distributed* on each side of the vertical axis is of practical value (as right different from left) only as a residue of experiences on fixed exterior points.

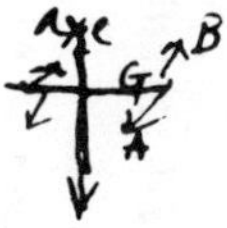

And *on the other hand:* the vertical axis considered separately turning on itself, a generating line at a right angle e.g., will always determine a circle in the 2 cases 1st turning in the direction A, 2nd direction B.—

Thus, *if it* were still possible, in the case of the vertical axis at rest., to consider *2 contrary directions* for the generating line G., the figure engendered (*whatever it may be*), can no longer be called left or right of the axis—

As there is gradually less differentiation from axis to axis., i.e. as all the axes gradually disappear in a fading verticality the front and the back, the reverse and the obverse acquire a circular significance: the right and the left which are the 4 arms of the front and back. melt. *along the* verticals.

the interior and exterior (in a fourth dimension) can receive a similar identification. but the axis is no longer vertical and has no longer a *one-*dimensional appearance

[2. LAWS AND GENERAL NOTES]

General notes. for a hilarious Picture.

Beer professor (litany of the chariot)
Principle of subsidized symmetries. (its application in the mvts. of the handler and of the hanged figure; see the Pendu femelle)
In general, the picture is the apparition of an appearance (see explanation)

Put the whole bride under a glass case, or into a transparent cage.

Contrary to the previous notes, the bride no longer provides gasoline for the cylinder-breasts. (Try for a better wording than "clyinder-breasts")

Of hygiene in the bride; or of the Diet in the bride.

give the juggler only 3 feet because 3 points of support are necessary for stable equilibrium, 2 would give only an unstable equilibrium

Painting of precision, and beauty of indifference

Solidity of construction:

Equality of superposition: the principal dimensions of the general foundation for the bride and for the bachelor mach. are equal.

Directions:

the Form 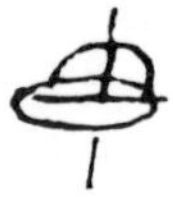 = space–

the numb. 3. taken as a refrain in duration–(numb. is mathematical duration.

Always or nearly always give reasons for the choice between 2 or more solutions (by ironical causality).

Ironism of affirmation: differences from negative ironism dependent solely on Laughter.

Laws, principles, phenomena

–*Phen,* of *stretching in the unit of length*–

–*Adage of spontaneity* = *The bach. grinds his choc. himself*

–*Phen. or principle of oscillating density,* a property of the substance of brand bottles.

–Emancipated metal of the rods of the sleigh

–Friction reintegrated *in ~~reverse~~* (emancipated metal)

Establish a society in which the individual has to pay for the air he breathes (air meters; imprisonment and rarefied air, in case of non-payment simple asphyxiation if necessary (cut off the air)
on condition that (?)
Ordinary brick satiates the knot.
to be tired of

Razor blades which cut well and razor blades which no longer cut
The first have "cuttage" in reserve
—Use this "cuttage" or "cuttation"

The Clock *in profile.* and the *Inspector* of Space.

Musical Sculpture

Sounds lasting and leaving from different places and forming a sounding sculpture which lasts.

Identifying
To lose the *possibility of recognizing 2 similar objects*—2 colors, 2 laces, 2 hats, 2 forms whatsoever to reach the Impossibility of sufficient *visual* memory, to transfer from one like object to another the *memory* imprint.
—Same possibility with sounds; with brain facts

[3. LANGUAGE]

Conditions of a language:

The search for "*prime words*" ("divisible" only by themselves and by unity).

Take a Larousse dict. and copy all the so-called "abstract" words. i.e., those which have no concrete reference.

Compose a schematic sign designating each of these words. (this sign can be composed with the standard stops)
These signs must be thought of as the letters of the new alphabet.
A grouping of several signs will determine
(utilize colors—in order to differentiate what would correspond in this

[literature] to the substantive, verb, adverb declensions, conjugations etc.)

Necessity for *ideal continuity*. i.e.: each grouping will be connected with the other groupings by a *strict meaning* (a sort of grammar, no longer requiring a pedagogical sentence construction. But, apart from the differences of languages, and the "figures of speech" peculiar to each language—weighs and measures some *abstractions* of *substantives, of negatives, of* relations of subject to verb, etc, by means of standard signs. (representing these new relations: conjugations, declensions, plural and singular, adjectivation inexpressible by the *concrete alphabetic* forms of languages living now and to come.).

This alphabet very probably is only suitable for the description of this picture.

[4. READYMADES]

Specifications for "Readymades".

by planning for a moment to come (on such a day, such a date such a minute), "*to inscribe* a readymade"—The readymade can later be looked for.—(with all kinds of delays)

The important thing then is just this matter of timing, this snapshot effect, like a speech delivered on no matter what occasion but *at such and such an hour*. It is a kind of rendezvous.

—Naturally inscribe that date, hour, minute, on the readymade as *information*.

also the serial characteristic of the readymade.

Reciprocal Readymade = Use a Rembrandt as an ironing-board—

Piggy Bank (or canned goods)

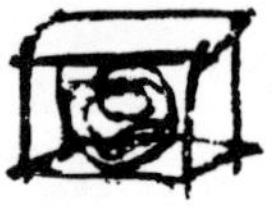

Make a readymade with a box containing something unrecognizable by its sound and solder the box

already done in the semi Readymade of copper plates and a ball of twine

Make a sick picture or a sick Readymade

buy a pair of ice-tongs as a Rdymade

Limit the no. of rdymades yearly (?)

: shadows cast by Readymades.

shadow cast by 2,3,4, Readymades. *"brought together"*

(Perhaps use an enlargement of that so as to extract from it a figure formed by an equal [length] (for ex.) taken in each Readymade and becoming by the projection a part of the cast shadow

for ex. 10 cm in the first Rdymade
10 cm " " 2nd "
etc.

each of these 10 cm. having become a part of the cast shadow

Take. these "having become" and from them make a tracing without of course changing their position in relation to each other in the original projection.

[5. CHANCE]

3 Standard Stops =

canned chance–
1914.

The Idea of the Fabrication

straight horizontal
–If a thread one meter long falls from a height of one meter straight on to a horizontal plane twisting *as it pleases* and creates a new image of the unit of length.–

—Regime of gravity—

Ministry of coincidences.
Department (or better):
Regime of Coincidence
Ministry of gravity.

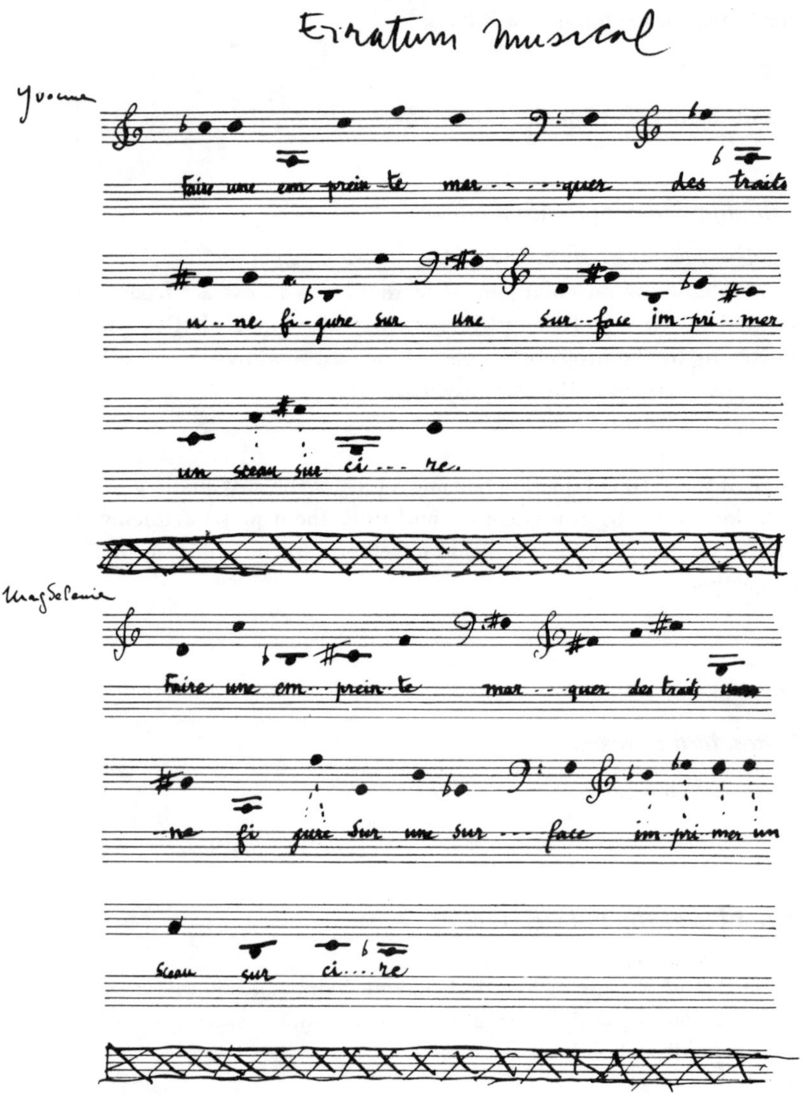

Musical Erratum

Yvonne	To make an imprint mark with lines a figure on a surface impress a seal on wax.
Magdeleine	To make an imprint mark with lines a figure on a surface impress a seal on wax.
Marcel	To make an imprint mark with lines a figure on a surface impress a seal on wax.

Painting or Sculpture.

Flat container. in glass—[holding] all sorts of liquids. Colored, pieces of wood, of iron, chemical reactions. Shake the container. and look through it.

Use a radiator and a piece of paper (or something else) moved by the heat above.

photo. 3. performances—probably with a background giving a better indication of the displacements and deformations.

perhaps use that for the splash

[6. SKILL]

Shots

From more or less far; on a *target*. This target in short *corresponds* to the vanishing point (in perspective.)

The figure thus obtained will be the projection (*through skill*) of the principal points of a 3 dim'l body.—With maximum skill, this projection would be reduced to a point (the target).

With ordinary skill this projection will be a demultiplication of the target. (Each of the new points [images of the target] will have a coefficient of displacement. This coefficient is nothing but a souvenir and can be noted conventionally (The different shots tinted from black to white according to their distance)—
In general, the figure obtained is the *visible* flattening (a stop on the way) of the demultiplied body

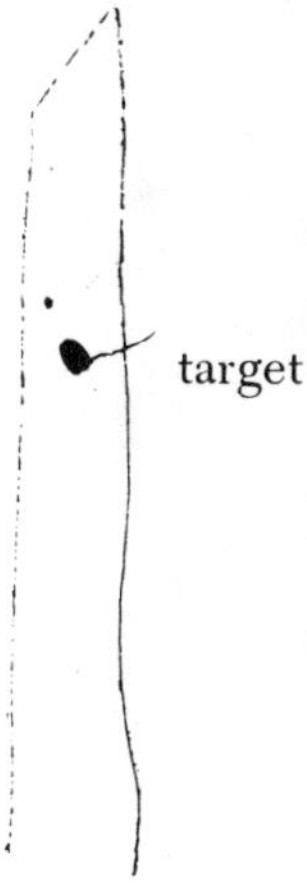

Cannon 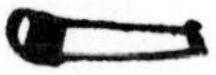 match with tip of fresh paint

Repeat this operation 9 times—3 times by 3 times from the same point

A
3 shots

B
3 shots

C
3 shots

A.B.C. are not in a plane and represent the schema of any object whatever. of the demultiplied body

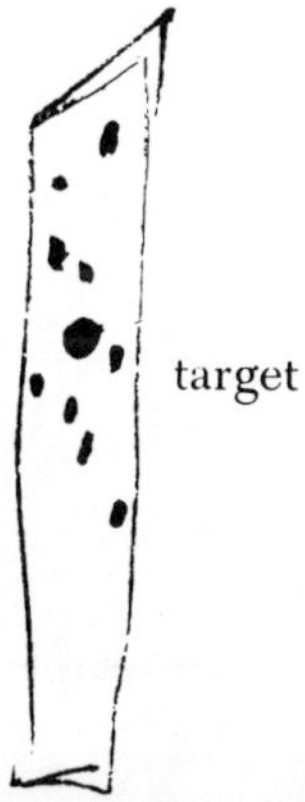

Wind—for the draft pistons
Skill—for the holes
Weight—for the standard stops
to be developed.

By perspective (or any other conventional means . . .) the lines, the drawing are *"strained."* and *lose* the nearly of the "always possible"— with moreover the irony to have *chosen* the body or original object which *inevitably becomes* according to this perspective (or other convention)

[7. TOP INSCRIPTION]

Top inscription

obtained with the draft pistons. (indicate the way to "prepare" these pistons.).

Then "place" them for a certain time. (2 to 3 months) and let them leave their imprint as 3 *nets* through which pass the commands of the pendu femelle (commands having their alphabet and terms governed by the orientation of the 3 nets [a sort of triple *"cipher"* through which the milky way supports and guides the said commands]

Next remove them so that nothing remains but their firm imprint i.e. the *form* permitting all combinations of letters sent across this said triple form, commands, orders, authorizations, etc. which must join the shots and the splash

Kind of milky way *flesh color* surrounding unevenly densely the 3 Pistons (i.e. there will be a transparent layer on the glass then the 3 Pistons then another layer of milky way) This flesh-like milky way to be used as a support for the inscription which is concerned with the cannon shots (at A)

3 Photos of a piece of white cloth-*piston of the draft;* i.e. cloth accepted and rejected by the draft.

(To avoid any play of light, make symmetrical marks, on the cloth flat before the photo in the form of points or small squares equal and at equal distances from each other [perhaps cut out]; after the photo, the group of marked squares disSymmetrically arranged, will present on a flat surface a conventional representation of the 3 *draft pistons.* May. 1915.

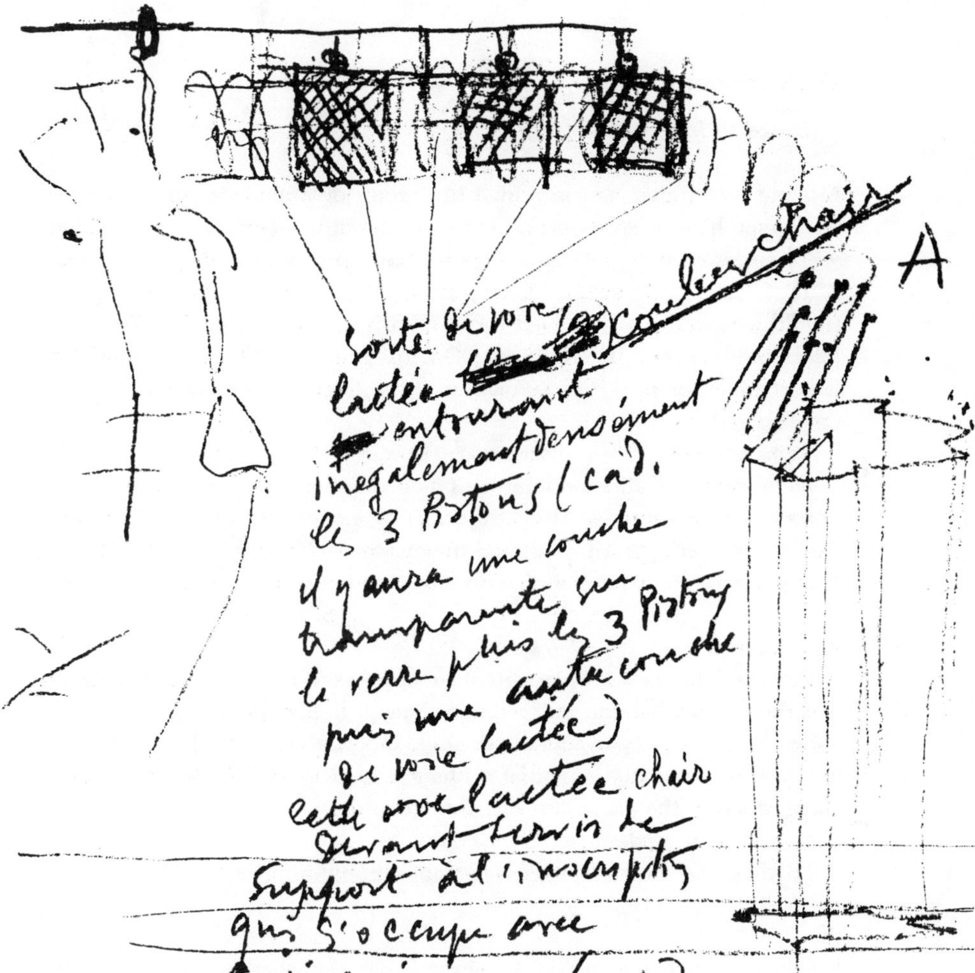
Sorte de voie
couleur chair
lactée
entourant
inégalement densément
les 3 Pistons (c.à.d.
il y aura une couche
transparente sur
le verre puis les 3 Pistons
puis une autre couche
de voie lactée)
cette voie lactée chair
devant servir de
support à l'inscription
qui s'occupe avec
les tirés du canon (en A)
A

Milky Way

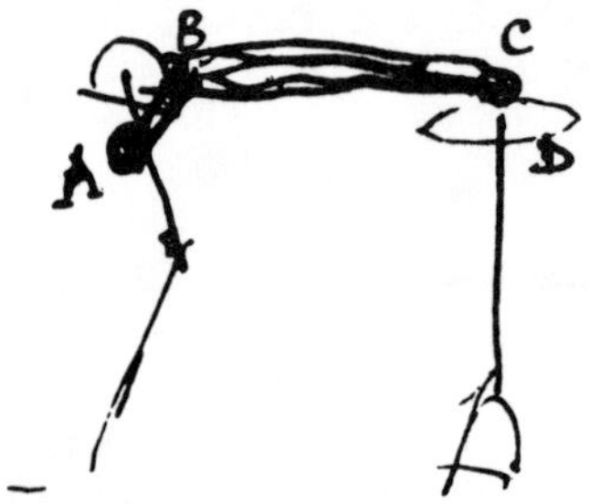

[*Blossoming*] *ABC*..

To make an *Inscription* of it
(title,).

Moving inscription. i.e. in which the group of alphabetic units. should no longer have a strict order from left to right.—each *alphabetic unit* will be present only *once* in the group ABC. and will be displaced from A to C and back again.—Since, from A towards C, the inscription should, according to the need for equilibrium of the plate D, displace a [stabilizer] (a ball or anything). On this plate D. At A. there will be [a sort of *letter box*] (alphabet) which will go towards B and C. (to develop and study)

Representation of this inscription: Photographic method

Determine the alphabetic units. (their number, form, significance. .).

represent sculpturally this inscription *in movement*. and take a snapshot. have it enlarged to the final dimensions.—With the negative of the enlargement: have prepared with silver bromide—the large plate glass and make a print. directly. on the back. (ask a photographer for information—).

Perhaps look for a way to obtain superimposed prints.—i.e. a first print —of the first alphabetic unit (for instance). hyposulphite.—make a second print of the second alphabetic unit. superimposing itself on the first. but printing only the essential without a background (the transparent background of the glass) 3rd 4th, 5th etc. units.

all that to be studied. for the execution.

(Perhaps have a *half-tone block* made. simply to print,).???

Perhaps use a less transparent (ground glass or oiled paper or varnish on the glass) allowing a provisional opacity made by the splashes from upstream and down.

[for the top "Inscription"].

blossoming. *1914*

[8. THE BRIDE]

The Bride stripped bare by the bachelors 1

2 principal elements: 1. Bride
2. Bachelors

Graphic arrangement.
a long canvas, upright.
Bride above—bachelors below.

The bach. serving as an architectonic base for the bride the latter becomes a sort of apotheosis of virginity.

—steam engine on a masonry substructure on this brick base. a solid foundation, the bachelor-machine fat lubricious—(to develop.)

At the place (still ascending) where this eroticism is revealed (which should be one of the principal cogs in the bachelor machine.

This tormented gearing gives birth to the desire-part of the machine 2
This desire-part—then alters its mechanical state—which from steam passes to the state of internal combustion engine.

(Develop the desire motor, consequence of the lubricious gearing.)

This desire motor is the last part of the bachelor machine. Far from being in direct contact with the Bride. the desire motor is separated by an air cooler. (or water).

This cooler. (graphically) to express the fact that the bride, instead of being merely an asensual icicle, warmly rejects. (not chastely) the bachelors' brusque offer this cooler will be in transparent glass. Several 3
plates of glass one above the other.,

In spite of this cooler. there is no discontinuity between the bach. machine and the Bride. But the connections. will be. *electrical.* and will thus express the stripping: an alternating process. Short circuit if necessary—

Take care of the fastening: it is necessary *to stress* the introduction of the new motor: the bride.

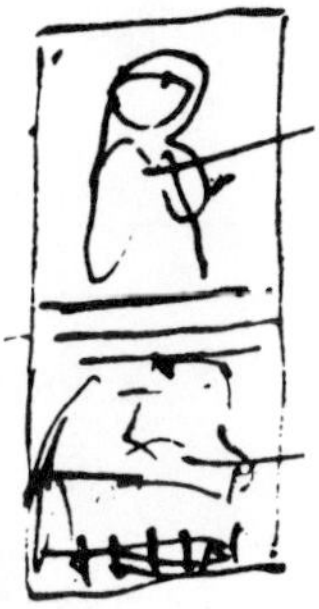

Bride.

In general, if this bride motor must appear as an apotheosis of virginity. i.e. ignorant desire. blank desire. (with a touch of malice) and if it (graphically) does not need to satisfy the laws of weighted balance. nonetheless. a shiny metal gallows could simulate the maiden's attachment to her girl friends and relatives. (the former and the latter corre- 4
sponding graphically to a solid base. on firm ground, like the masonry base of the bachelor machine. which also rests on firm ground

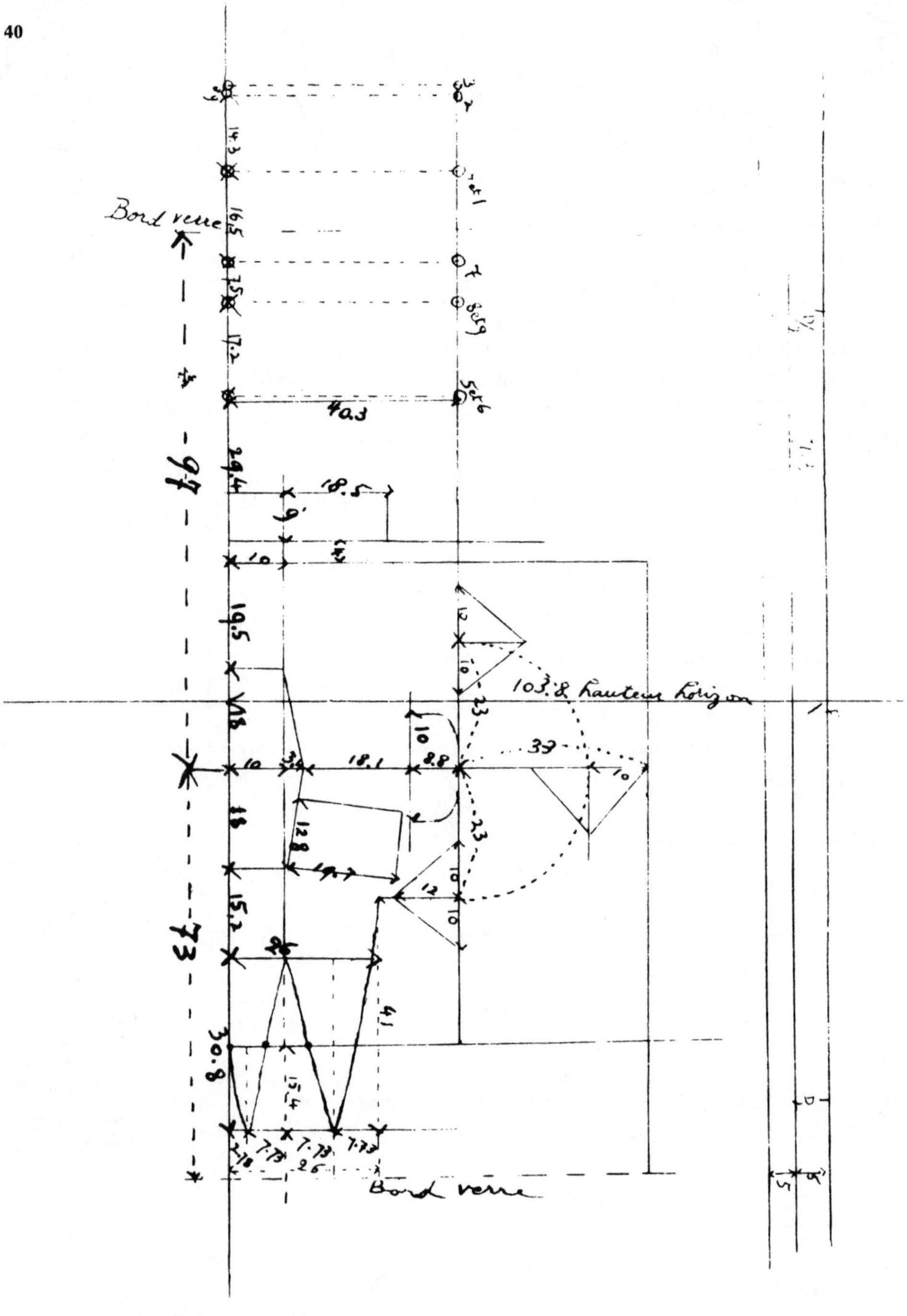

Bachelor Apparatus (Elevation)

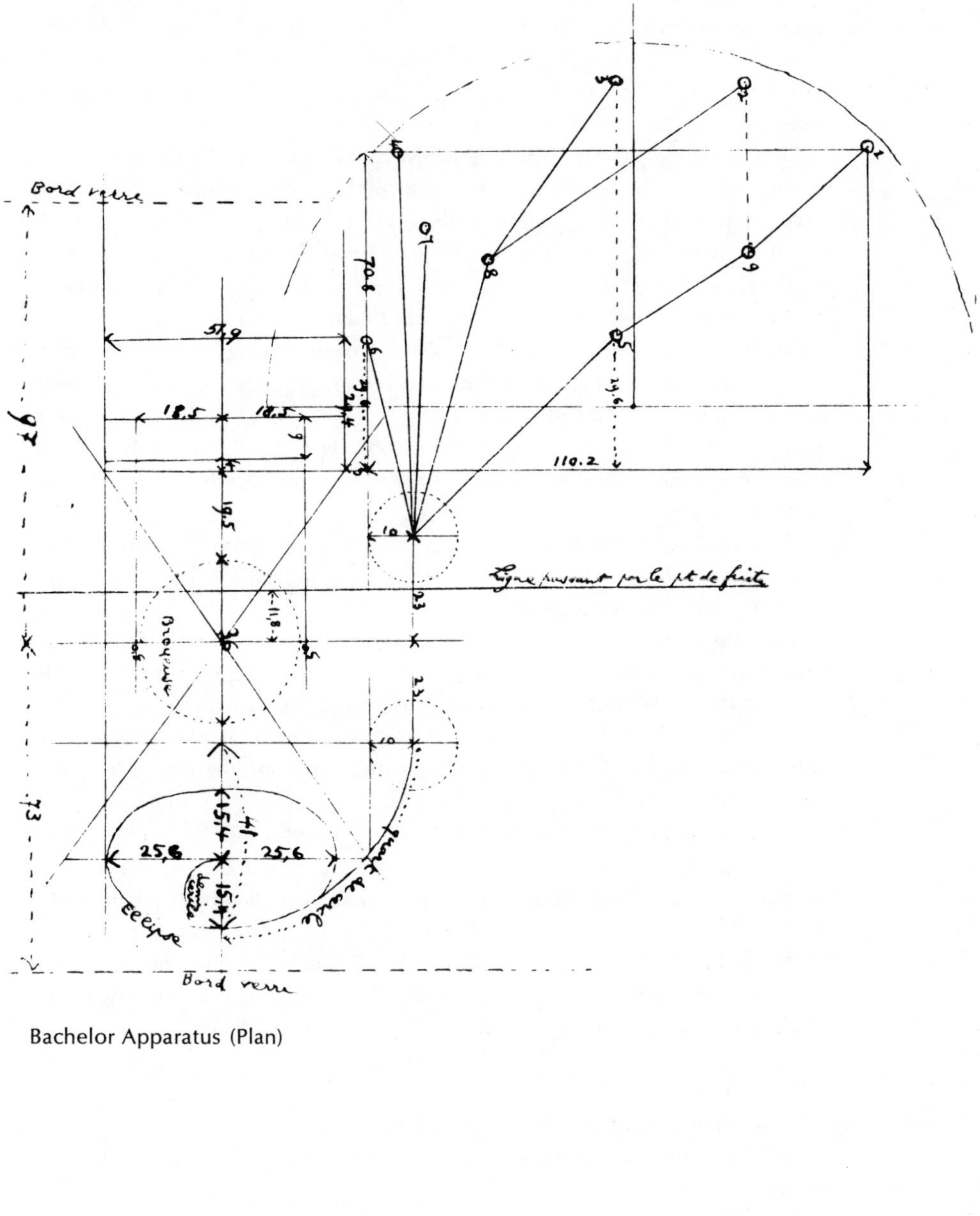

Bachelor Apparatus (Plan)

The Bride basically is a motor. But before being a motor which transmits her timid-power.—she is this very timid-power—This timid-power is a sort of automobiline, love gasoline, that, distributed to the quite feeble cylinders, within reach of the *sparks of her constant life*, is used for the blossoming of this virgin who has reached the goal of her desire—(Here the desire-gears will occupy less space than in the bachelor machine.—They are only the string that binds the bouquet.)

The whole graphic significance is for this cinematic blossoming.

5 This cinematic blossoming is controlled by the electrical stripping (see the passage of the bach. machine to the bride)

This cinematic blossoming which expresses the moment of the stripping, should be grafted on to an arbor-type of the bride. This arbor type has its roots in the desire-gears. but *the cinematic effects of the electrical stripping, transmitted* to the motor with quite feeble cylinders, leave (plastic necessity) the arbor-type at rest—(graphically, in Munich I had already made 2 studies of this arbor type) and do not touch. the desire gears. which by giving birth to the arbor type, find within this arbor type the transmission of the desire to the blossoming into stripping voluntarily imagined by the bride desiring.

This electrical stripping. sets in motion the motor with quite feeble cylinders which reveals the blossoming into stripping by the bach. in its action on the clockwork gears.

6 Grafting itself on the arbor type—the cinematic blossoming (controlled by the electrical stripping) This cinematic blossoming is the most important part of the painting. (graphically as a surface)

It is, in general, the halo of the bride, the sum total of her splendid vibrations: graphically, there is no question of symbolizing by a grandiose painting this happy goal—the bride's desire; only more clearly, in all this blossoming, the painting will be an inventory of the elements of this blossoming, elements of the sexual life imagined by her the bride-desiring. In this blossoming, The bride reveals herself nude in 2 appearances: the first, that of the stripping by the bachelors. the second appearance that voluntary-imaginative one of the bride. On the coupling of these 2 appearances of pure virginity—On their collision, depends the whole blossoming, the upper part and crown of the picture.

Thus

7 Develop graphically

1st the blossoming into the stripping by the bach

2nd the blossoming. into the imaginative stripping by the bride-desiring.

3rd From the 2 graphic developments obtained find their conciliation. which should be the "blossoming" without causal distinction.

Mixture, physical compound of the 2 causes (bach. and imaginative desire) unanalyzable by logic.

THE BRIDE'S VEIL

The last state of this nude bride before the orgasm which may (might) bring about her fall graphically, the need to express in a completely different way from the rest of the painting, this blossoming.

1st *Blossoming into the stripping by bach.*

Electrical control

This blossoming-effect of the electrical stripping should, graphically, end in the clockwork movement (electrical clocks in railway stations) Gearwheels, cogs, etc (develop expressing indeed the throbbing jerk of the minute hand. 8

The whole in mat metal—(fine copper, steel silver,

2nd Blossoming as stripping voluntarily imagined by the bride-desiring.

This blossoming should be the refined development of the arbor type.

It is born, as boughs on this arbor type.

Boughs frosted in nickel. and platinum. As it gradually leaves the arbor, this blossoming is the image of a motor car, climbing a slope in low gear. (The car wants more and more to reach the top, and while slowly accelerating, as if exhausted by hope, the motor of the car turns over faster and faster, until it roars triumphantly.

3rd Blossoming-crown (Composed of the 2 preceding). 9

The 1st blossoming. is attached to the motor with quite feeble cylinders.

The 2nd to the arbor-type, of which it is the cinematic development.

The arbor type—has its roots in the desire-gear, a constituent, skeletal part of the bride.

The motor with quite feeble cylinders is a superficial organ of the bride; it is activated by the love gasoline, a secretion of the bride's sexual glands and by the electric sparks of the stripping. (to show that the bride does not refuse this stripping by the bachelors, even accepts it since she furnishes the love gasoline and goes so far as to help towards complete nudity by developing in a sparkling fashion her intense desire for the orgasm.

Thus the motor with quite feeble cylinders a constituent but superfi- 10
cial organ of the bride, is the 2 foci of the blossoming ellipse. (the 1st focus the center of the blossoming into stripping by the bach. 2nd focus, center of the voluntarily imagined blossoming into stripping of the bride. 2nd focus, actuating the desire gears (the skeletal part of the bride) giving birth to the arbor type etc.

The Bride. skeleton.

The bride, at her base, is a reservoir of love gasoline. (or timid-power). This timid-power, distributed to the motor with quite feeble cylinders,

II in contact with the sparks of her constant life (desire-magneto) explodes and makes this virgin blossom who has attained her desire.

Besides the sparks of the desire-magneto, the artificial sparks which are produced by the electrical stripping should supply explosions in the motor with quite feeble cylinders.

Hence, this motor with quite feeble cylinders has 2 strokes. The 1st stroke (sparks of the desire-magneto) controls the immobile arbor type. This arbor-type is a kind of spinal column and should be the support for the blossoming into the bride's voluntary stripping. The 2nd stroke (artificial sparks of the electrical stripping) controls the clockwork machinery, graphic translation of the blossoming into stripping by the bachelors. (expressing the throbbing jerk of the minute hand on electric clocks.)

III The bride accepts this stripping by the bachelors, since she supplies the love gasoline to the sparks of this electrical stripping; moreover, she furthers her complete nudity by adding to the 1st focus of sparks (electrical stripping) the 2nd focus of sparks of the desire-magneto.

Blossoming

The Bride stripped bare by her bachelors, even

—Agricultural machine—
—(a world in yellow)—
preferably in the text
?

In reply to your esteemed letter of the . . . inst. I have the honor . . .
M. Duchamp 1913. [this business] has much to offer . . .
not on the title page

Apparatus
instrument for farming

The *principal forms* of the bachelor machine are imperfect: rectangle, circle, parallelepiped, symmetrical handle, demi-sphere = i.e. they are mensurable (relation of their dimensions among themselves. and relation of these principal forms to their destination in the bachelor mach.) In the bride, the *principal forms* are *more or less large or* small, have no longer, in relation to their destination a mensurability: a sphere, in the bride will be of some radius or other (the radius given in the representation is fictitious and dotted.)

Similarly and better in the Pendu femelle and the [wasp], parabolas hyperbolas (or volumes deriving from them) will lose all character of mensurable position. The actual representation will be but one *example* of each of these *principal freed forms.* (an example without representational value, but *permitting the more or less*).

The pulse needle in addition to its vibratory mvt. is mounted on a wandering leash. It has the liberty of caged animals—on condition that it will provide (by its vibratory mvt. actuating the sex cylinder) the ventilation on the pole [at the drum]. This pulse needle will thus promenade in balance the sex cylinder which spits at the drum the dew which is to nourish the vessels of the filament paste and at the same time imparts to the Pendu its swinging in relation to the 4 cardinal pnts.
Wasp = Properties:

1st *Secretion* of love gasoline by osmosis

2nd *Flair* or the sense which receives *the waves* of *unbalance from the black ball* In relation to the Pendu's *upper part* (which distributes the orders of new balance to each of the poles.)

3rd Vibratory property determining the pulsations of the needle.

4th Ventilation. determining the swinging *to and fro* of *the pendu with its accessories.*

Reservoir.—concerning the nourishment layer of the wasp.

The reservoir will end at the bottom with a liquid layer from which the sex wasp will take the necessary dose to sprinkle the drum and to nourish the filament substance. This liquid layer will be contained in the oscillating bathtub (hygiene of the bride.)

Sex Cylinder—(*Wasp*).

Ventilation: Start from an interior *draft*—

~~the pulse~~ needle should ~~have its source in the life center.~~ of the bride. (The bride ~~has a life center~~—the bachelors have not. They live on coal ~~or other~~ raw material drawn not from them ~~but from their not them.~~

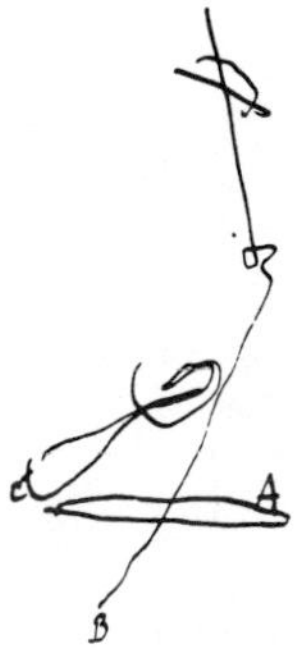

B and C (as they sway.) just. strike the circle A. B below, C above—The above and the below. should be used in the decisions or inscriptions transmitted through the draft pistons.

[9. THE PENDU FEMELLE]

The Pendu femelle is the form in *ordinary perspective* of a Pendu femelle for which one could perhaps try to discover the true form—

This comes from the fact that any form is the perspective of another form according to a certain *vanishing point* and a certain *distance*

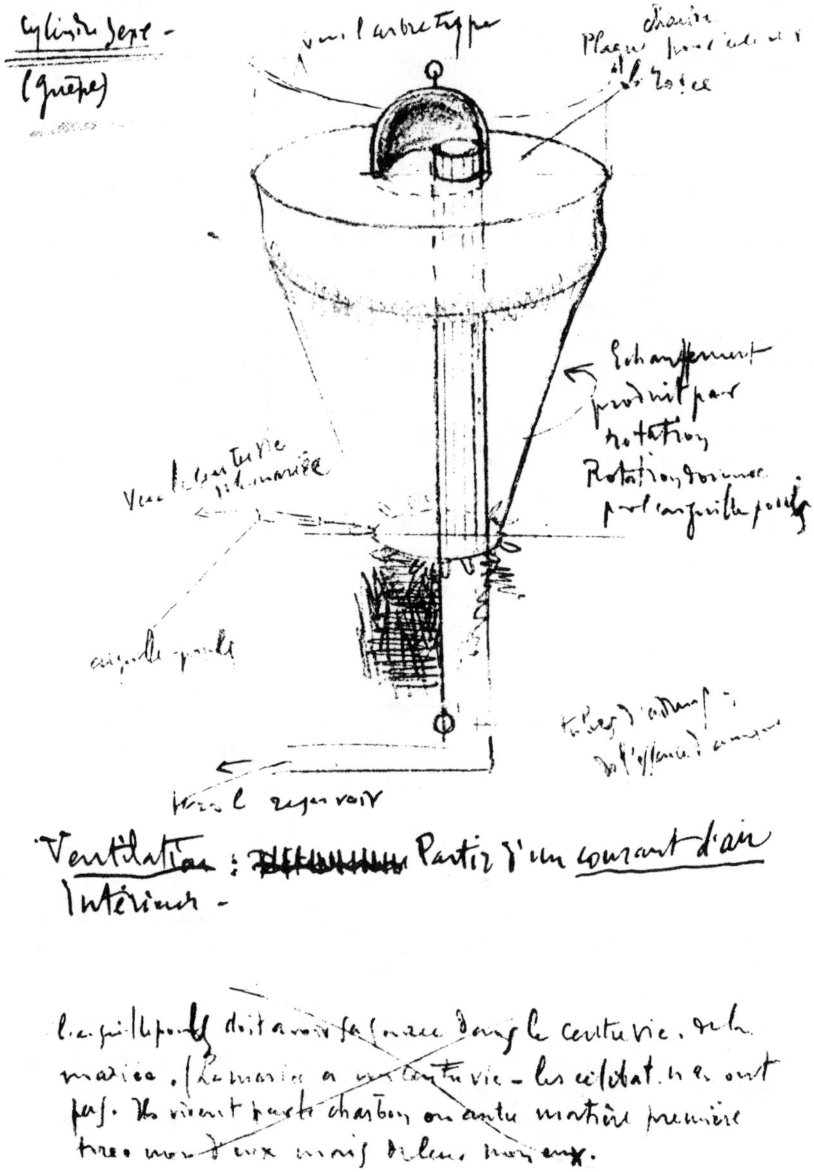

Wasp, or Sex Cylinder

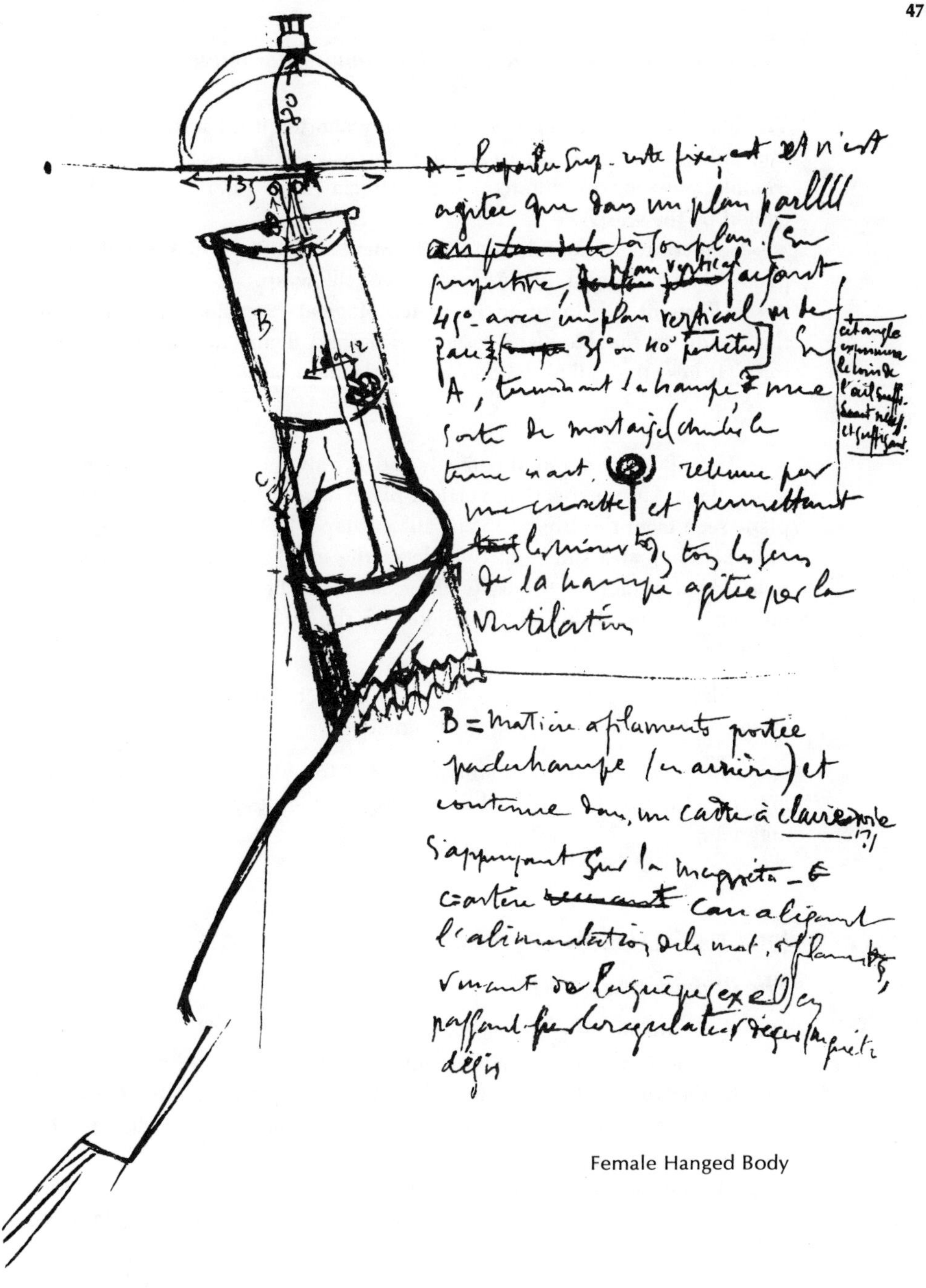

Female Hanged Body

In the Pendu; femelle—and the blossoming Barometer.

The filament substance might lengthen or shorten itself in response to an *atmospheric pressure* organized by the wasp. (filament substance *extremely sensitive* to differences of artificial atmospheric pressure controlled by the wasp).

—Isolated cage—containing the filament subst. in which would take place—the storms and the fine weathers of the wasp.

the filament substance in its meteorological extension (part relating the pendu *to the handler*) resembles a solid flame, i.e. having a solid force. It licks the ball of the handler displacing it as it pleases

A = The upper part remains fixed; and is only moved in a plane parllll to its plane. [In perspective, vertical plane at a 45° angle with a vertical plane seen from the front (35° or 40° perhaps)] [This angle will express the necessary and sufficient twinkle of the eye.] At A, terminating the pole a kind of mortice (look for the exact term, held by a bowl and permitting movement in all directions of the pole agitated by the air currents

B = Filament substance carried by the pole (behind) and contained in an *open* (?) frame resting on the magneto—

C = artery channeling the nourishment of the filament substance, coming from the sex wasp (?) while passing by the desire regulator (desire magneto

[10. THE ILLUMINATING GAS]

***The illuminating gas* (I)**

after the malic moulds: (*malic forms*)

From the top of each malic mould. the gas passes along the unit of length in a *tube of elemental section.* and, by the *phenomenon of stretching in the unit of length* the gas finds itself [congealed] solidified in the form of elemental rods.

Each of these rods, under the pressure of the gas in the malic moulds, leaves its tube and breaks, through fragility, into unequal *spangles. lighter than air.* (retail fog)

(graphically: 8 horizontal tubes—elemental section to be studied etc.)

to develop this relationship of one *length* to the *change of condition* of the body (illum. gas) submitted to this unit of length.

in the case of *stretching*, the unit of length is variable in relation to the *section* of the tube. Given the unit of length with an element. section the tubes with a double section will have a length twice (Playful Physics) the standard of the element. sect. (this to give importance not to the unit of length but to the phenomenon of *stretching* the gas.)

Exit of the spangles:
The gas cut thus in bits, each spangle, retaining in its smallest parts the *malic tint.* liberated at the mouth of the tubes, tends to rise.

The spangles are stopped (parasol *Trap*) in their ascent by the 1st parasol (sieve.) (see note on the *Trap.*)

The sieves (6 probably) are semi-spherical parasols, with holes. [The holes of the sieves parasols should give in the *shape of a globe* the *figure* of the 8 malic moulds, *given* schematic. by the 8 summits (polygon concave plane). by subsidized symmetry].

Orientation of the parasols:
The 1st is horizontal, and receives the spangles as they leave the tubes. If one joins the centers of the parasols with a line one obtains a half circumference from A to B.

the Network of Standard stops

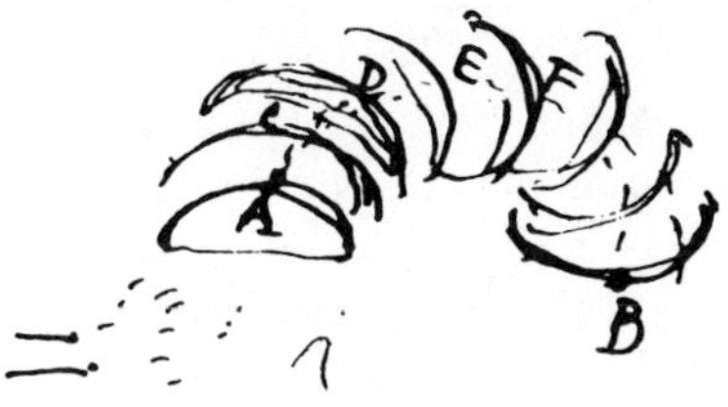

As in a Derby, the spangles pass through the parasols A,C D.EF . . . B. and as they gradually arrive at D,E,F, . . . etc. they are *straightened out* i.e. they lose their sense of up and down ([more precise term]).— The group of these parasols forms a sort of *labyrinth of the 3 directions.*—

The spangles dazed by this progressive turning. imperceptibly lose [*provisionally* they will find it again later] their *designation* of left, right, up, down, etc, lose their awareness of position.

The parasols. thus *straighten out* the spangles which, on leaving the tubes were free and wished to rise.

They *straighten them out* like a sheet of paper rolled up too much which one unrolls several times in the opposite direction.

to the point that: necessarily there is a change of condition in the spangles. They can no longer *retain their individuality* and they all *join* together after B.

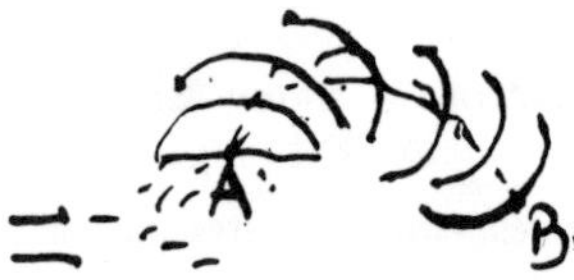

***The illuminating gas* (II).**

After B.

—change in the condition of the spangles.—

From their *dizziness* [provisional], from their *loss* of awareness of position, *obtained* by successive passing through the sieves and imperceptible change of direction of these sieves (change of direction of which the terminations are A and B), the spangles [dissolve]; the spangles splash themselves each to itself, i.e. change (little by little through the last sieves) their condition *from: spangles lighter than air, of a certain length, of elemental* thickness with a determination to rise, *into:* a liquid elemental scattering, seeking no direction, a *scattered suspension* on their way out at B, Vapor of inertia, snow. but keeping its liquid *character* through instinct for cohesion (the only manifestation of the *individuality* (so reduced!!) of the illuminating gas in its habitual games with conventional surroundings.

What a drip!

Ventilator—*Churn.* (perhaps give it a butterfly form

sediment of the inert illuminating gas in a dense liquid preserving the exterior qualities of the dissolved spangles—putting up a front (before this Ventilator) by exaggerating the cohesion.—by turning, the ventilator forces the gas to attach itself at ab, cd, ef. etc. in a condition resembling glycerine mixed with water. to be crossed out

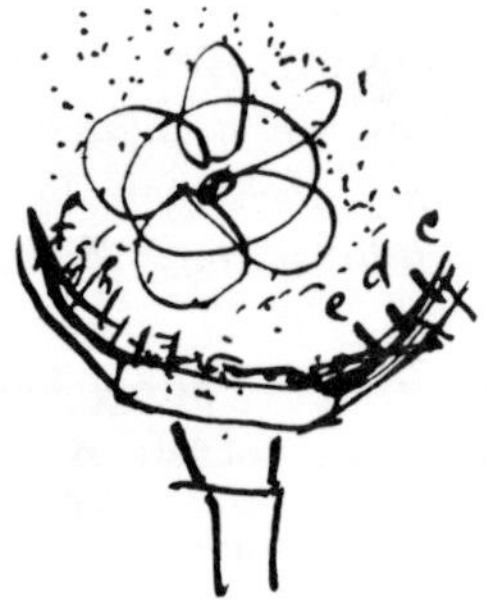

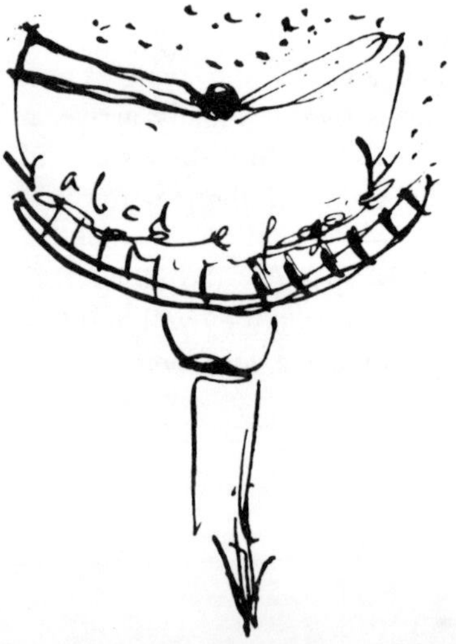

—Improvement of the [illuminating] gas to the slopes.—

—as a *"Commentary"* on the section Slopes. = have a photograph made of: *to have the apprentice in the sun*

[11. MALIC MOULDS]

Given the illuminating gas. Progress (improvement) of the illuminating gas up to the planes of flow

Malique moulds. (*Malic* (?))

By eros' matrix, we understand the group of ^{8} uniforms or hollow
receive the
liveries destined to give to the illuminating gas which takes 8 malic forms (gendarme, cuirassier etc.)

The gas *castings* so obtained, would hear the litanies sung by the chariot, refrain of the whole celibate machine, But *they* will never be able *to pass beyond the Mask* = They would have been as if enveloped, alongside their regrets, by a mirror reflecting back to them their own complexity to the point of their being hallucinated rather onanistically. (Cemetery of ^{8} uniforms or liveries)

Each of the 8 malic forms is *built* above and below a common horizontal plane, the plane of sex cutting them at the pnt. of sex. (refer to figure)

or

Each of the 8 malic forms is cut by an imaginary horizontal plane at a pnt. called the pnt. of sex.

Nine Malic Moulds, 1914-15

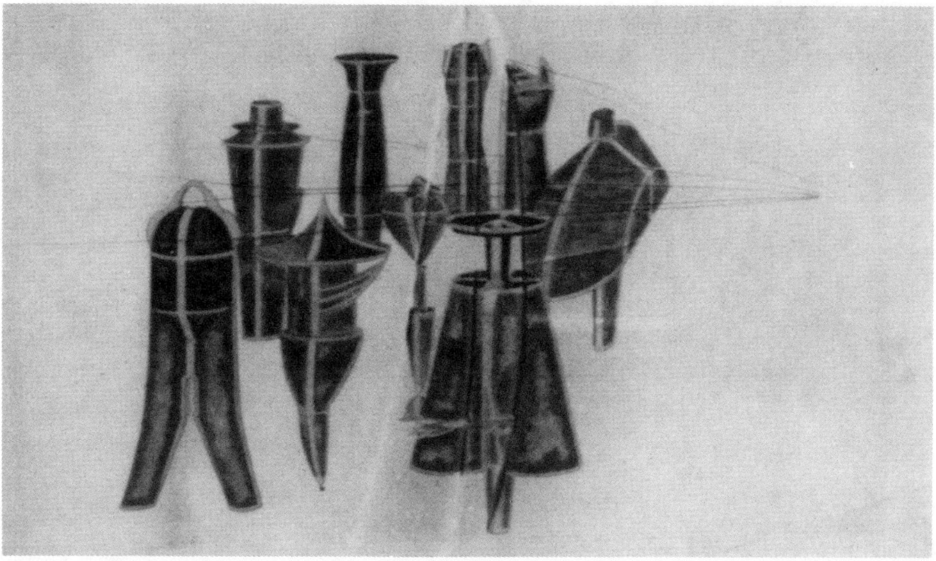

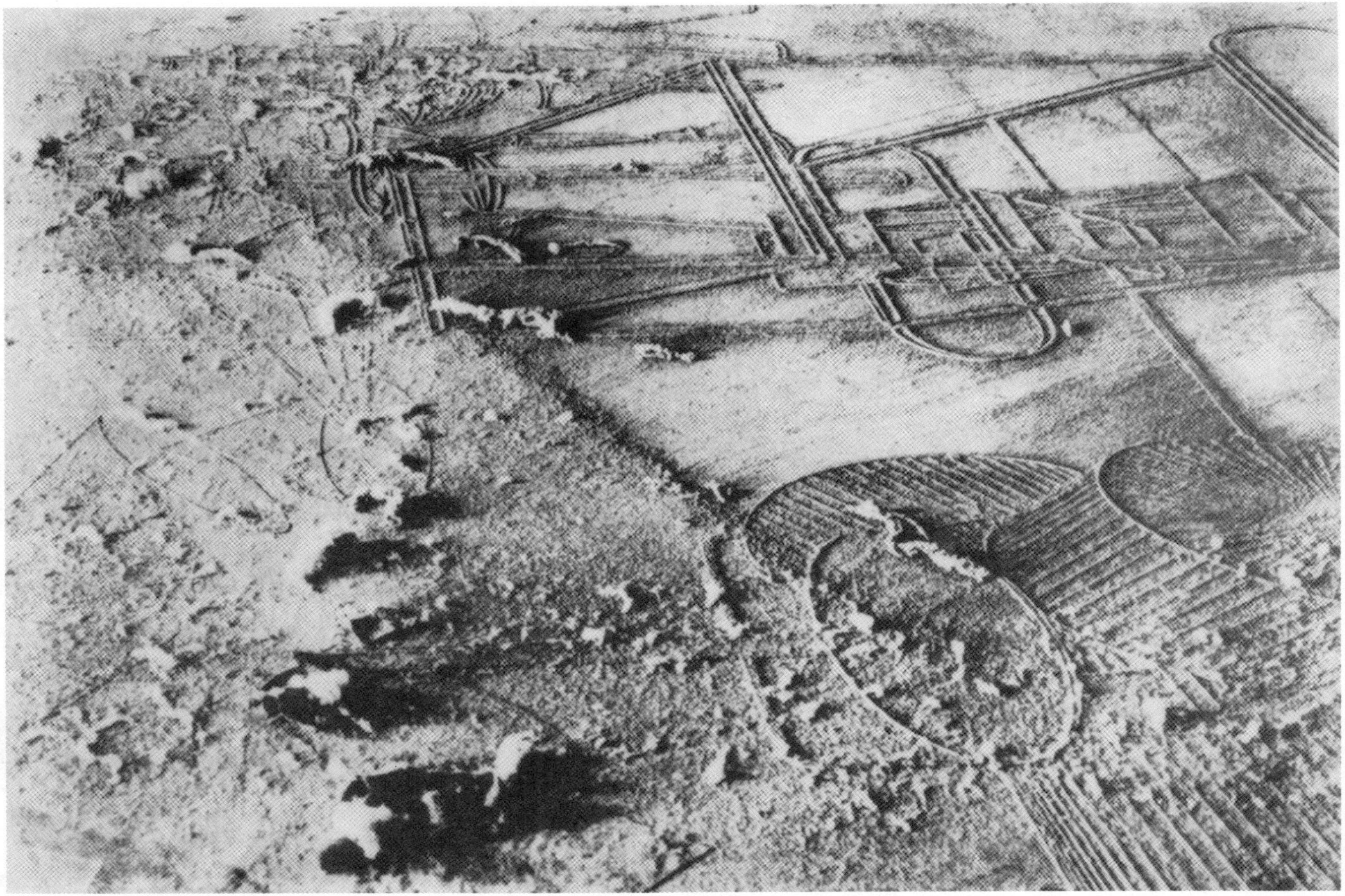

Dust Breeding. Photograph by Man Ray and Marcel Duchamp. The caption for this photograph, when it appeared in *Littérature,* no. 5, Oct. 1, 1922, was: "Behold the domain of Rrose Sélavy/How arid it is—How fertile—How joyous—How sad!" [Trans. E. P.]

Progress (improvement of the illuminating gas up to the planes of flow. (continued) the 24 capillary tubes

A *Each* malic form terminates at the head in 3 capillary tubes, the 24 therefore were supposed to *cut the gas in bits* and would have led it to disguise itself as 24 fine solid needles so that they will bcome when reunited once again in the 2 demisiphons, a fog made of a thousand spangles of frosty gas.

B At the head, [at the summit], of each malic mould 3 capillary tubes, *24 in all:* to cut the gas in bits, to cut *the gas* in long needles *already* solid, since before becoming an explosive liquid, *it* takes the form of a fog of solid spangles of frosty gas, all this by the phenomenon of *stretching in the unit of length*

When the 2 demisiphons (letter in fig.) would have been filled with the fog of spangles which are lighter than air, the operation of the liquification of the gas began through the sieve and the horizontal filter: each spangle of solid gas strives (in a kind of spangle derby) *to pass* the holes of the sieve with élan, reacting already to the suction of the pump.

[12. DUST BREEDING]

To raise dust on Dust-Glasses for 4 months. 6 months. which you close up afterwards hermetically = Transparency

—Differences. to be worked out

For the sieves in the glass—allow dust to fall on this part a dust of 3 or 4 months and wipe well around it in such a way that this dust will be a kind of color (transparent pastel) *Use of mica*

Also try to find several layers of transparent colors (probably with varnish) one above the other. the whole on glass.—

To be mentioned the quality of *the other side of the dust* either as the name of the metal or otherwise

[13. THE SIEVES]

After the 9 malic forms:

The sieves.

The *sieves* of the bachelor apparatus are a *reversed image* of *porosity.*

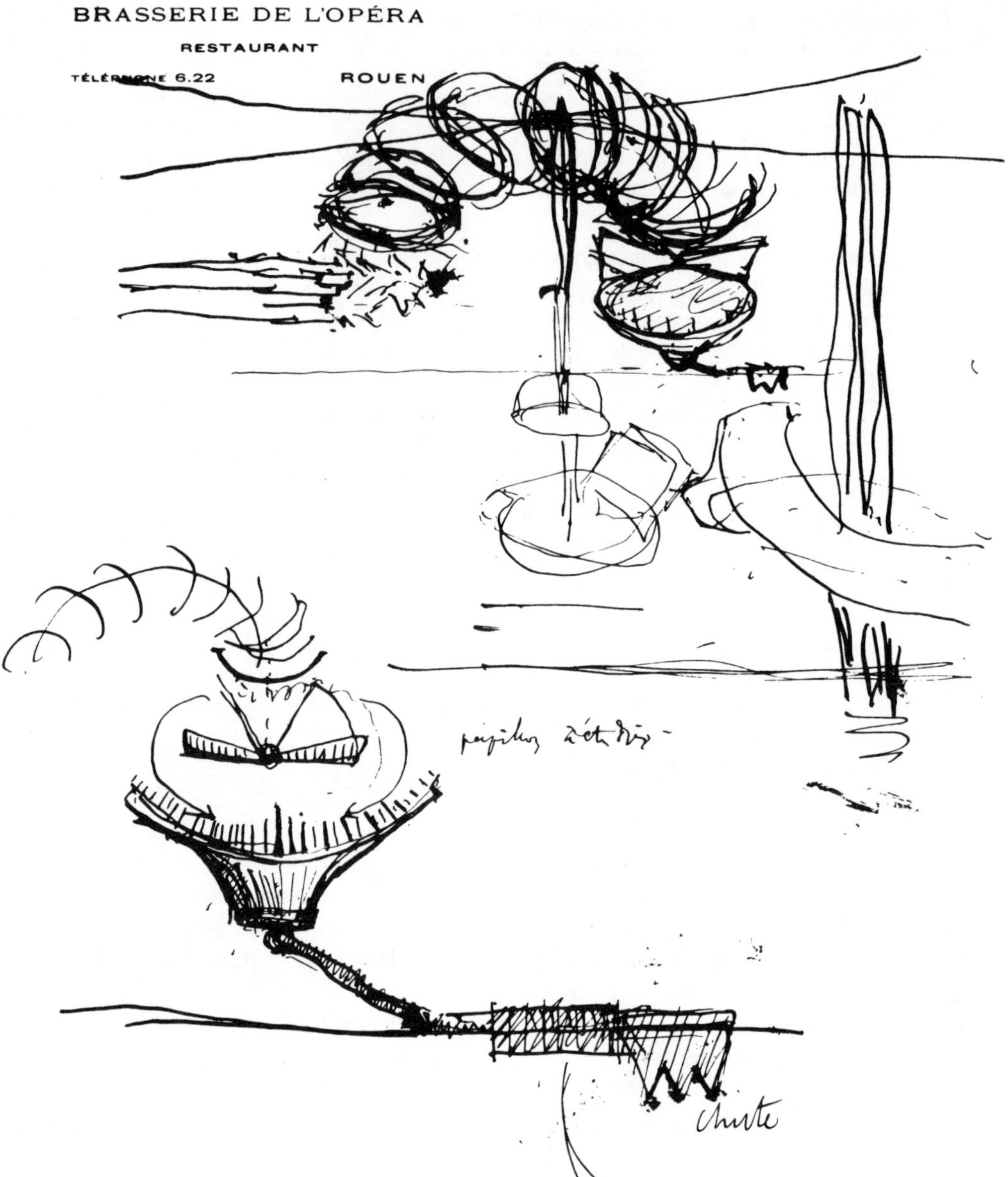

Sieves and Detail of the Butterfly Pump

the figures between parenthesis indicate the measures *not transposed* by the perspective.→ $\frac{D}{2}$ = 14 cm. 2.6

For the perspective construction of the intermediate circles A and B: SR given by division by 3 of the circumferences.—VT *parll.* to SR. *absol.*ʸ

perhaps form of funnels (*roofing and fish scales*).

All the numbers to divide by 2 to have the size of 1/10

see large final drawing made at Yport 1914.

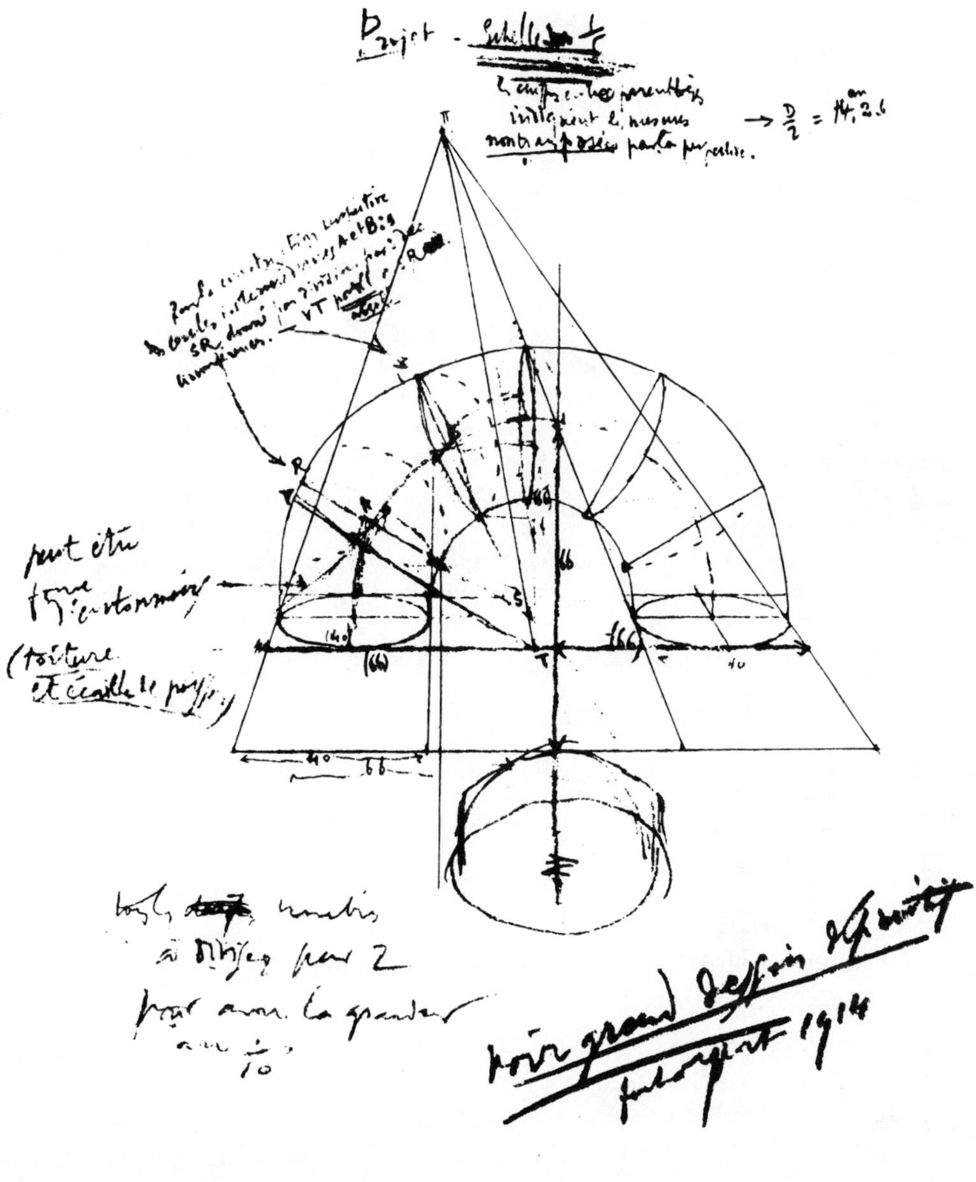

[14. CHARIOT]

~~*Chariot*~~ *Sleigh—Glider*

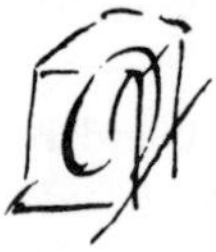

the litanies of the Chariot:
Slow life.
Vicious circle.
Onanism.
Horizontal.
round trip for the buffer.
Junk of life.
Cheap construction.
Tin, cords, iron wire.
Eccentric wooden pulleys.
Monotonous fly wheel.
Beer professor. (to be entirely redone).

draw the scheme of the chariot
The Chariot should be made of rods of *emancipated metal;* the chariot would have the property of giving itself without resistance of gravity to a force acting *horizontally* upon it. (see the fall of the weight, in the form of a bottle of Benedictine)

The sleigh mounted on runners dovetailed into an underground. rail, after having been drawn from A to B. returns to its 1st position by the phen. of *inversion of friction.* Principle: friction reintegrated The friction of the runner on the rail [instead of changing into heat] is transformed into a returning force equal to the going force. (This phen. in relation to the emancipation of the metal which forms the body of the rods of the sleigh

~~*Chariot*~~*—Sleigh—Glider*

Exposé of the Chariot (in the text = litanies of the chariot)
–Slow life–
–Vicious circle–
–Onanism–
–Horizontal–
–Buffer of life
–Bach. life regarded as an alternating rebounding on this buffer.
–Rebounding = junk of life

—Cheap construction
—Tin
—Cords
—Iron wire
—Crude wooden pulleys
—Eccentrics
—Monotonous fly wheel

Buffer of life = stopping the action not by brutal opposition but by extended springs slowly resuming their first position.

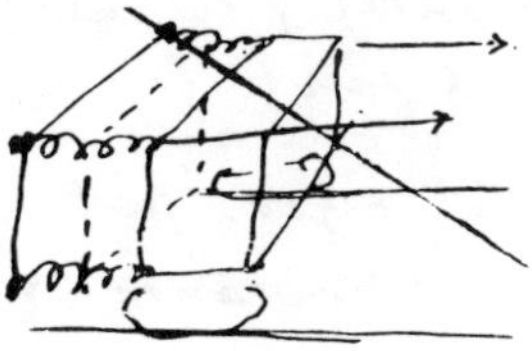

The metal or (material)—of the chariot is *emancipated.* i.e: that it has a weight but a force acting horizontally on the chariot does not have to support this weight (the *weight* of the metal does not *impede* a horizontal traction (to be developed)). The chariot is *emancipated horizontally.* it is free of all gravity in the horizontal plane (property of the metal of the rods which compose the chariot)

These rods are of this shape:

square section 1 cm section across the center
ordinary type. (size apparent on the final version

Color: yellow green. (like the queen in the King and Queen . . .) (Light cadmium and white) See also: for this color the Munich notes on the composition of the colors in the first studies.

The chariot is supported by runners which slide (oil etc.) in a groove
the cord, which has to pull the chariot under the blow of the bottle weight, is attached at A to the runner by a temporary knot.
Interior multiplication of the mvt. of the mill wheel *to obtain speed.*
Projection of the chariot
length = to the drop of the bottle weight at *o*
Behind (at the left of the picture) the chariot is brought back into position by the Sandow.
In the picture the sandows will be at rest (*almost relaxed*)
axle of the mill wheel
Hook
Cord pulling the chariot

le métal ou (matière) du chariot est ~~émancipé~~. c.à.d. qu'il a un poids mais qu'une force agissant horizontalement sur le chariot n'a pas à supporter ce poids (le poids du métal ne s'oppose pas à une traction horizontale développée) le chariot est émancipé horizontalement. il est libre de ~~toute~~ pesanteur dans le plan horizontal (propriété du métal des tiges qui composent le chariot)

Ces tiges sont de forme : 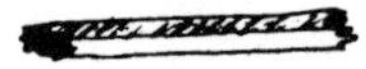

Section carrée 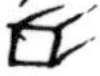

type courant.

plus [illegible] section [illegible] carrée. [illegible]

Couleur : jaune vert. (comme la reine du Roi et la Reine . . . .) (cadmium clair et blanc)

voir aussi pour cette couleur les notes de munich sur la composition des couleurs des premières études.

Le chariot est supporté par des patins qui glissent (huile etc.) dans une gouttière

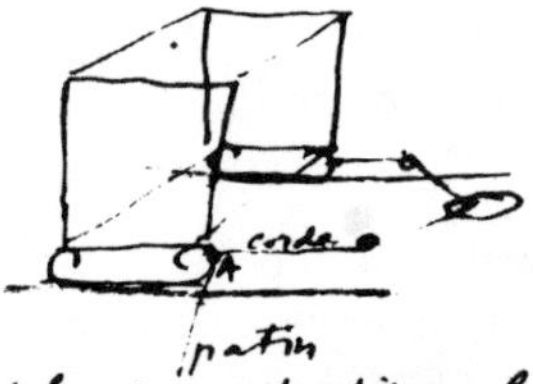

La corde, devant tirer le chariot sous le coup du poids bouteille, s'attache en A au patin par un nœud provisoire.

Multiplication intérieure

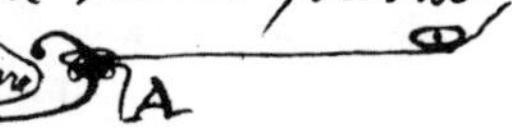

retour de la roue du moulin pour obtenir rotage

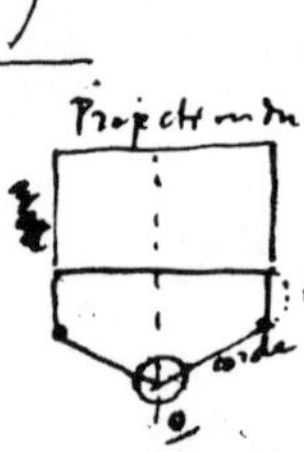

En arrière (à gauche du tableau) le chariot est ramené en position par le Sandow.

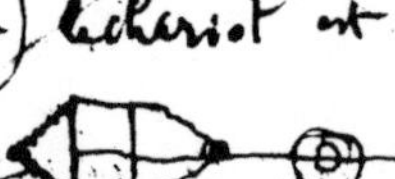

Dans le tableau les Sandows seront au repos. (presque détendus)

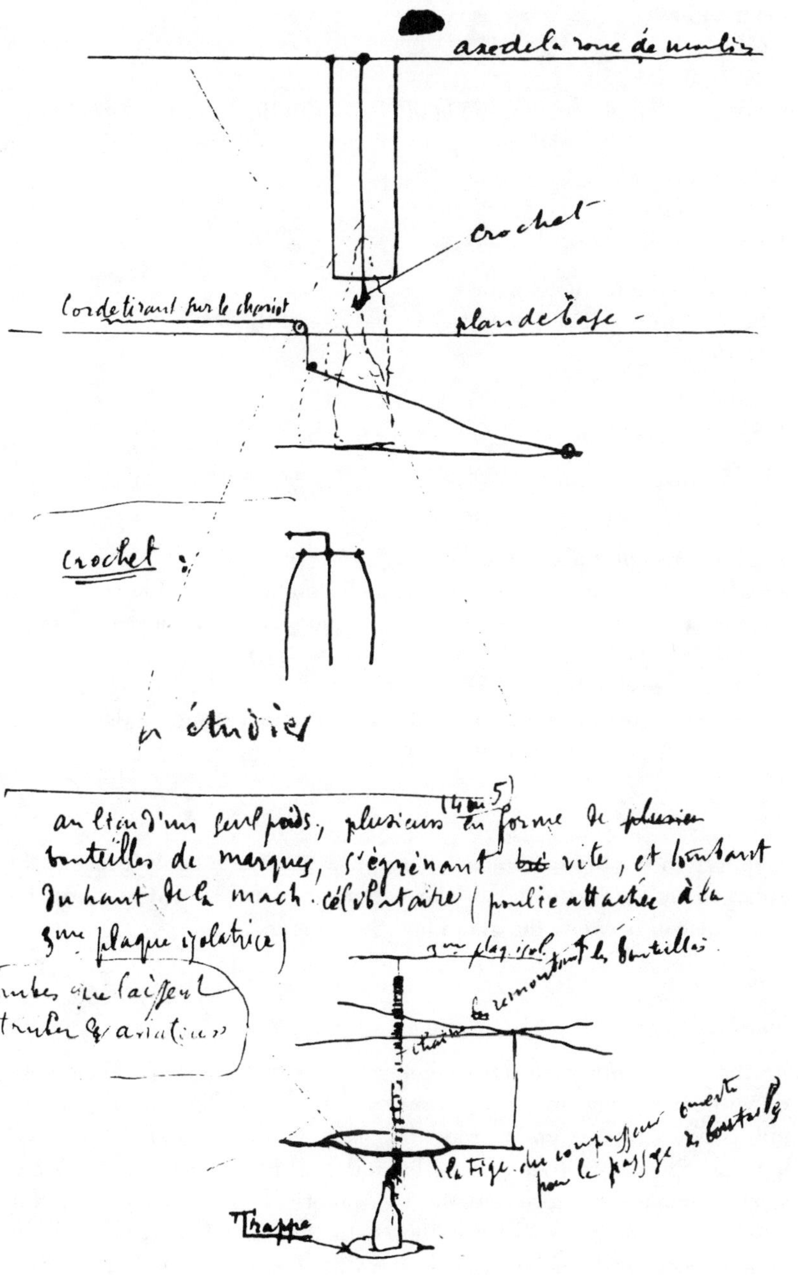
axe de la roue de moulin
crochet
corde tirant sur le chariot
plan de base
crochet :
à étudier
au lieu d'un seul poids, plusieurs (4 ou 5) en forme de plusieurs bouteilles de marques, s'égrénant très vite, et tombant du haut de la mach. célibataire (poulie attachée à la 2me plaque isolatrice)
2me plaq. isol.
remontant les bouteilles
chaîne
la tige du compresseur ouverte pour le passage des bouteilles
Trappe

Chariot

plane of base
Hook:
to be studied
instead of a single weight., several (*4 or 5*) in the form of brand bottles, dropping quickly, and falling from the top of the Bachelor Mach. (pulley attached to the 3rd isolating plate)
3rd isol. plate
bombs which aviators let fall

—chain raising the bottles.
—the compressor rod opened for the passage of the bottles
Trapdoor

[15. WEIGHT]

[*More simply*]*:*

the glider goes and comes.
It goes: a weight falls and makes it go
It comes: By friction of the runners the metal of the glider responds elastically i.e. the glider resumes a little more slowly its first position, as it sends back in the air the *weight.* und so weiter.
By condescension, this weight is denser going down than going up
[find a concrete object which could respond to this changing density]

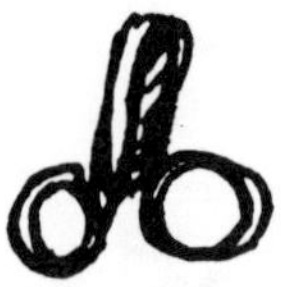

hook

falling from the top of the bachelor apparatus take a hook—considerably enlarged. and functioning in the basement—which it enters through 2 holes. placed between the glider and the grinder

hook

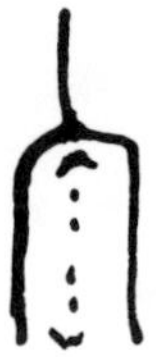

At the top of the glass (from below) = a sort of fork [heavier going down than coming up (*so as to save the power of the waterfall*)] must fall astride the axle going from the glider to the grinder. This fork is high enough not to touch this (this fork will be an ordinary hook considerably enlarged) axle and the two points of the fork will penetrate into the basement through two holes—In this basement it actuates the glider by its fall It makes it come towards the grinder. and at the same time opens the scissors.

It rises again to the top by means of the chain engaged on the axle of the water mill. which turns a sprocket with

(A an increased gear ratio so that it goes faster.
B fork

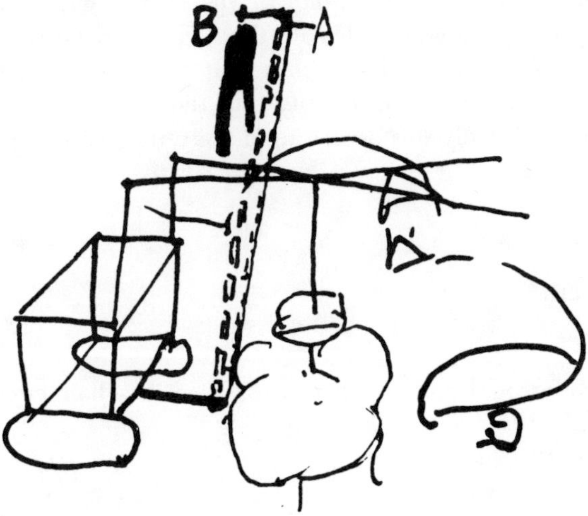

the Hook which falls between Grinder and Glider and which makes the glider glide, Is made of a substance of *oscillating density*. This hook therefore has an indeterminate, variable, and uncontrollable weight.— It is by this oscillating density that the choice is made between the 3 crashes: according to the strength of the fall of the hook the decelerations or accelerations (caused by the continual changes of density,) the right is chosen rather than the left or alternatively or the center.

Bottle of ~~Benedictine as a form~~ of the Weight.

4 Weights in the form of Brand bottles.
The chariot should, while reciting its litanies, go from A to B. and return *fig.*
from B to A. at a *jerky* pace; it appears in the *costume of Emancipation, hiding in its bosom the landscape of the water mill,* *paragraph*

It necessarily follows that a lead weight in the form of a bottle of Benedictine acting normally on a system of cords attached to the chariot, would force it to come from A to B. much too far-fetched

The springs x and x' . . . . restore it immediately afterwards to its initial position (A).

Song: of the revolution of the bottle of Bened.

—After having *pulled* the chariot by its fall, the bottle of Benedictine lets itself be raised by the hook C; it falls asleep as it goes up; the dead point wakes it up suddenly and with its head down. It pirouettes and, falls vertically according to the laws of gravity.

Molecular or (Body) composition of the bottles with lead bottoms, *such* that it is impossible to calculate their weight. = Great density and in perpetual mvt. not at all fixed like that of metals (Oscillating density). It is by this oscillating density that the choice is made between the 3 crashes It is truly this oscillating density that expresses the liberty of indiff.

[16. WATERFALL]

Waterfall.

A sort of waterspout coming from a distance in a half circle over the malic moulds

(seen from the side)

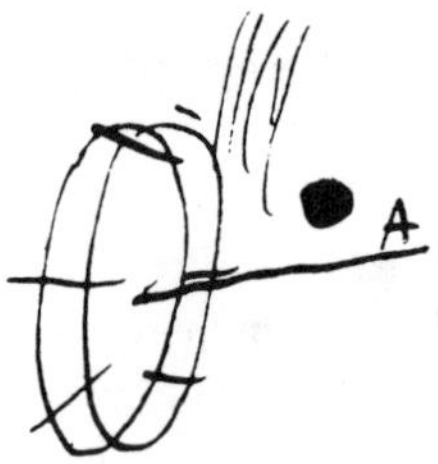

Water Mill (landscape—).

Given the waterfall

Draw it full size—
A ≡ *axis* of the wheel *which* should drag the bottle of Benedictine.
the bottles

Speed of the mill wheel

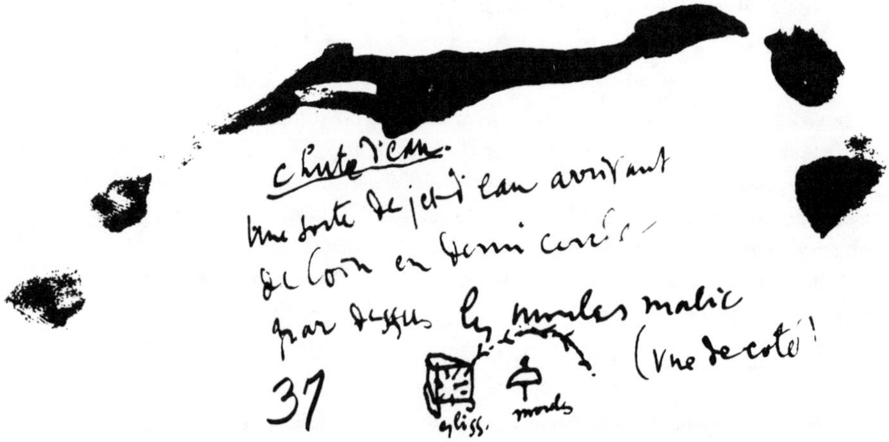

[17. SPLASH]

after the 3 crashes =
Splash. and not vertical channeling of the encounter at the bottom of the slopes.

Planes of flow Slopes of *flow?*

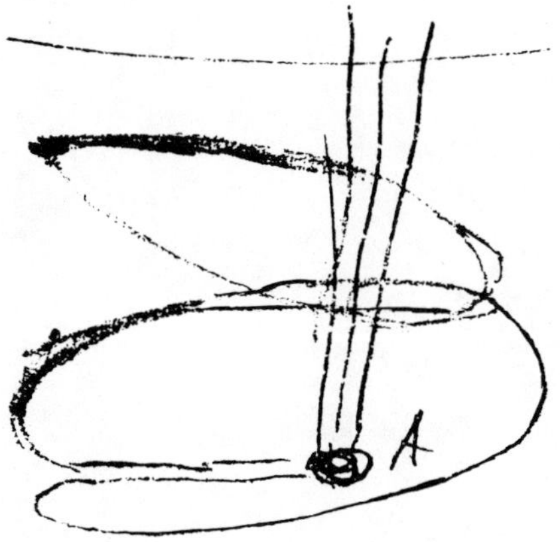

in the form of a toboggan but more of a corkscrew. and the splash at A —is an uncorking The group may be described in the sense of model-uncorking.

The fall of A of the three-crashes helps the uncorking—

The splash (nothing in common with champagne) ends the series of bachelor operations and transforms the combination of the illuminating gas and the scissors into a single continuous support, support which will be regularized by the 9 holes.

[18. THE OCULIST WITNESSES]

Weight with holes

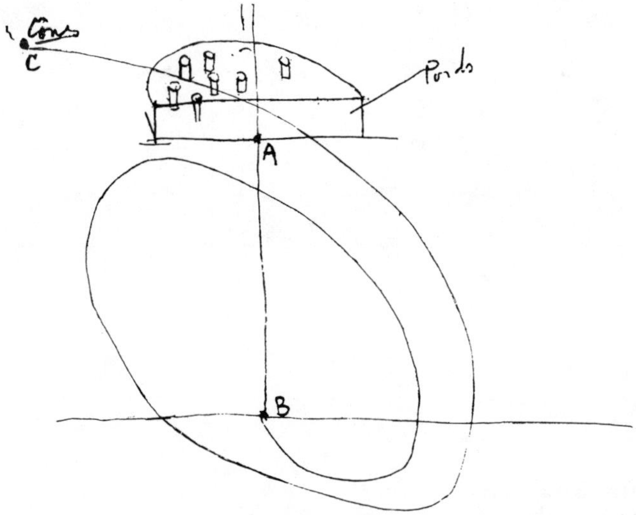

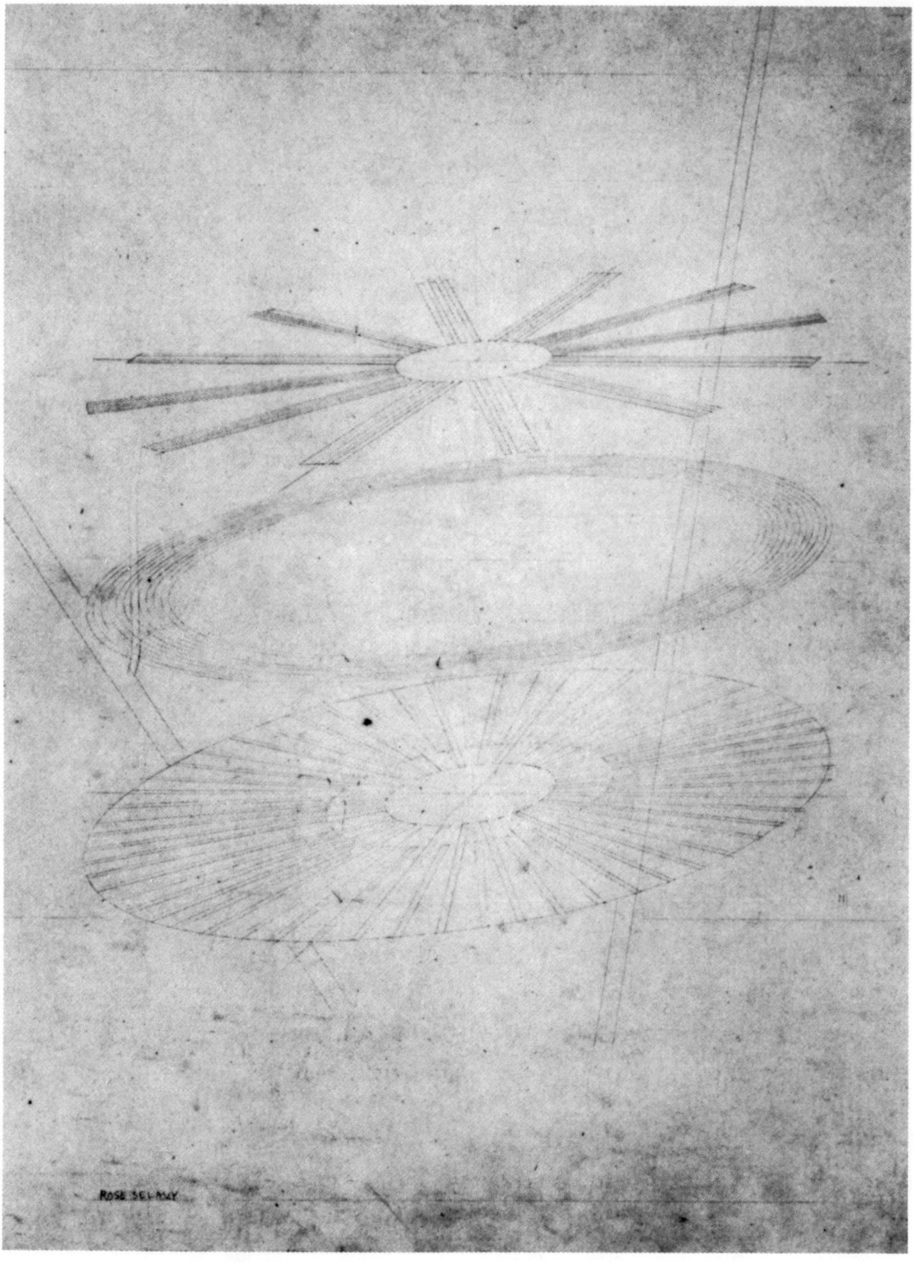

Oculist Witnesses, 1920

The weight with holes should rise to the *same* height AB as the juice descending in an oval.—Whence consequences in the splash (points C and A at the same height above the horizontal plane in which is B.)

Oculist's charts—Dazzling of the splash by the oculist's charts.

Sculpture of drops (points) which the splash forms after having been dazzled across the oculist's charts, each drop acting as a point and sent back mirrorically to the high part of the glass to meet the 9 shots =

Mirrorical return—Each drop will pass the 3 planes at the horizon between the perspective and the geometrical drawing of 2 figures which will be indicated on these 3 planes by the Wilson-Lincoln system (i.e. like the portraits which seen from the left show Wilson seen from the right show Lincoln—)

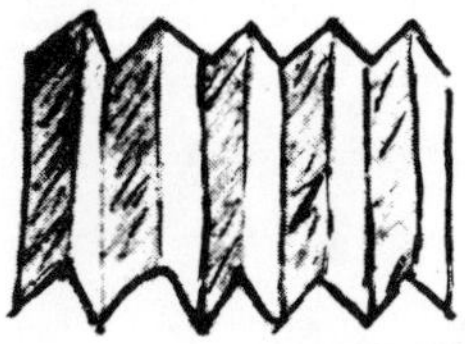

seen from the right the figure may give a square for example from the front and seen from the right it could give the same square seen in perspective—

The mirrorical drops not the drops themselves but their image pass between these 2 states of the same figure (square in this example)

(Perhaps use prisms stuck behind the glass.) to obtain the desired effect)

Parts to look at cross-eyed, like a piece of silvered glass, in which are reflected the objects in the room.

[19. HANDLER OF GRAVITY]

Handler of gravity

[Suppress the center]
Make the rod as a spring (to be studied:
perhaps—??
Handler
[Tender] of gravity
these 2 terms are complementary.

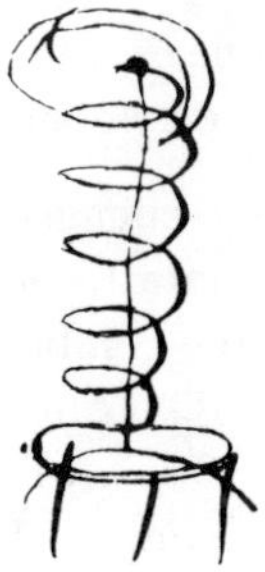

Study the 3 falls:

After the center one, the *mobile* will splash the gas which has become liquid and arrived at the bottom of the slopes

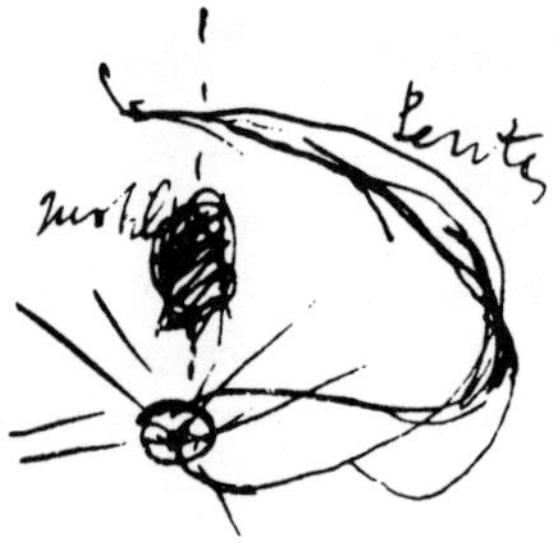

Direct these splashes which should be used for the manoeuvering of the handler of gravity.

(Boxing match.)

[20. BOXING MATCH]

(the 3 pts., A,B,C, are in the same vertical plane)

—Boxing Match = Trajectory of the combat marble:

A. Departure—Contact of the marble at the 1st Summit—Unfastening of the clockwork and fall to B.

B. 2nd very sharp attack—contact at the 2nd Summit and release of the 1st Ram.—Fall to C.

C. Direct to the 3rd Summit—Release of the 2nd Ram.

1st and 2nd Rams descending after the contact of the combat marble to the 2nd and 3rd Summits. This descent carries with it the garment of the bride which the rams support. The juggler of centers of gravity, having his 3 points of support on this garment dances to the will of the descending rams controlled by the stripping.

—A spring in red steel actuating the whole clockwork—The cogwheels by means of a rack, push the fallen rams up again.

T and T' release hinges of the rams which losing their support by the contact of the combat marble at X and X', fall down.

R and R'—R engaged position of the red transmission with the rack System—R' unfastened position in consequence of the contact at the 1st Summit of the combat marble; DG moves to D'G and like a door gently returns to DG (Automatic closure F) leaving time for the marble to produce the 2 following releases.

Marcel Duchamp, 1913

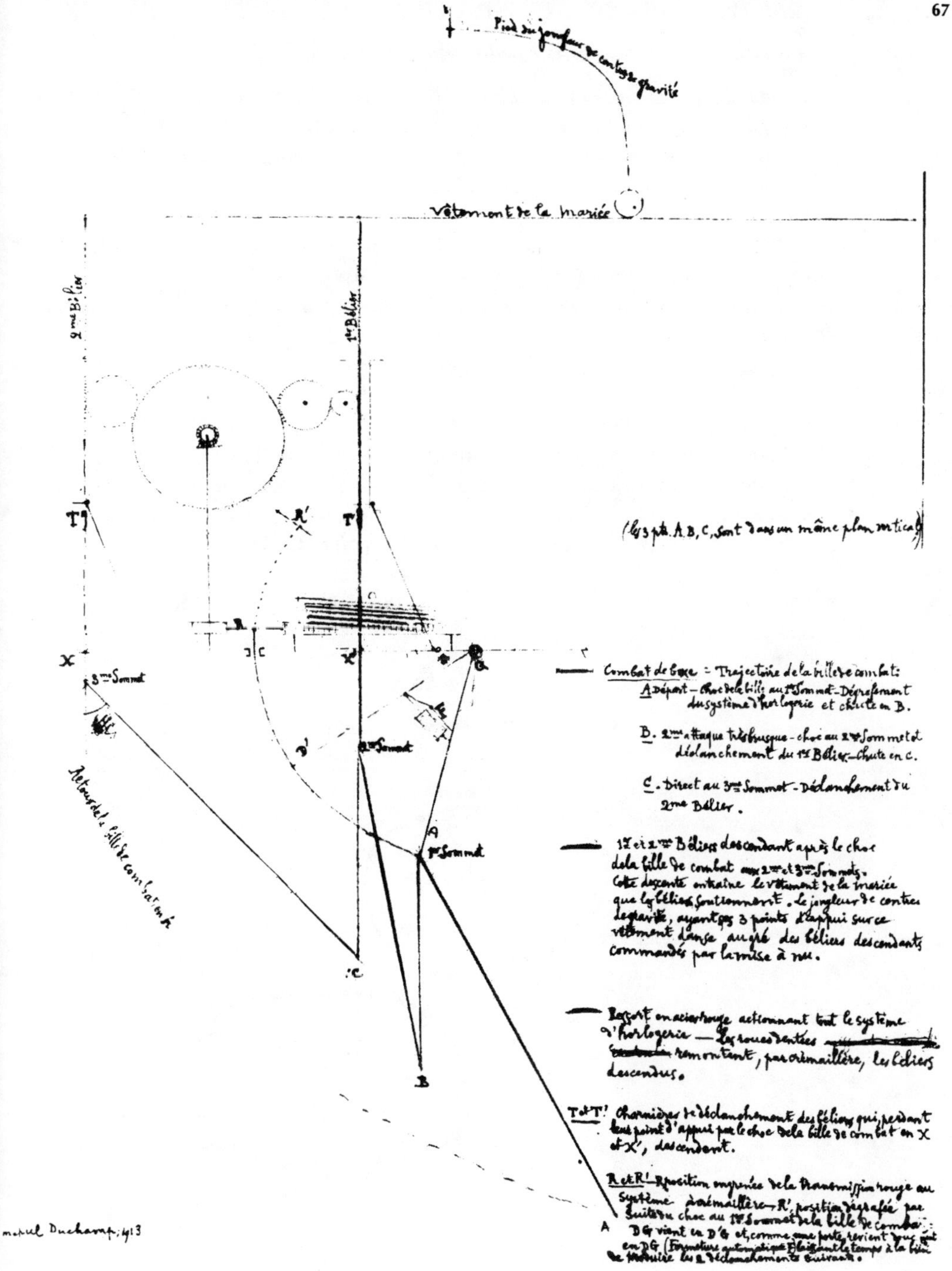

Boxing Match

[21. THE CHOCOLATE GRINDER]

the Chocolate Grinder is essentially composed. . .

The *chocolate* of the rollers, *coming* from one knows not where,
Would deposit itself after grinding, as milk chocolate. . . . .

The *necktie* (insert a letter referring to a diagram) with brilliant shimmering would have been of aluminum foil stretched and stuck down, *but the 3 rollers always turn beneath.*

The *Bayonet*—(X) Helps to hold up the compression bar and the large scissors and the isolating plates. *First-class article.*

The grinder is mounted on a Louis XV nickled chassis.

Reconsider it.

Adage

Principle of [*spontaneity*] (which explains the gyratory mvt. of the grinder without other help)

The bachelor grinds his chocolate himself—

commercial formula, trade mark, commercial slogan inscribed like an advertisement on a bit of glossy and colored paper (have it made by a printer)—this paper stuck on the article "Chocolate Grinder"

The necktie will owe its elegance to its thickness—½ cm or 1 cm at the most

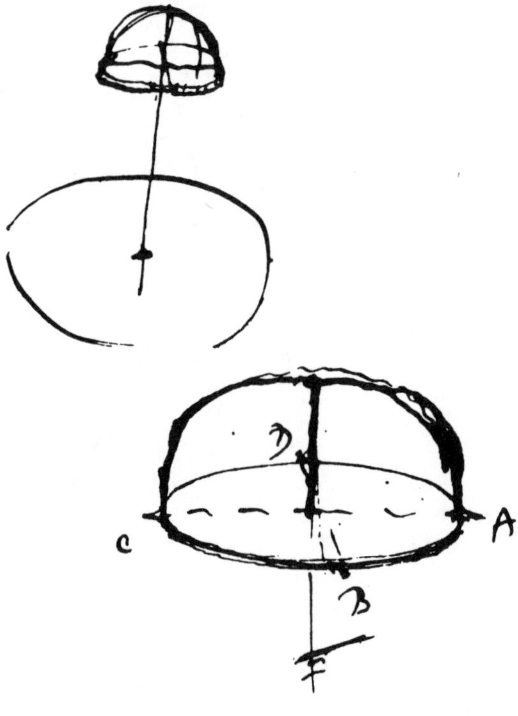

resplendent
It will be brilliant *above*.

perhaps 4 points on the sides, A B C D. *very pointed* (*like all neckties*)

[to be put in the text]

Description of the necktie:

1st resplendent in color

2nd provided at the 4 corners with very sharp points (like all neckties.

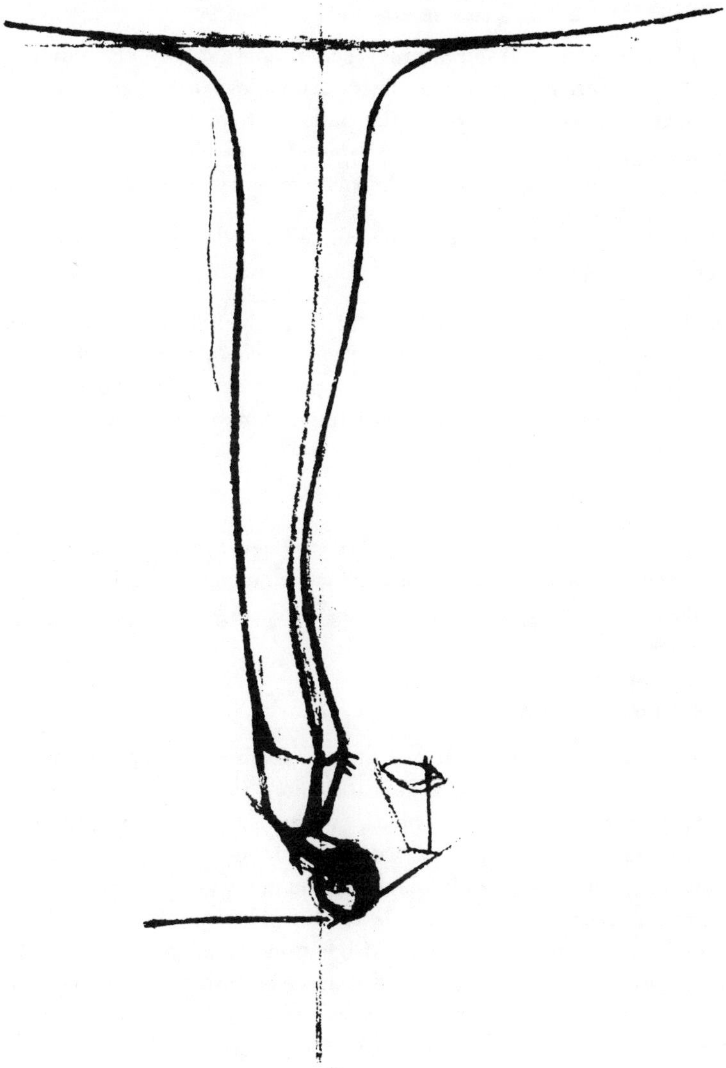

Study for the Louis XV Chassis (Chocolate Grinder's Leg), 1913

[22. COLOR]

Given *an object in chocolate.*

1st its appearance = retinal impression (and other sensory consequences)

2nd its apparition.

in negative a) of the surface

The *mould* of a chocolate object is the *negative apparition* of the *plane*

in the conditional tense. if one . . .

(with one or several curvatures) generating 1st (by elementary prllll-ism) the *colored* form of the object. 2nd *the mass of elements of light (chocolate type elements)*: in the passage from the *apparition* (mould) to the *appearance, the plane,* composed of elements of *chocolate type* light determines the apparent chocolate mass by *physical dyeing.*

in negative

a) The *negative* apparition (determined *for the colored form conventionally* by the linear perspective, but always in an environment of n-1

for ex. in negative

dimens. for an object of n dimens.); In the same way this *negative apparition,* for the phenomenon of *physical dyeing,* is determined by the source of light becoming in the *apparent* object lighted mass (*native colors.* = apparition in negative of the *apparent* colors of the substance of the objects.)

–Provisional color = The malic forms. They are provisionally painted with red lead *while waiting* for each one to receive its color, like croquet mallets.

Breeding of Colors.

–In the greenhouse–[On a glass plate, colors seen transparently].

Mixture of flowers of color i.e. each color still in its optical state:

Perfumes (?) of reds, of blues, of greens or of grays heightened towards yellow blue red or of weaker maroons. (the whole in scales.). These perfumes with physiological rebound can be neglected and extracted in an imprisonment for the fruit.

Only, the fruit still has to avoid being eaten. It's this dryness of "*nuts and raisins*" that you get in the ripe imputrescent colors (rarefied colors.).

Interior lighting.

Instead of an extra solar light falling at an angle of 45°.

determine the luminous effects (lights and shadows) of an interior source, i.e., that each substance in its chemical composition is endowed with a *"phosphorescence"* (?) and lights up like luminous advertisements not quite. its *light* is not independent of its color.—In short the color effect of the whole will be the appearance of matter having a source of light in its molecular construction.

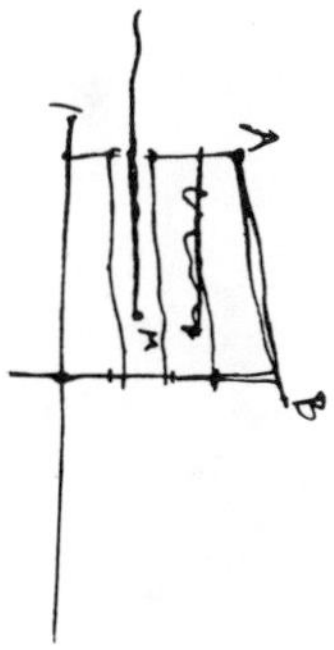

The substance of each part is both a *source of light* and a *color.* (in other words *the apparent color of each part is the source of visibility in color of that* part (with no reflections on the other parts)

try to find a way to distribute the "distance between molecules" ? according to *the form* of each part (roundness, flatness *Begin with darkness* (black background) or rather picric yellow) *Strictness of a Huguenot sort.*

The whole picture seems to be in papier mâché because the whole of this representation is the sketch (*like a mould*) for a *reality which would be possible by slightly distending* the laws of physics and chemistry.

[23. COMB]

Classify combs by the number of their teeth

Rattle.

with a kind of comb, by using the space between 2 teeth as a unit, determine the relations between the 2 ends of the comb and some intermediary points (by the broken teeth).

Use, as a proportional control, this comb with broken teeth, on another object made up, also of smaller elements (smaller so that it can accommodate this control. For example: lead wires more or less thick, laid one against the other in one plane (like hair). Then, develop the comb, i.e. so that it works abnormally on a plane of lead wires [or then turning on a point, or even a curved comb i.e. not flat or with teeth of unequal lengths; or even the action of these different models of comb on a thick material (lead wires) and no longer just flat]. etc.

Sept. 1915

Cast Shadows

probably to relate to the notes on 4-dim'l perspective.

after the bride. . . .
make a picture. of *shadows cast*
by objects 1st on a plane.
2nd on à surface of
such (or such) curvature
3rd on several transparent surfaces
thus one can obtain a hypophysical
analysis of the successive transformations
of objects. (in their form-outline—)
To do this 1st determine—the sources
of light (gas, electricity, acetylene [for the differentiation
of the colors] etc). 2nd determine their number
3rd their situation with respect
to the receiving planes.
Obviously, the object will not
be just any object. it shall have
to be constructed sculpturally in 3 dim.
—*the execution* of the picture by
means of luminous sources.
and by drawing the shadows on these planes.
simply following the
real outlines projected . . .

all this to be completed and
specially to relate with the subject?

Isometric projections: see book

This for the upper part of the
glass included between the horizon and the 9 holes

cast shadows formed by the splashes coming from below
like some jets of water which weave forms in their
transparency.

Possible

Possible

The figuration of a possible.
(not as the opposite of impossible
nor as related to probable
nor as subordinated to likely)

the *possible* is only
a *physical "caustic"* [vitriol type]
burning up all aesthetics or callistics

A l'Infinitif

Speculations

Can one make works which are not works of "art"?

On reverse side: 1913

The question of shop windows ∴
To undergo the interrogation of shop windows ∴
The exigency of the shop window ∴
The shop window proof of the existence of the outside world ∴
When one undergoes the examination of the shop window, one also pronounces one's own sentence. In fact, one's choice is "round trip." From the demands of the shop windows, from the inevitable response to shop windows, my choice is determined. No obstinacy, ad absurdum, of hiding the coition through a glass pane with one or many objects of the shop window. The penalty consists in cutting the pane and in feeling regret as soon as possession is consummated. Q.E.D.

Neuilly, 1913

Recopy and correct
I. Show case with sliding glass panes—place some *fragile* objects inside.
—Inconvenience—narrowness—reduction of a space, i.e. way of being able to experiment in 3 dim. as one operates on planes in plane geometry—
—Placing on a table the largest number of *fragile* objects and of different shapes but without angles and standing upright on a level base of some width i.e. providing some stability.—*Assemble as many objects as possible on the table in height* and consequently avoid the danger of their falling, of breaking them,—but nevertheless *squeeze them together as much as possible* so that they fit together one into the other (in height I mean). . . . .
Perhaps: make a good photo of a table thus prepared, make *one* good print and then break the plate.—
—Same exercise in a box. 1° Make a kind of background with the same objects this time lying on their rounded parts in semi-stability, *prop*

them up one with the other. 2° Put a paper on top and remake a second *layer* above, using the *holes* left by the layer underneath, and continue thus.

—Shoe polish. Red and yellow

II. With a glass-front highboy closed by sliding glass panes on ball bearings etc.—one obtains the figure of a space, a figure analogous to the figure of a plane 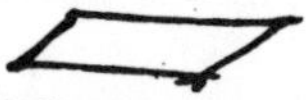 in geometry, i.e. one can use this figure of a space and demonstrate as one demonstrates theorems by constructing, on paper, lines corresponding to the hypothesis. Do not be tempted to make the ridiculous comparison—objection—that a table or a glass pane for example is to the drawing 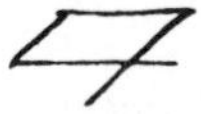 what this glass-front highboy is in relation to . . .

find inscription for Woolworth Bldg.
as readymade

Jan. 1916

2 "similar" objects i.e. of different dimensions but one being the replica of the other (like 2 deck chairs, one large and one doll size) could be used to establish a *4-dim'l* perspective—not by placing them in relative positions with respect to each other in space[3] but simply by considering the optical illusions produced by the difference in their dimensions.

Make a painting or sculpture as one winds up a reel of moving picture film. With each turn, on a large reel (several meters in diameter if necessary), a new "shot" continuing the preceding turn and tying it into the next one—This kind of continuity may have nothing in common with moving picture film or even resemble it.

Construct one and several musical precision instruments which produce mechanically the *continuous* passage of one tone to another in order to be able to record without hearing them sculptured sound forms (against "virtuosism," and the physical division of sound which reminds one of the uselessness of the physical color theories).

On reverse side: 1913

A thing to be looked at with one eye
— — — — — —with the left eye
— — — — — — — — right—
What one must hear with one ear

— — — — — the right ear
— — — — — — left —

to put in the Crash—splash.

One could base a whole series of *things to be looked at with a single eye* (left or right).
One could find a whole series of things to be heard (or listened to) with a single ear.

Use ground glass behind which one lays mat black paper
(silvered effect)
(in the opticeries)

Buy a book about "*knots.*" (Sailor's knot and others).

Have a room entirely made of mirrors which one can move—and photograph mirror effects . . .

Photo.
Photo: Wall (morning)
: My portrait in the bathroom mirror
: 3 rolls of lead wire on an inclined plane (sort of race)
: piles—heaps—of similar things (stretcher keys) (sponges 10th St.)

Lead embossed, hammered or "tufted" is less dense

Use tooth paste
make a test on the glass
also Brilliantine, Cold cream etc. ?

Not solid

Soapy water + strong tea = in varying doses—brown yellow, light greenish

Milky way
or Louis XV images like the legs of the Grinder

The clouds are rather of soap (*shaving*)

Do not forget the painting of Dumouchel: Pharmacy—snow effect, dark sky, dusk, and 2 lights on the horizon (pink and green).

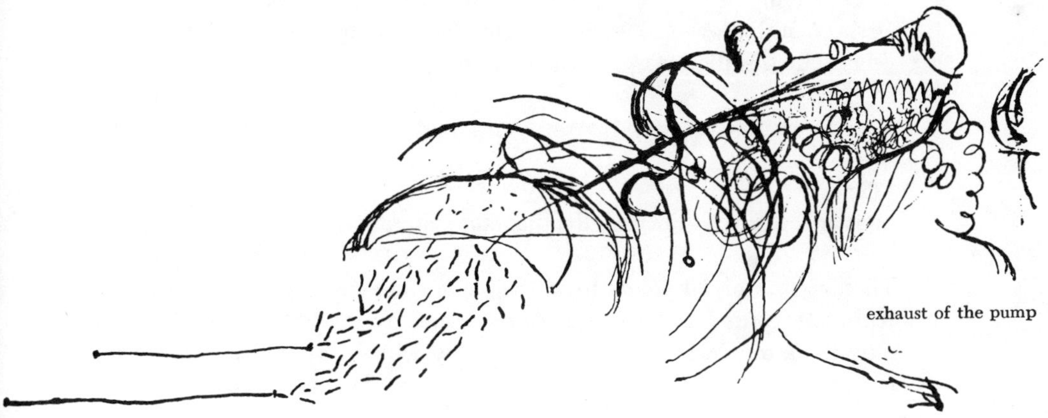

Try to argue on the *plastic* duration

Reference is to readymade, *Pharmacy,* 1914. [Cleve Gray]
This is written alongside a sketch for *The Glass* showing "gas with cones." [C.G.]
I mean space into time. [M.D., 1965.]

Dictionaries and Atlases

Dictionary

—of a language in which each word would be translated into French (or other) by several words, when necessary by a whole sentence.

—of a language which one could translate *in its elements* into known languages but which would not reciprocally express the translation of French words (or other), or of French or *other* sentences.

—Make this dictionary by means of cards

—find how to classify these cards (alphabetical order, but which alphabet)

Alphabet—or rather a few elementary signs, like a dot, a line, a circle, etc. (to be seen) which will vary according to the position etc.

—Sound of this language, is it speakable? No.

Relation to shorthand.

"Grammar"—i.e. How to connect the elementary signs (like words), then the *groups* of signs one to the other; what *will become of the ideas* of action or of being (verbs), of modulation (adverbs)—etc.?

Buy a dictionary and cross out the words to be crossed out. Sign: revised and corrected

Look through a dictionary and scratch out all the "undesirable" words. Perhaps add a few—Sometimes replace the scratched out words with another. Use this dictionary for the written part of the glass.

For the dictionary look for the equivalent of colors which cannot be seen.
"Theory"
10 words found by opening the dictionary at random by A
— — — — — — — — — by B
These 2 sets of 10 words have the same difference of *"personality"* as if the 10 words had been written by A and by B with an intention. Or else, it matters little, there would be cases where this "personality" may disappear in A and B. That is the best case and the most difficult.

Dictionary—
with films, taken close up, of parts of very large objects, obtain photographic records which no longer look like photographs of something. With these semi-microscopics constitute a dictionary of which each film would be the representation of a group of words in a sentence or separated so that this film would assume a new significance or rather that the concentration on this film of the sentences or words chosen would give a form of meaning to this film and that, once learned, this relation between film and meaning translated into words would be "striking" and would serve as a basis for a kind of writing which no longer has an alphabet or words but signs (films) already freed from the "baby talk" of all ordinary languages.
—Find a means of filing all these films in such order that one could refer to them as in a dictionary.

Make a *list of surnames—French* or English (or other language) or mixed—with Christian names (alphabetical order or not)—etc.

A kind of illuminatistic Scribism in painting (A plastic for plastic retaliation)

A kind of *pictorial Nominalism.* (Check)

On reverse side: 1914

A geographic "landscapism"—"in the manner" of geographic maps
—but
The landscapist from the height of an acroplane—Then the field trip (400 km.) Notes taken i.e. for example number of houses in each village, or then again number of Louis XV chairs in each house—The geographic landscape (with perspective, or without perspective, seen from

above like maps) could record all kinds of things, have a caption, take on a statistical look.—
There is also "geological landscapism": Different formations, different colors—A mine of information!
Meteorological landscapism (Barometry, thermometry, etc.)

See similar detailed reference to a dictionary in *The Green Box.* [C.G.]

Color

On the more or less final drawing, paint very *lightly in black and white* the perspective lighting (convention of a light source more distant than the sun having an indifferent value of "black and white"). This background must disappear under the *value* (colored) of the *substance* of each part. Determine thus each substance by its color composition—(White 1, black ½, vermilion ¼, etc.). Except for certain substances (like chocolate, the water[fall] etc. which have a physical equivalent that should be approximated as closely as possible without atmospherization); except for these substances the others will all have I. a *name* (on ite, on in, or other ending?) II. a *chemical composition* (blend) which will be that of the color blend. III. a visual appearance—(1° colored and 2° different molecular *composition*—hardness, porosity, etc.) for each substance *which* will be designated by schematic and conventional notation (without evoking, however, the different parallel lines of architects). IV. Properties.

Over this second coat, shade again in black and white (spatter).

Classification of colors to be used to achieve "*pure tone*"

Yellow
- lemon
- Indian
- Naples light
- Naples
- orange

Red
- minimum (to protect certain metallic parts from oxidation) vermilion

Avoid lakes

Black
- ivory
- lamp (usually to be mixed with dark earth color to avoid cracking)

Blue

Prussian (usually with black—with yellow for special greens)

Avoid blue in mixtures because of its imbecile atmospheric tendency

Ochre

yellow } find other ochres or earth colors
red }

Green

light (for light metals)

Emerald

Bistre

(try)

To obtain *"exactitude"*—dye canvas black (or make black by other means) before painting, so that a line ruled with a point into the thickness of paint while it is still half wet will show up black and will underline.

As in geographic maps, as in architects' drawings or diagrams with color wash, need of a color key: *substantive meaning* of each color used—(e.g. for certain metals, for wood, etc., determine the *conventional color* used.

Picric acid and tincture of iodine etc. to tint surfaces not part of the machine—*Use of screen*—See triturators and liquefiers.

—Prussian and Vermilion

Beautiful black—Prussian blue and bistre

ˣThe background or factitious atmosphere could be done in graphite (to enhance the overall effect through the contrast of oil painting and graphite).

ˣTo obtain "exactitude"—glue to the *finished* canvas threads of different *thickness—color* to accentuate the lines (or intersections)—planes (this thread will be held in place by the varnish)

ˣFor the execution of the final canvas: cut out some *stencils* in opaline or thick gelatine. Ahead of time prepare a background as exactly as possible, indicating the shadows and allowing the last coat (the one to be stenciled) to have little thickness.

steel

raw

worked

nickel

nickel plated } difference of shine
pure nickel }

platinum
somewhat mat shine
copper
mat
red
yellow
polished
aluminum
mat—dark
iron
blue violet of iron
to be used for architectures
iron
ultramarine, black, lake, Prussian blue, white (on light background)
steel white, yellow, black, ochre (dark background)
nickel white, cobalt, gray, green (on dark background)
platinum white, cobalt, green, black (dark background)
aluminum white, Prussian blue, yellow, ochre
wood
glass transparent colorless juice
mica yellow transparent juice
copper yellow, red, black, white, raw Sienna

Experiments:
nickel white, lemon yellow-green (graduated to yellow-blue gray for the shadows)
platinum white, brilliant yellow, black
aluminum white, black, brilliant yellow, Prussian blue
steel white, black, Prussian blue, brilliant yellow
iron
Father
Bergmann
Gress
Vorel
M. Blocman
Gosselin
wood various essences
pine
oak
varnished mahogany
mica transparent yellow
glass ground
transparent
colored (special uses)

See afterwards mixtures of pure color and its complementary color
also: Prussian blue and vermilion

Beautiful black: Prussian blue and bistre
mixing of pure color and its complementary color

Ground glass and rust of different metals as colors to use in the *"splasher"*

Graphite + quick-drying linseed oil = steel shade

B. Prussian blue and vermilion
B. Prussian blue and bistre

Use of screen
Use a *blue* in the "splash"—but only the blue of the blue-print paper which architects use—match in oil paint the blue of the paper
Washable colors—(for the colors of the glass)

The Bride. 2nd Study (Munich)
Pink: Light burnt ochre and white
Brown backgrounds: pure raw Sienna with a little Light burnt ochre and some white
Light yellow: Light ochre and white
Machinery: Gold ochre
Bridge: Cyprus burnt umber
Greens: Light ochre and black. Little of green earth

Notes for "The Bride stripped bare by the Bachelors."
(Study: the Passage of the Virgin to the Bride)
Bride: The pink leitmotif obtained by White (silver) and the light burnt ochre. A bit of gold ochre.
The reds have more light burnt ochre.
The deep perspectives obtained by black and burnt Sienna and gold ochre and also Cyprus burnt umber (a bit of light burnt ochre to redden).
On the left—the greenish is obtained by Verona green earth with light burnt ochre and black.
In the center the dark contains a lot of Cyprus burnt umber.

to do:

Bachelors: To obtain the dark, use Prussian blue which will warm and contrast sufficiently with the Bride.

Find the papers about colors considered in the sense of coloring light

sources and not differentiations within a uniform light (sunlight, artificial light, etc.)
Come back to:
Supposing several colors—light-sources—(of that order) exposed at the same time, the optical relationship of these different coloring sources is no longer of the same order as a comparison of a red spot with a blue spot in sunlight. *There is a certain inopticity, a certain cold consideration, these colorings affecting only imaginary eyes* in this exposure. (The colors about which one speaks. A little like the passage of a present participle to a past one.

These references to colors are often in German here. M.D. says that at this time he was using Behrendt oil colors. [C.G.]
I mean the difference between speaking about red and looking at red. [M.D., 1965.]

Further References to The Glass

Recipes—obtain (general form to describe certain parts):
e.g. One obtains the shots by . . .
To obtain . . . take . . .

Silver (like a mirror) a part of the crash-splash. Make inquiries from technical point of view. With the ground glass part and the Rust—
—Rust appearing through the ground glass—and also Rust alone. Glue a magnifying glass on. Kodak lens.

Package of white cards. Stack of cards—to be used in the inclined ramp. (Slopes of flow or Crash-splash). Make in actual size and photograph.
Dec. 1915

Perspective[4]
Principal forms, imperfect and freed
The principal forms of the bachelor apparatus or utensil are *imperfect:* Rectangle, circle, square, parallelepiped, symmetrical handle; demi-sphere.—i.e. these forms are *mensurated* (interrelation of their actual dimensions and relation of these dimensions to the destination of the forms in the bachelor utensil.)
In the Bride—the *principal forms* will be more or less large or small, no longer have mensurability in relation to their destination: a sphere in the Bride will have *any* radius (the radius given to represent it is "fictitious and dotted.")
Likewise, or better still, *in the Pendu Femelle* parabolas, hyperbolas (or volumes deriving from them) will lose all connotation of men—surated position.

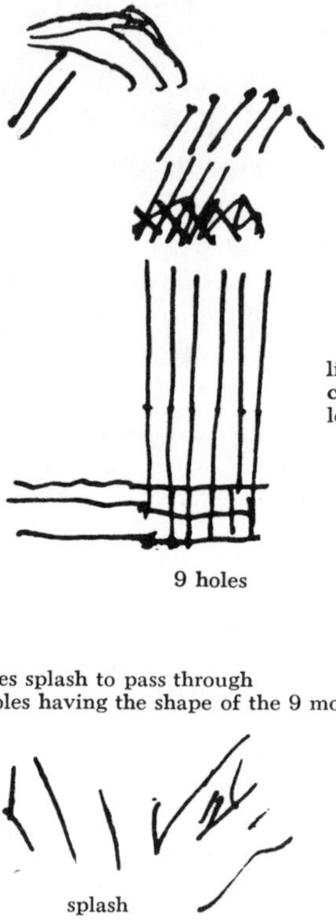

Their actual representation will be only an *example of each one of these freed forms* (an example without representational value but *permitting a maximum of plus or minus*)

Reference here is to parts of *The Glass.* [C.G.]

The object referred to here is in The Museum of Modern Art, New York. [C.G.]

Reference is to part of *The Glass* that was never executed, called *Toboggan* (Ramp). [M.D., 1965.]

The 9 molds are the 9 *Malic Molds.* [C.G.]

Note close correspondence to a page of the *Green Box.* [C.G.]

Appearance and Apparition

Appearance }
Apparition } of a chocolate object for ex.

1° The appearance of this object will be the sum of the usual sensory evidence enabling one to have an ordinary perception of that object

(see psychology manuals)

2° Its apparition is the mold of it
i.e.
a) There is the *surface apparition* (for a *spatial* object like a chocolate object) which is like a kind of mirror image *looking* as if it were used for the making of this object, like a mold, but this mold of the form is not itself an object, it is the image in n-1 dimensions of the essential points of this object of n dimensions. The 3-dim'l appearance comes from the 2-dim'l apparition which is the mold of it (external form).
b) As another part of the mold there is the apparition in *native colors.* The native colors are not colors (in the sense of blue, red etc. reflections of lighting X coming from the outside)—They are luminous sources producing active colors—i.e. a surface of native-chocolate color will be composed of a sort of chocolate phosphorescence completing the molded apparition of this chocolate object—
Thus on the one hand the 2-dim'l form of native chocolate color seems to be the mold, to give birth on the other hand to the chocolate object in 3 dim.
These *native colors in the apparition* determine the real colors which change because of the exterior lighting *in their appearance by physical inner dye.*—They are generally related to substances. There is *one* single native chocolate color which serves to determine all chocolates.

Given *The object,* considered in its physical appearance (*color, mass, form.*) Define (graphically i.e. by means of pictorial *conventions*) the *mold* of the *object.*
By mold is meant: from the point of view of form and color, the *negative* (photographic); from the point of view of mass, a plane (generating the object's form by means of elementary parallelism) composed of elements of light, (this light of equal intensity manifesting itself in color-source differences (and not colors subjected to a source of light exterior to the object).
e.g. The mold of a chocolate object is the *negative apparition* of the plane with several curvatures (determined conventionally (perspectively e.g. by a 3-dim'l space) by its position in a *space* containing this object and an archetype) generating **explain negative apparition**
1° the colored form of this object
2° the mass of light elements called chocolate elements, a sort of *physical dye* which determines: in the transition from *apparition* (mold) to *appearance* (chocolate object) the chocolate color, the chocolate mass, undergoing all the optical transformations in different lightings.

I The object is illuminant. Luminous source. The *body* of the object is composed of luminous molecules and becomes the source of the *lighted* objects' substance (e.g. the chocolate emanating is the atomic mold of the opaque chocolate substance having a physical existence *verified* (?) by the 5 senses.—The emanating object is an *apparition.*

Native color: the color that is in the molecules. [M.D., 1965.]
This section is more detailed than a similar one in the *Green Box.* [C.G.]
Physical dye, as opposed to chemical dye, is the molecular essence. [M.D., 1965.]

Perspective

Perspective.
See Catalogue of Bibliothèque St. Geneviève
the whole section on Perspective:
Niceron, (Father Fr., S.J.)
Thaumaturgus opticus

Linear Perspective[3]

Plane view
D indicates the distance
from (point of sight)
Projected in perspective:
AD, FD, GD, CD are the *verticals*

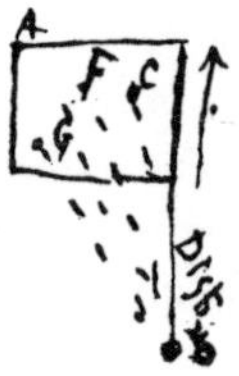

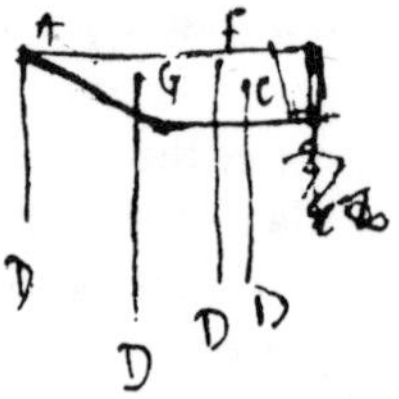

? see photos made for the perspective
of the standard stoppages and the
red fellows

Right and Left	plane[2]
Top and Bottom	space[3]

Right, Left = plane[2]
Top, Bottom = space[3]

Gravity and center of gravity make for horizontal and vertical in space[3]
In a plane[2]—the vanishing point corresponds to the center of gravity, all these parallel lines meeting at the vanishing point just as the verticals all run toward the center of gravity. *Physically*—the eye is the sense of perspective. In this, *perspective resembles color* which like it cannot be tested by touch. Gravity is not controlled physically in us by one of the 5 ordinary senses. We always reduce a gravity experience to an auto-cognizance, real or imagined, registered inside us in the region of the stomach.

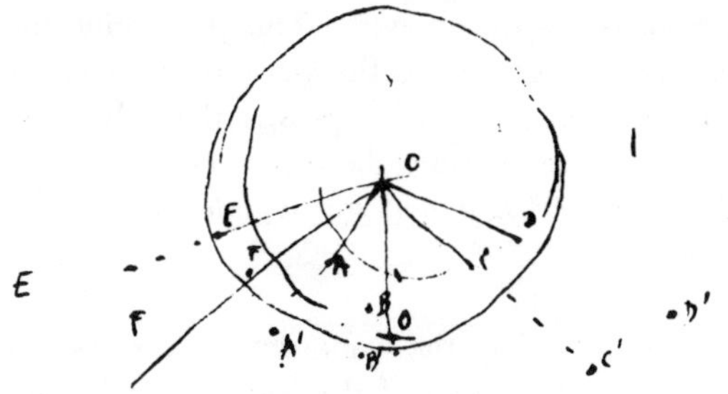

Pseudo sphere (Projections from the center)

Resemblance—
between a perspective view and a circle—
the vanishing point and the center—
To what in a perspective view would the
circle itself correspond?

Horizon

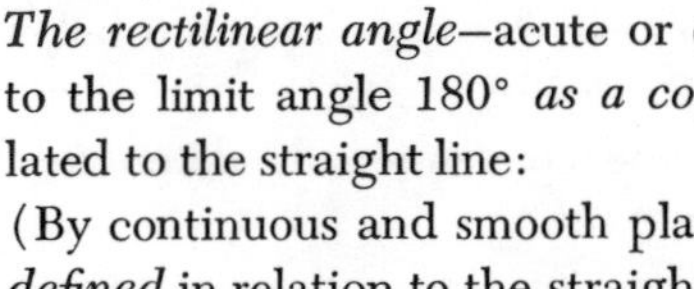

etc.

In the plane seen from the height of the 3rd dimension
The rectilinear angle—acute or obtuse—is related to the *right angle* and to the limit angle 180° *as a continuous and smooth plane curve* is related to the straight line:
(By continuous and smooth plane curve one should understand a curve *defined* in relation to the straight line, circle, ellipse, etc.)
How to represent or imagine the *angle* which compares to the right angle and to the limit angle 180° as a curve continuous but not smooth compares to the straight line.
(*To help define the notions: angle, straight line, curve, etc.*)

The mirror = Shadow projected in 3 dims. Comparison of a 3 sided mirror with a shadow projected by a body on a cube—This real image of the mirror has 3 virtual dimensions because the mirror is a plane—
(incomplete?)

On reverse side: Paris May 27, 1913 (not M.D.'s writing)

Use transparent glass and mirror for perspective^4
analogy: perspective^4: the 3-dim'l perspective representation of an *object*^{4} will be perceptible to the eye^3 *just as* the perspective of a cathedral is perceptible to the *flat eye*^{2} (and not to the eye^3). This perception for the eye^2 is a wandering-perception (relating to the sense of distance)—An eye^2 will only have a tactile perception of a perspective^3. It must wander from one point to another and measure the distances. *It will not have a view of the whole* like the eye^3. By analogy: wandering-perception by the eye^3 of perspective^4.

Difference between *"tactile exploration"* or the wandering in a plane by a 2-dim'l eye around a circle, and the vision of this very circle by the same 2-dim'l eye fixing itself at a point. Also: difference *between "tactile exploration," 3-dim'l wandering* by an ordinary eye around a sphere *and* the vision of that sphere by the same eye fixing itself at a point (linear perspective). Also: the same difference exists in the *4-dim'l* domain: there is a "tactile exploration" in the 4 dimensions and a 3-dim'l *visual* perspective perception of the 4-dim'l body. This 3-dim'l visual perspective perception is only distinguishable to the 4-dim'l eye. The 3-dim'l eye will not distinguish it clearly (just as a 2-dim'l eye only sees the projected segment of a circle). A 3-dim'l tactile exploration, a wandering around, will perhaps permit an imaginative reconstruction of the numerous 4-dim'l bodies, allowing this perspective to be understood in a 3-dim'l medium.

On reverse side: Paris gas bill dated Sept. 14, 1914

Construction of a 4-dim'l eye

From—: A circle (when seen by a 3-dim'l eye moving above and below until the visual ray falls in the plane which contains the circle) undergoes many changes in shape conventionally determined by the laws of linear perspective.

To—: (For the 3-dim'l eye a sphere remains always the same whatever the point of sight.)

But a sphere (for the 4-dim'l perception moving in a 4-dim'l space until the rays^4 become visual rays for the ordinary 3-dim'l eye) undergoes many changes in shape, from 3-dim'l sphere gradually decreasing in volume without decreasing in radius, to simple plane circle.

On reverse side: Paris gas bill dated Nov. 11, 1914

Light and shade exist for 4 dim'l as for 3,2,1.

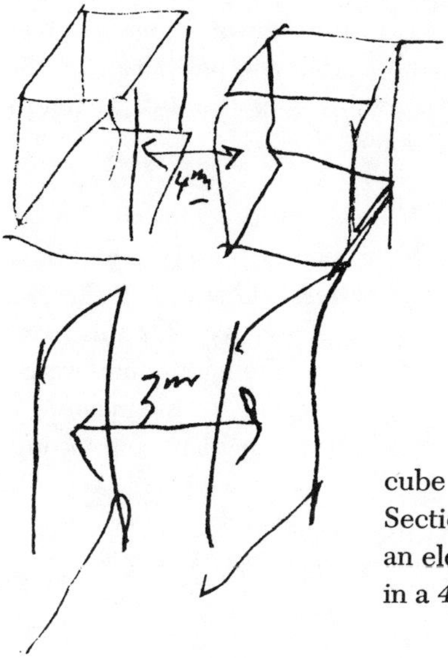

cube
Section of
an element
in a *4 dim'l medium.*

Perspective[3] starts in an initial *frontal plane without deformation*
Perspective[4] will have a cube or 3 dim'l medium as a starting point which will not cause deformation i.e. in which the object[3] is seen *circumhyperhypo-embraced* (as if *grasped with the hand* and not seen with the *eyes*)

—Just as a point intersects a curve and does not intersect a plane, so a curve of infinite length or *surface element* intersects a volume and does not intersect a 4-dim'l "solid." But either a plane or a surface intersects this 4-dim'l solid.
—This 4-dim'l solid will be bounded by 3-dim'l volumes.
The shadow cast by a 4-dim'l figure on our space is a *3-dim'l* shadow (see Jouffret "Geom. à 4 dim." page 186, last 3 lines.)
Three-dimensional sections of four-dimensional figures by a space: by analogy with the method by which architects depict the plan of each *story* of a house, a four-dimensional figure can be represented (in each one of its *stories*) by three-dimensional sections. These different stories will be bound to one another by the 4th dim.

Construct all the 3-dim'l states of the 4-dim'l figure the same way one determines all the planes or sides of a 3-dim'l figure—in other words:
A 4-dim'l figure is perceived (?) through an ∞ of 3-dim'l sides which are the sections of this 4-dim'l figure by the infinite number of spaces (in 3 dim.) which envelope this figure.—In other words: one can *move* around the 4-dim'l figure according to the 4 directions of the continuum. The number of positions of the perceiver is ∞ but one can reduce to a finite number these different positions (as in the case of *regular* 3-dim'l figures) and then each perception, in these different positions, is a 3-diml' figure. The set of these 3-dim'l perceptions of the 4-dim'l figure would be the foundation for a reconstruction of the 4-dim'l figure.

By analogy the flat being[2] has a *length.* This length is symmetrically set on each side of an axis whose imaginary extension in the plane will pass through a pole common to all the individual axes[2] determining the *flat equilibrium* corresponding to the equilibrium of gravity[3]. (Is this axis[2] a compass or a 2-dimensional water gauge????) In the continuum[4] verticals and horizontals lose their "fundamental" meaning, (basic meaning) —(just as the flat being[2] does not know whether the plane supporting him is horizontal or vertical).

The "red fellows" are the *Malic Molds.* [M.D., 1965.]
3 sided mirror: a full-length 3 sided mirror in a hinged frame. [M.D., 1965.]

The Continuum

On the 4-dim'l *vision.*
In the 4-dim'l continuum the *plane* is always *seen* as a line. It has no more perspective development.
The line is *seen* as a point.
Express how a volume is *seen.* (Define this *perception of the whole.*)
The 3-dim'l body when seen in the 4-dim'l continuum is *seen as a whole.*
(does it have a reverse and a front side like the plane seen in space?)

Definition of a space for a 4-dim'l perception.
What *representation* can one give of a 3-dim'l space in a 4-dim'l continuum?
One represents a finite plane in a 3-dim'l space thus:

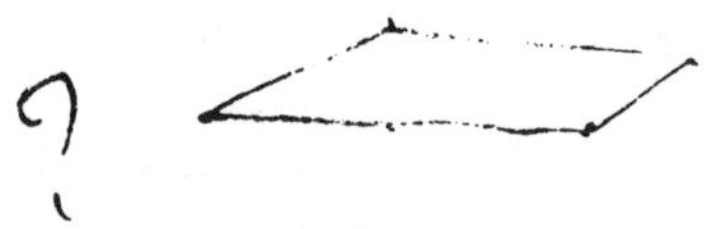

sph sph sph sph

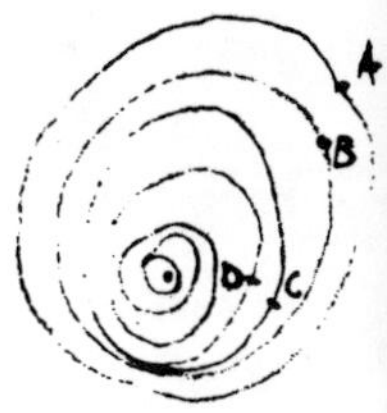

A B C D are the spherical points of the 4-dim'l line. This continuous line made of different spherical points has no *thickness* in the continuum. Its length in the continuum is determined by the different lengths of radius of the successive spheres from 0 to infinity.

Analogies between Perspectives^3 and^4
The *vanishing point* of lines corresponds to the *vanishing line* of planes^2 in a perspective^4
On the vanishing line in perspective^3 there are several vanishing points (meeting of different groups of horizontal parallels). By analogy, there will be several vanishing *lines* all belonging to the same vanishing plane, and becoming the intersecting lines of the different groups of parallel horizontal planes.

Analogy between:
Reflection in a plane mirror and the *3-dim'l section* of a 4-dim'l body by a 3-dim'l space—
For an ordinary eye, a point in a space^3 hides, conceals the 4th direction of the continuum—which is to say that this eye can try to perceive physically this 4th direction by going around the said point. From whatever angle it looks at this point, this point will always be the border line of the 4th direction.
—Just as an ordinary eye going around a mirror will never be able to perceive anything but the reflected 3-dim'l virtual image and nothing from behind—

The plane of the mirror is a convenient way of giving the idea of 3-dim'l infinite space. It is at this plane that the 3-dim'l infinity stops. (There is no contradiction in putting it this way since it is only to familiarize the mind with the ideal representation of the 4-dim'l continuum).
Incorrectly speaking, the line which seems to stop at the mirror's plane should simply cross through and continue to infinity in its own 3-dim'l continuum. It would not enter the 4-dim'l continuum which would contain the line without being *intersected* by it (as a point is contained in a plane without intersecting it.)

Comparison. From: A point does not intersect a 3-dim'l continuum; a curve does.
By analogy, given a cube—its reflection in a mirror—one could say that a straight line perpendicular to the plane of the mirror will not intersect the cube's image (will not hide the cube's image). Because the eye goes around the curve without thickness. This curve will stop at the mirror's

plane.—On the contrary, a plane or any opaque surface touching the mirror will cut or hide from the observer's eyes a part of or the whole *image* of the cube in the mirror. The 4-dim'l continuum is *essentially* the mirror of the 3-dim'l continuum.

Elemental parallelism: repetition of a line equivalent to an elemental line (in the sense of similar at any point) in order to generate the surface. Same parallelism when passing from plane to volume: Sort of parallel multiplication of the n-dim'l continuum, to form the n + 1 dim'l continuum. The process by parallelism is a posteriori. Indeed: knowing the 3-dim'l world, we have, starting from the point, drawn the line by means of elemental parallelism; from the line, by means of elemental parallelism, we have constructed the plane, and thus from the plane to the volume. But this operation already assumed the knowledge or intuition of the 3-dim'l world. Therefore:
Will the passage from volume to 4-dim'l figure be produced through parallelism? Yes. But this elemental parallelism being a geometric process requires an intuitive knowledge of the 4-dim'l continuum. One can give the following definition for a 4-dim'l continuum. (By analogical reasoning, it is an enumeration of a few characteristics common to all the n-dim'l continuums rather than a definition): A representation of the 4-dim'l continuum will be realized by a multiplication of closed volumes evolving by elemental parallelism along the 4th dimension. Of course one has still to define by intuitive knowledge the *"direction"* of this 4th dim.
Hence the *mirror*?

Find a 2-dim'l time, 3-dim'l, etc.

Analogy
In connection with the representation on paper of an angle^4 (2 spaces intersecting along a plane as hinge).

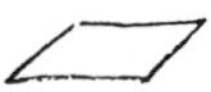

Difficulty of getting away from space^3. In order to draw or represent a space^3 as one draws a plane^2 seen from space^3, one would have to draw a space^3 (seen) from a continuum^4.

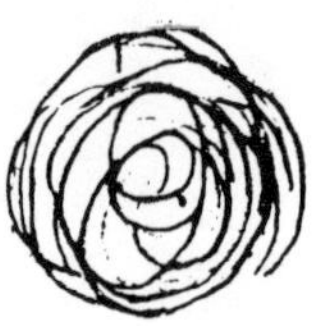

When I represent a space^3 by means of a 3-dim'l sphere (or a cube^3) I am comparable to a flat individual A who sees the *section* of a drawn plane P. The individual A can move to A^1. He measures, while moving, the 4 sides of the quadrangle but at each stop he only sees a *projection* of the quadrangle on an imaginary axis perpendicular to his visual ray.

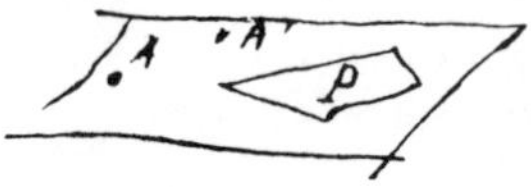

The vision[3] of a plane P. corresponds in the continuum to a *grasp*[4] of which one can get an idea by holding a penknife clasped in one's fist, for example

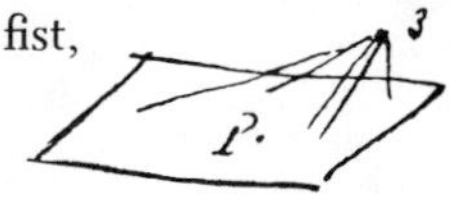

For the representation of the angle[4], 2 mirrors intersecting (at an obtuse angle) depict 2 spaces intersecting along a hinge-plane. For the eye[3] in space[3] this hinge-plane is only seen through its intersection with space[3], i.e. the intersection line of the 2 mirrors. *The hinge-plane of the 2 spaces*[3] *is hidden behind this line* and gives a clear picture to the eye[3] moving from right to left without ever being able to catch any part of this plane.

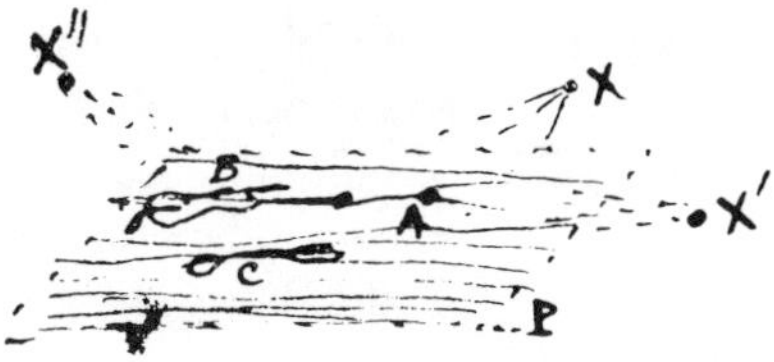

4-dim'l Perspective
Analogies
I. In a 3-dim'l continuum

A.B.C.: 3 plane objects on plane P.
X X' X'': three different points of sight
For a 3-dim'l individual, the 2-dim'l retinal image is different at each point of sight (X X' X'' etc.)—(Hence linear perspective).

II. In a 4-dim'l continuum

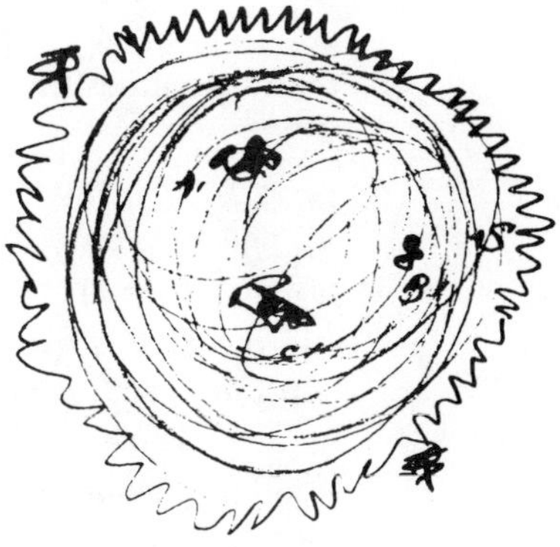

A' B' C': 3 *solid objects* in 3-dim'l space S.
Define the grasp
a starting point
for this grasp,
etc.

For a 4-dim'l individual the 3-dim'l *tactile grasp-image* (like a penknife in one's fist) will differ when the (point? where the grasp? starts?) moves 4-dimensionally.

In a continuum, 2 straight lines intersecting do not determine a plane —they *merge* (parallel lines also merge).
In a continuum—the plane reduces to its own section: the straight line.
In a continuum—2 intersecting planes do not determine a space—they

merge along a plane perpendicular to their common intersecting line.
Hence:
In a continuum, any space is perceived by a 4-dim'l sense of touch as a sort of projection on a plane recording the different 3-dim'l coordinates. —The perceived object is no longer the point, as to the ordinary sense of touch, but rather a sort of tactile expansible *sphere* assuming all 3-dim'l shapes.

Self-evident truths:

In a space, 2 straight lines intersecting determine a plane or 2-dim'l continuum

In a space, 3 straight lines intersecting at a common point determine a 3-dim'l space

In a plane, 3 straight lines intersecting do not determine a space. Therefore in a space^4 lines intersecting do not determine a *continuum.*

In the continuum

The 4-dim'l eye is such that an infinite plane surface (for ex.) does not *intersect* the continuum.
This 4-dim'l eye can be depicted (3-dim'lly) as a *closed spherical retina* which would receive at the same time the picture of all the 3-dim'l features of the surface. This 4-dim'l picture of the surface is not an enumeration (to infinity) of the 3-dim'l features of the surface; it is a retinal formula synthesizing this surface.

In the plane, the 2-dim'l native is either on one side of an infinite straight line or on the other side. Therefore this line is for him a Dedekind cut (Poincaré) creating 2 distinct plane fields.
—In the 3-dim'l space we *must* cross a plane in order to *know* its 2 sides.
—In the 4-dim'l continuum a 4-dim'l body will *be such* that if sectioned by a median space^3 the 2 separate 4-dim'l parts will be symmetrical about this median space^3.
The 4-dim'l native when perceiving this symmetrical 4-dim'l body will go from one region to the other by *crossing instantaneously* the median space^3.

One can imagine this instantaneous crossing of a space^3 by recalling certain effects with 3-sided mirrors in which the images disappear (behind) new images.

Space

The space or 4-dim'l field is a continuum the basic element of which is a sphere of infinitely small radius ($R = 1$ rather than $R = 0$).

(That which may be termed) the *4-dim'l straight line* is defined by *the whole set of successive spheres with larger and larger radii* starting from point 0, center of the *first elemental sphere.* This straight 4-dim' line = 3-dim'l space and does not get out of that space.
In space this 4-dim'l line is located in function of its elemental sphere. It answers completely the question of continuity without deviation in relation to a 4-dim'l perception.
As part of the 4-dim'l continuum it remains of a 3-dim'l nature and is perceptible to the beings living in the 3-dim'l space, to such a point that they cannot step out of it (physically).
For the ordinary eye in a space^3 any point is the end of a line (whether straight or not) coming from a continuum^4. The eye could go endlessly around the point (in the 3-dim'l), it will never be able to perceive any part of this 4-dim'l line other than the point where it meets the 3-dim'l medium.

Relation of space^3 to continuum^4
A plane in the continuum^4 intersects a *space^3* along a line–i.e. every line of space^3 is the possible section (visible to the eye^3) of one or more planes coming from the continuum.

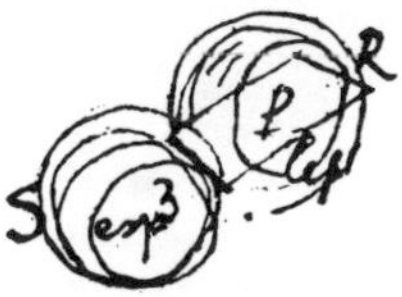

P forms a part, in the continuum, of a space^3 R making an angle^4 with space^3 S

It is certain that every point of space^3 conceals, hides, is the end of a line of the continuum. One would like to go around this point and perceive this 4th direction which comes (at this point) into contact with space^3–
A line of space^3 also conceals a plane; it is like the section of this plane, the only one visible to the eye^3.

In the same way a plane is certainly the intersection of 2 spaces^3 (see angles^4). But an object^3 in a space^3 does not conceal. It is on the contrary attacked, cut up by all the *lines, volumes, planes of the continuum^4*
1 2 3
ending, in its space^3, at its construction in points, planes, lines.
1 2 3

Each ordinary 3-dim'l body, inkpot, house, captive balloon is *the* perspective projected by *numerous* 4-dim'l bodies upon the 3-dim'l medium. There are 3-dim'l bodies which correspond to fewer perspective projections (in the 4 to 3-dim'l region) than others. One would have to construct / determine those which are the projection of a single 4-dim'l body (4-dim'l Perspective).

Angles^4*:*

2 spaces^3 R and S intersect in the continuum along a *hinge-plane. The angle*^{4} *is thus determined by 2 spaces*^{3} *as sides and one plane*^{2} *as hinge.*

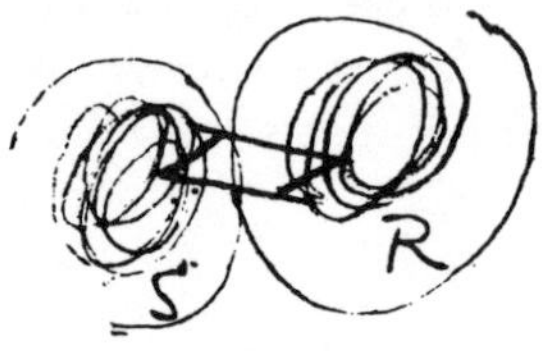

On an infinite line let us take two points, A, B. Let us rotate AB about A as hinge. AB will generate some sort of surface, i.e. either curved, broken or plane.

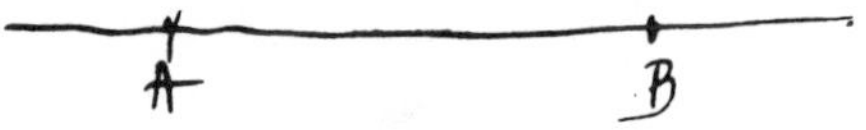

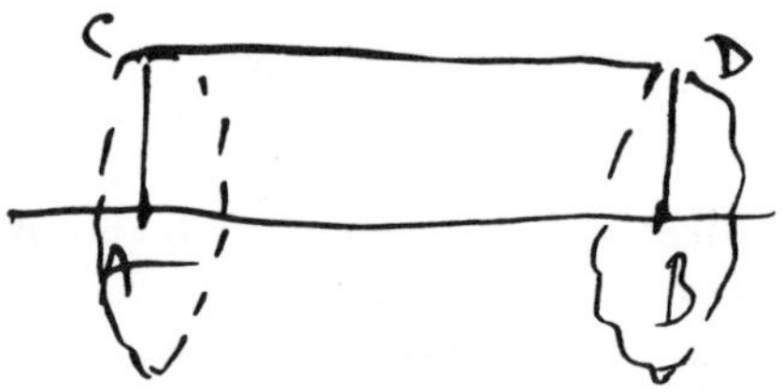

Let us rotate the plane surface ABCD about AB as hinge. It will generate a volume.

Thus a *finite* 3-dim'l continuum is generated by a *finite* 2-dim'l continuum *rotating* (in the general sense) about a finite 1-dim'l hinge. *Thus a 4-dim'l finite continuum is generated by a finite 3-dim'l continuum rotating (here the word loses its physical meaning—see further on) about a 2-dim'l hinge.*

A 2-dim'l hinge = infinite surface.

Finite hinge = closed section in this plane.

This closed section is by the way one of the sides of the volume or finite 3-dim'l continuum.
This volume of 3-dim'l continuum must rotate about the plane section as hinge. But the word rotate must lose here its physical meaning because it is obvious that if we let this plane section rotate about an axis, we will only generate 3-dim'l continuums. By analogy with the preceding operation (hinge-line of a rotating surface), we shall find that the hinge-line does not move (or, if we allow ourselves a physical representation, rotates about itself in its infinite 1-dim'l continuum without moving in this continuum).
Therefore the plane section as hinge must *not move* or *"rotate" only about itself without generating any volume,* and *without moving in its infinite 2-dim'l continuum.*

Consequences:
e.g.: The intersection of a cube by the hinge-surface will be a square: this square must not move on the infinite surface, must remain motionless and, notwithstanding, *rotate about itself as square section of a surface.*

What meaning can one give to this last sentence:
When the hinge-line was rotating about itself each point on this line carried in its revolution a line perpendicular (at this point) on the hinge. By analogy each line of the hinge-square-surface will carry a plane perpendicular to the square. By line of the hinge-square-surface I mean element of the surface, just as by point I meant element of the line.

Starting with a sphere (having a radius of 10 cm. for ex.) This sphere, 3-dim'l continuum, is a Dedekind cut in a n-dim'l continuum composed of the virtual images of that sphere repeated to infinity, i.e. composed of the positions in a 3-dim'l continuum which this sphere can occupy, and of all the unities that

1. Any object in the geometric 3-dim'l space is located by the mensuration of *every one* of its 3 dimensions. This mensuration of its shape which is an arithmetic (or chronic) formula determines *Its Reality* by the *constant* ratio of its 3 dimensions with respect to one another.
This 3-dim'l Reality leads to the infinite repetition of images greater than, equal to or smaller than the object, but each of these images, in infinite number, is subject to the constant ratio of the 3 dimensions of the prototype object.
2. The innumerable (infinite a priori) set of these virtual images compose a 4-dim'l continuum and not only the 3-dim'l continuum (geo-

metric infinity). In fact: the geometric infinity is indeed a continuum whose 3 dimensions are considered in their *indefinity* since they start from the axiomatic point. On the contrary the continuous set of virtual images starts from a geometric 3-dim'l volume and the *virtual images which constitute it* are the transposition of a 3-dim'l object. Our senses, very accustomed to physical space, hardly allow the conception of a 5-dim'l continuum for ex., which would be a set of *supravirtual images* of the virtual image already given by the 3-dim'l object in its 4-dim'l conception.

3. Objection: What is the meaning of this word *4th* dimension since it does not have either tactile or sensorial correspondence as do the 1st, the 2nd, the 3rd dimension.

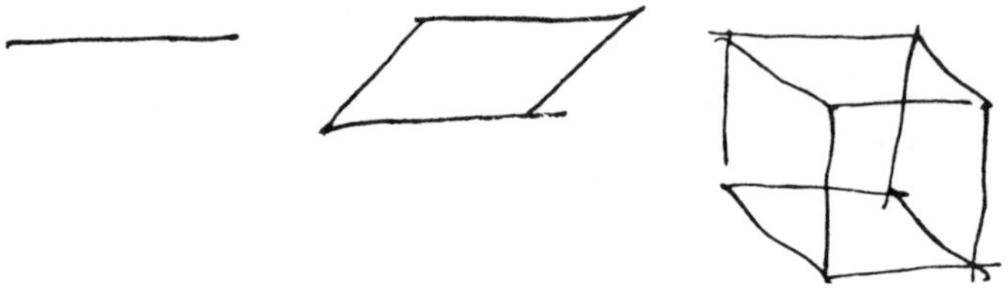

For a 5th dimension one can hypothetically imagine that the constant ratio which determines every virtual image in the 4-dim'l continuum ceases to be constant and yet does not therefore cease to be a *ratio. Explain.*

Also, the 4-dim'l continuum: Poincaré's explanation about n-dim'l continuums by means of the Dedekind cut of the n-1 continuum is not in error. It is on the contrary confirmed and it is by even basing oneself on this explanation that one can justify the name of 4th dimension given to this continuum of virtual images in which the Dedekind cut could only be obtained by means of the 3-dim'l prototype object considered *in its geometric infinity.*

The reflection (virtual images)
in a mirror

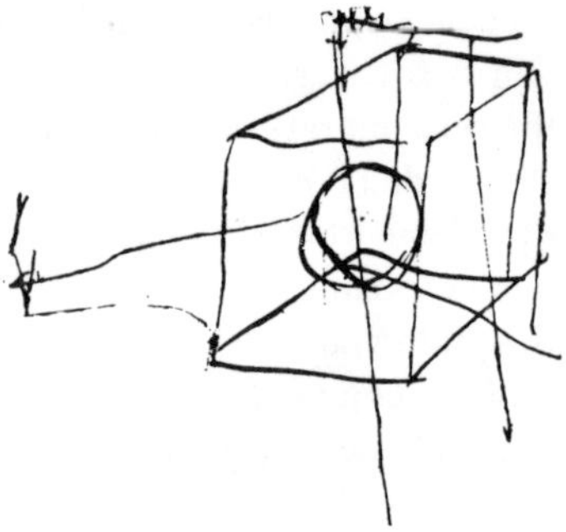

From the 2-dim'l perspective giving the appearance of the 3-dim'l continuum, construct a 3-dim'l (or perhaps a 2-dim'l perspective) of this 4 dim'l continuum.
Echo. Virtual sound

Virtuality as 4th dimension. Not the Reality in its sensorial appearance, but the virtual representation of a volume (analogous to the reflection in a mirror).

Multiplicity to infinity of the virtual images of the 3-dim'l object. These images being the smallest to infinity and the largest to infinity.

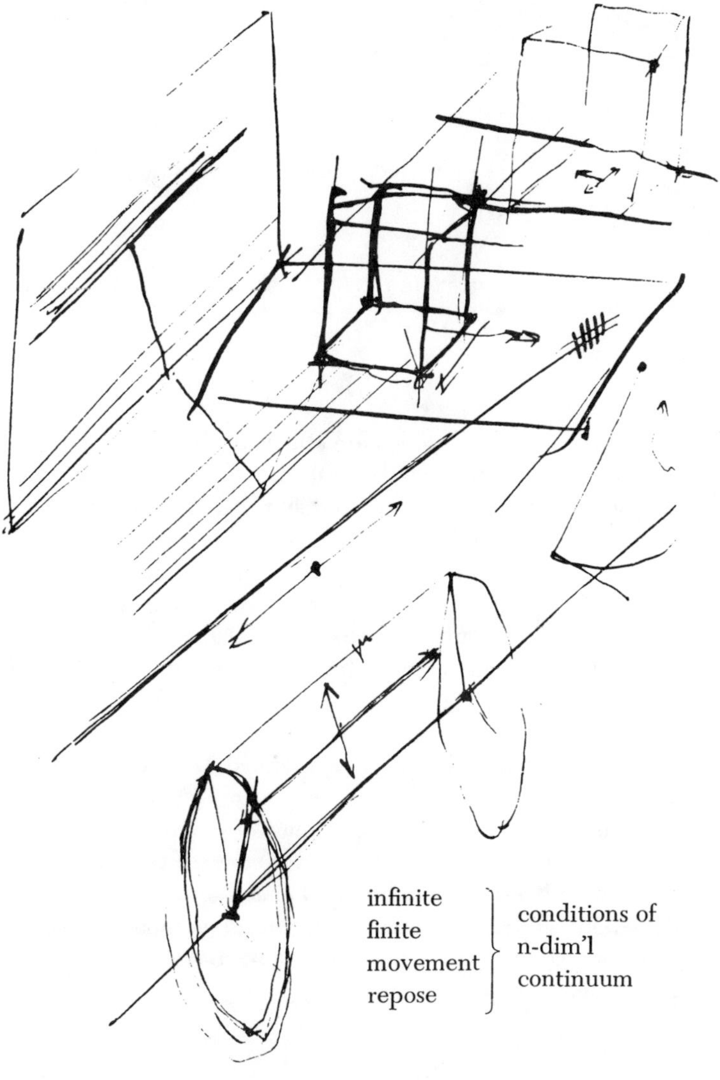

infinite finite movement repose	conditions of n-dim'l continuum

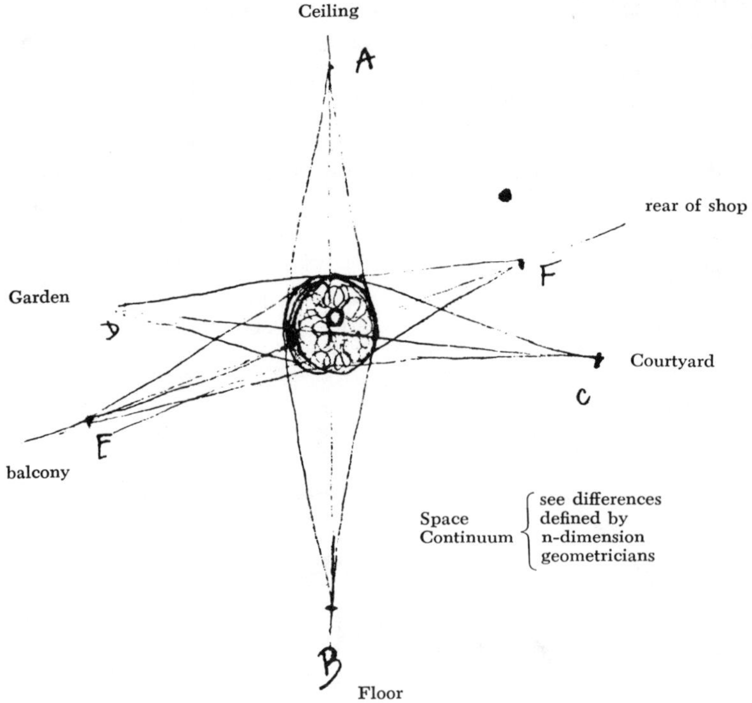

A B C D E F. Points in space to which are attached (from one side, one end) the threads tangent to the new body 0. From the point of contact these threads wind up "snail-like" and stretch towards a new point of gravity.

Hence the body 0:1° is tangent to space. 2° Its shape is determined by this new point (temporarily point of gravity), whose *property of distraction* only applies on the confines of space i.e.: at the limit the shape of the body 0 is the resultant of the 2 forces (attraction in space and distraction in the continuum).

Graphically this force of distraction is represented by the threads of contact.

Try to find the other properties of the new point of gravity e.g. Lack of *uniformity in the obedience movement* of body 0 toward the center, i.e. this movement can be *alternative* and body 0 enjoys an alternative freedom. The deviations of time measuring this *freedom* followed by an equal time deviation during which body 0 is *determined* by the center under *certain* conditions. (Find the certain.)

These time deviations are made of 2- or 3-dim'l periods (see special development of the dial seen in profile in the "*revolver chewer.*")

A clock seen in profile so that time disappears, but which accepts the idea of time other than linear time. [M.D., 1965.]
M.D. suggests reading J. W. Dunne's *Experiment in Time* and *Serialism*. See Robert Lebel's *L'Inventeur du Temps Gratuit,* Le Soleil Noir, Paris 1964, for which M.D. made a "pliage" of a clock seen in profile (*Le Pendule de Profil*). See also the Green Box: The Clock *in profile,* etc. [C.G.]

Rrose Sélavy & Co.

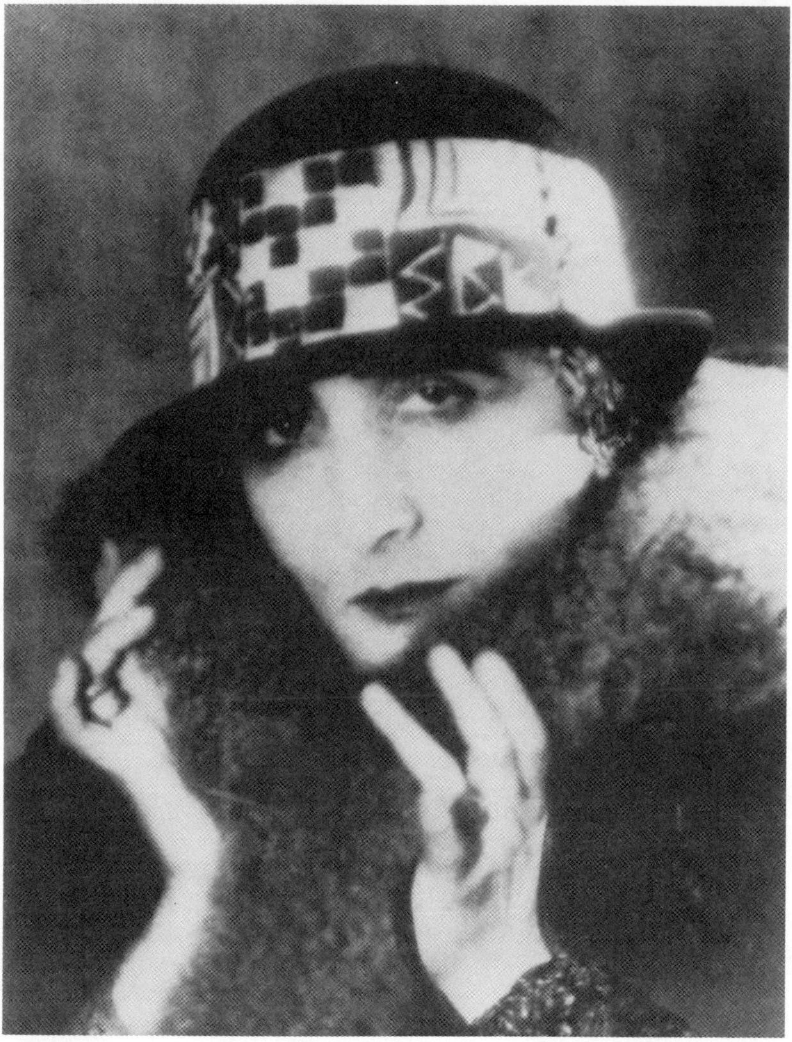

Rrose Sélavy by Man Ray, 1921

PRECISION OCULISM

RROSE SÉLAVY

New York–Paris

COMPLETE LINE OF

WHISKERS AND KICKS

This calling card announced Duchamp–Sélavy and her dual speciality: precision oculism and whiskers and kicks. The invented name Rrose Sélavy ("eros c'est la vie" or "arroser la vie"–drink it up, celebrate life) has received ample commentary elsewhere; cf. Duchamp's own explanation in Pierre Cabanne's *Dialogues with Marcel Duchamp* (New York: Viking Press, 1971), pp. 64–65. As for the optical part of the specialty, it was an important preoccupation of Duchamp's, producing mixed results, including the Op Art movement and the near decapitation of Man Ray when one of the spinning glassplate machines went berserk on its trial run.

In addition to the serious side of the firm's business there is, as usual with Duchamp, a built-in alternate and less serious possibility. "Oculiste" sounds like "au culiste" and it contains the word "cul," ass. Duchamp's doctored *Mona Lisa* was, of course, entitled L.H.O.O.Q., which when pronounced in French yields "elle a chaud au cul" or "she has a hot ass." So Sélavy advertises herself as a specialist in precision ass and glass work.

The firm's headquarters are first in New York and then Paris; but a patriotic Frenchman offended by the billing could console himself by recalling Duchamp's answer as to why he became an American citizen: the passport was handy because his bags were opened less often, allowing him to smuggle cigars from country to country with relative ease.

The whiskers and kicks probably have reference to what was added to the *Mona Lisa* in addition to the caption–a moustache and a goatee–as well as to the fact that Duchamp hardly ever misses a chance to boot us in the rear when we are reverently bent over examining or explicating his work. One of his Ready-mades, called "trébuchet" or "trap," was a coatrack nailed to the floor, inviting accidents. Duchamp obviously enjoyed verbal traps or trips as well and *Rrose Sélavy* abounds in them.

Rrose Sélavy trouve qu'un incesticide doit coucher avec sa mère avant de la tuer; les punaises sont de rigueur.

[Rrose Sélavy finds that an incesticide must sleep with his mother before killing her; bed bugs are de rigueur.] [E.P.]

This note was published for the first time in *Littérature* (nouvelle série, no. 5, Paris, 1 October, 1922). It has been frequently reproduced, for example in the program for the Matinée of the Comédie des Champs Elyseés: "Breton will Speak on Black Humor." In André Breton's *Anthologie de l'humour noir* the following variant is found: "An incesticide must sleep with his 'relative' before killing her; bed bugs are required." Roger Shattuck suggests two imaginative translations: ". . . bugging required" or "We all have our ticks."

Most of these notes appeared in one or all of the following publications: *Littérature 5, Anthologie de l'humour noir, The Wonderful Book, The Box in a Valise*. The following abbreviations will identify the location: *L., A.H.N., W.B., V.* Duchamp put nine of these short sayings–some slightly modified–in white spirals on black cardboard discs in 1925 and 1926. They were used in the short film, *Anémic Cinéma,* which he made with Man Ray and Marc Allégret.

Rrose Sélavy et moi esquivons les ecchymoses des Esquimaux aux mots exquis.

Reproduced in *391* (Paris, July 1924) and inscribed on an *Anémic Cinéma* disc, it was also engraved on a copper ring of the *Precision Optics Rotary Demisphere,* 1925. The *W.B.* variant reads: "Nous estimons les ecchymoses. . . ."

Question d'hygiène intime:
Faut-il mettre la moelle de l'épée dans le poil de l'aimée?

[Question of intimate hygiene:
Should you put the hilt of the foil in the quilt of the goil?] [E.P.]

First published in *Le Coeur à barbe* (Paris, 1922) where the word "conseil" or recommendation is substituted for "question." In *A.H.N.* and the discs the question becomes: "Have you already put . . . ?" The above translation is a regional variation.

Abominables fourrures abdominales.

[Abominable abdominal furs.] [E.P.]

Initially published in *L.;* it reappears in *V.*

Parmi nos articles de quincaillerie paresseuse, nous recommandons un robinet qui s'arrête de couler quand on ne l'écoute pas.

[Among our articles of lazy hardware we recommend a faucet which stops dripping when nobody is listening to it.] [E.P.]

Reprinted in *V.,* in the discs, and in *A.H.N.* with a single change, "le" robinet. The inscription also appears in an etching of a urinal entitled "An Original Revolutionary Faucet: 'Mirrorical Return?' " *A Collection of Galleria Schwarz Catalogs* (Milan, 1965).

La mode pratique, création Rrose Sélavy:
La robe oblongue, dessinée exclusivement pour dames affligées du hoquet.

[For practical wear, a Rrose Sélavy creation:
The oblong dress, exclusively designed for ladies afflicted with the hiccups.] [E.P.]

This appears in the program for the Breton speech on Black Humor at the Comédie des Champs Elysées. One of several variations is "Teinturerie Rrose Sélavy: robe oblongue pour personne affligée du hoquet. Marcel Duchamp," Catalogue de l'Exposition de dessins surréalistes—"Les Quatre Chemins," 1935. Duchamp does have some clothing designs to his credit—vests and aprons—each with its own Duchampian significance.

La différence entre un bébé qui téte et un premier prix d'horticulture est que le premier est un souffleur de chair chaude et le second un choufleur de serre chaude.

There seems to be no need to translate this little spoonerism (about the difference between nursing babies and hot-house cauliflowers) which also appears, slightly modified, on a disc. It is a mild and amusing exercise for Duchamp, whose posers are usually more on the order of the difference between the man leaving church and the lady getting out of the tub, the first with his soul full of hope. . . . Or the groups of acrobats and cheerleaders, the first showing a cunning array of stunts. . . .

Nous livrons à domicile: moustiques domestiques (demi-stock).

[We make home deliveries: domestic mosquitoes (half-stock)] [E.P.]

Reprinted in *V*. Variants: "Moustiques domestiques demistock" (*Intervention surréaliste,* nouvelle série, no. 1, juin 1934, p. 32); "Nous livrons des moustiques domestiques (Demi-stock)"; W.B.; A.H.N., followed by "Pour la cure d'azote sur la côte d'Azur—" [for the nitrogen cure on the Côte d'Azur]. This was a disc for *Anémic Cinéma.*

Des bas en soie . . . la chose aussi.

[Silk stockings . . . the thing too.] [E.P.]

This first appears in *W.B.,* then in *A.H.N.* and *V.* In the *Dictionnaire abrégé du surréalisme* (Paris: Galerie des Beaux-Arts, 1938) it becomes the following entry: "Bas—Des bas en soie . . . la chose aussi." One suposes that "the thing" is both "en bas" and "en soie," enclosed perhaps in what the French call an "English hood," and probably not pertaining to the Kantian, Hegelian, and existentialist "en-soi."

A charge de revanche; à verge de rechange.

Reprinted in *V.* and in *A.H.N.* with a single change: "A charge de revanche et à verge de rechange." Duchamp simply switches some letters of nearly identical words. "A charge de revanche" means returning the favor and a "verge de rechange" has to do with finding a replacement penis.

A coups trop tirés.

[Ball too often.] [E.P.]

First appeared in *W.B.* It was reprinted in *A.H.N.* and in *V.* The disc reads "Inceste ou passion de famille, à coups trop tirés." "A couteaux tirés" means to be at daggers drawn, while the slang expression for having a lay is "tirer un coup."

Litanie des saints
Je crois qu'elle sent du bout des seins.
Tais-toi, tu sens du bout des seins.
Pourquoi sens-tu du bout des seins?
Je veux sentir du bout des seins.

This "Litany of the Saints" first appeared in *L,* no. 5, and then in *V.* Any attempt at translation is unrewarding since this is a play on words, the French words "seins," breasts, pronounced like "saints," and "des saints," which sounds much like both "dessein" (design, plan, scheme, project) and "dessin" (drawing or sketch). In addition "du bout" is close to "debout," standing up. Finally, this is not unlike the grammatical exercises found in texts for learning French.

Opalin ô ma Laine.

"Opaline; oh my wool" was first printed in *L.* Duchamp is simply playing with masculine and feminine endings.

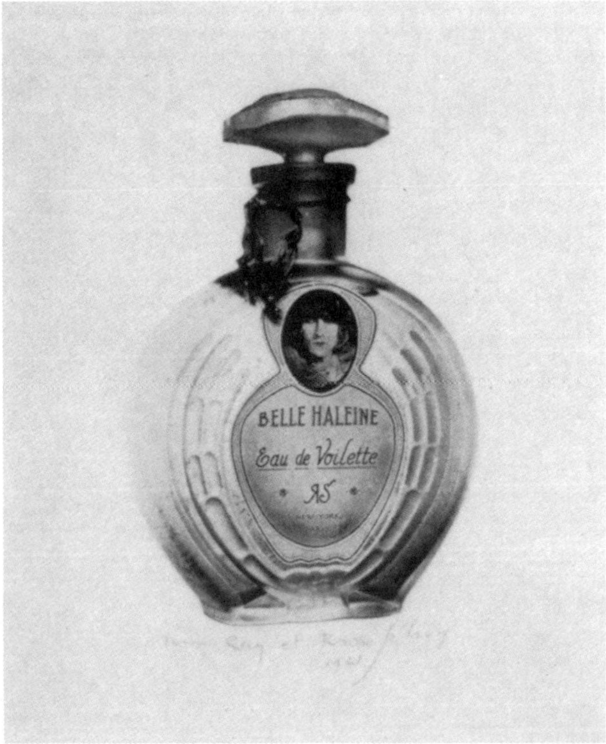

Beautiful Breath,
Veil Water, 1921

Avoir de l'haleine en dessous.

An *A.H.N.* variant reads: "There is he who takes the photograph and she who has 'de la haleine' underneath." The pair in question are Man Ray (the photographer) and Marcel Duchamp. The reference is to Man Ray's photograph, "Belle Haleine, Eau de Voilette," 1921 which presents Duchamp in drag on a perfume bottle with the Belle Haleine caption. There is confusion between "Belle Haleine" (Sweet Breath) and *La Belle Hélène* (a popular Offenbach operetta). In addition "les dessous en laine" are woolen underwear, so the beauty might have woolies or odor underneath—or perhaps both.

Un mot de reine; des maux de reins.

First appearance in *W.B.*, then in *A.H.N.* and *V.* The queen's word ("mot de reine") and the backaches ("maux de reins") seem to be phonically and not logically connected. Duchamp is playing with a transformation of words from singular to plural and from masculine to feminine. There might, however, be more involved here; David Ball suggests that the queen's witty saying ("mot") may be acceptable *once;* but in the plural ("des maux"—"des mots") they are a pain in the backside.

Caleçons de musique (abréviation pour: leçons de musique de chambre).

Lesson ("leçon") is contained in the word "caleçons" (shorts) so the wild abbreviation for chamber music becomes "caleçons de musique" or musical shorts.

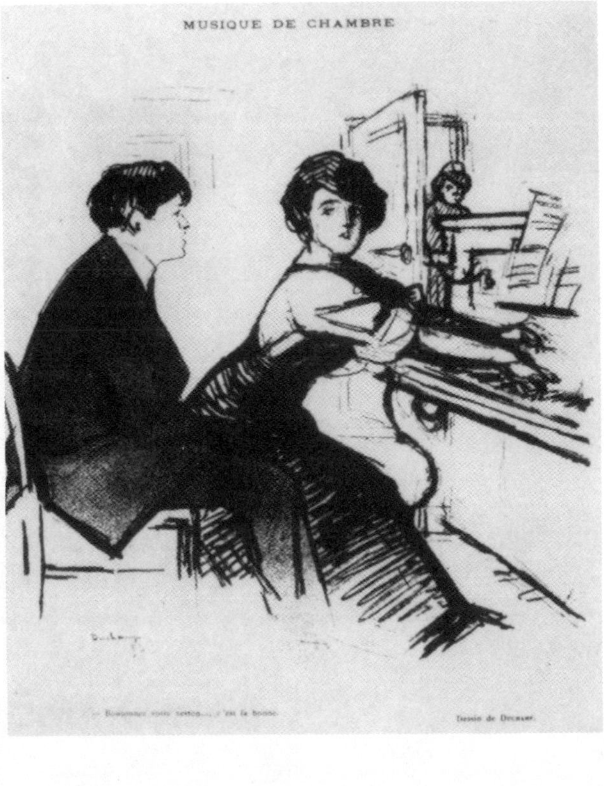

Chamber Music, 1909-10

Le meilleur des savons est le savon aux amendes honorables.

[The best of the soaps is honorable amends soap.] [E.P.]

In French the words for almonds and amends are pronounced the same. Another possibility, suggested by David Ball, is based on the fact that "passer un savon à quelqu'un" means to bawl someone out—after which one might want to make honorable amends.

Il faut dire:
La crasse du tympan, et non le Sacre du Printemps.

[One must say:
Grease of eardrum and not Rite of Spring.] [E.P.]

This first appears in *Le Coeur à barbe,* Paris, 1922, then in *V*. An *A.H.N.* variant reads: "Sacre du Printemps, crasse de tympan." "Crasse" (grease) is the anagram of "Sacre" (Rite), a deflation which must have delighted Duchamp. Some surrealists followed this lead, Michel Leiris transforming "patrie" (fatherland) to "tripaille" (tripe) and "catholicism" to "ism of your colic" in a 1925 issue of *La Révolution Surréaliste*. However, it appears that the fun-making at the Rite of Spring was not original with Duchamp. Very well known in 1913, it was attributed to Willy, Colette's husband (cf. Luc Etienne, *L'Art du Contrepet* [Paris: J. J. Pauvert]).

La bagarre d'Austerlitz.

[The brawl at Austerlitz.] [E.P.]

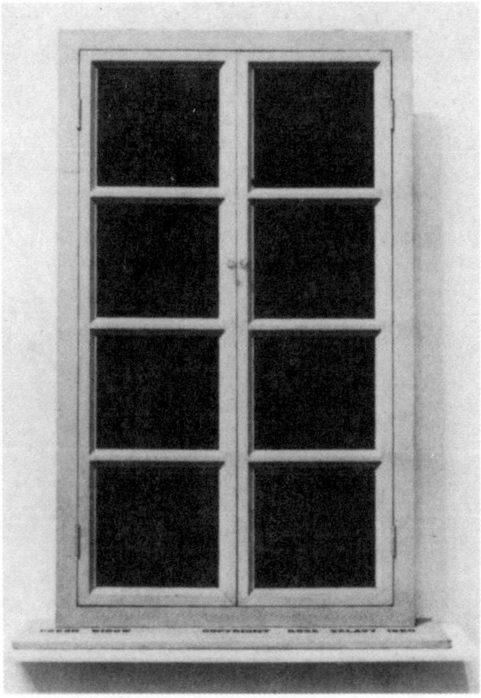

"Fresh Widow," 1920

"La Bagarre d'Austerlitz," 1921, is a Duchampian French window set in imitation brickwork, bearing the white marks left by glaziers on newly installed windows. There are multiple meanings possible. First, the Napoleonic battle at Austerlitz was quite a brawl. Second, "la bagarre" sounds a good bit like "la gare" (the station) and indeed the Gare d'Austerlitz is an important Paris terminal. One critic, David Antin in *ARTnews*, Oct. 1972, goes so far as to suggest that the title can be broken down to "la Bague, Garde d'Austères Lits" (the Ring, Keeper of Austere Beds), thus linking this window with another, the "Fresh Widow" who obviously sleeps in an austere bed. Antin remarks that the Battle of Austerlitz produced a good many widows.

My niece is cold because my knees are cold.

This appeared in English in the *W.B., A.H.N.,* and *V.*

Daily lady cherche démêlés avec Daily Mail.

[Daily lady will dally with Daily Mail.] [Ron Padgett]

The lady advertising for these diurnal involvements appeared in *A.H.N.* and *V.* A related and modified printed Ready–made (Eliot variant) might be:

> When evening quickens faintly in the vale,
> Wakening the appetites of love in some
> And to others bringing the Boston Daily Male . . . [E.P.]

Une cinq chevaux qui rue sur pignon.

This too defies translation. The "cinq chevaux" was an early and popular Citroën car–a French equivalent of the Ford Model T. "Ruer sur" means to rush at: "Avoir pignon sur rue" means to have a house of your own, but "pignon" also means gear pinion. Thus the sentence admits all possibilities and rules out none. It re–appears in *V.* and as "Une 5CV qui rue sur pignon" in *A.H.N.*

Une nymphe amie d'enfance.

This appears first in *W.B.* and subsequently in *A.H.N.* In English it reads "A nymph childhood friend" but again the French pronunciation allows several intriguing possibilities. "Nymphe amie" is close to the French word for nymphomania. "Infamie" and "en famille" are two other possibilities.

Ovaire toute la nuit.

[We never clothe.] [Ron Padgett]

This all–night ovary turns up again in *V.* Duchamp slightly modifies "ouvert," open: thus the common expression "ouvert toute la nuit" becomes "ovaire toute la nuit." He is also taking off on a popular 1922 novel, *Ouvert la nuit,* by Paul Morand, a very conventional novelist. In an unpublished "roman à clé" Du–champ's friend Francis Picabia invented a character very much resembling the author of *Ouvert la nuit,* who was called Pierre Moribond.

Se livrer à des foies de veau sur quelqu'un.

A French idiom, "se livrer à des *voies de fait* sur quelqu'un" means to give someone a sound beating. Here "voies de fait becomes "foies de veau," veal liver.

Le système métrite par un temps blenorrhagieux.

Duchamp slightly modifies two words, denying us the words we would expect. After "système" we would look for "métrique" and not "métrite." "Blennorragique" might be a pendant for "métrique," rather than the invented "blenorragieux." This first appears in *W.B.,* is reprinted in *A.H.N.,* and included in *V.* with "blenhorragieux" becoming "blennoragieux." "Métrite," a medical term, designates an inflammation of the uterus. "Blenhhorragie" comes from the Greek "blenna" meaning mucous, and "rhage," erruption, and is a medical term for a contagious and embarrassing genital–urinary disease which the French call "chaude–pisse." "Un temps blenorragieux" also sounds like "un temps bien orageux" or stormy weather, accompanied, one might suppose, by a clap of thunder.

Du dos de la cuillère au cul de la douairière.

"From the back of the spoon to the rump of the dowager" was first printed in *391*, no. 18 (Paris, juillet, 1924), reprinted in *A.H.N.* and, with "cuillère" becoming "cuiller," in *V.* This is pure nonsensical wordplay unless one admits a hidden connection between the spoon's bottom and that of the dowager.

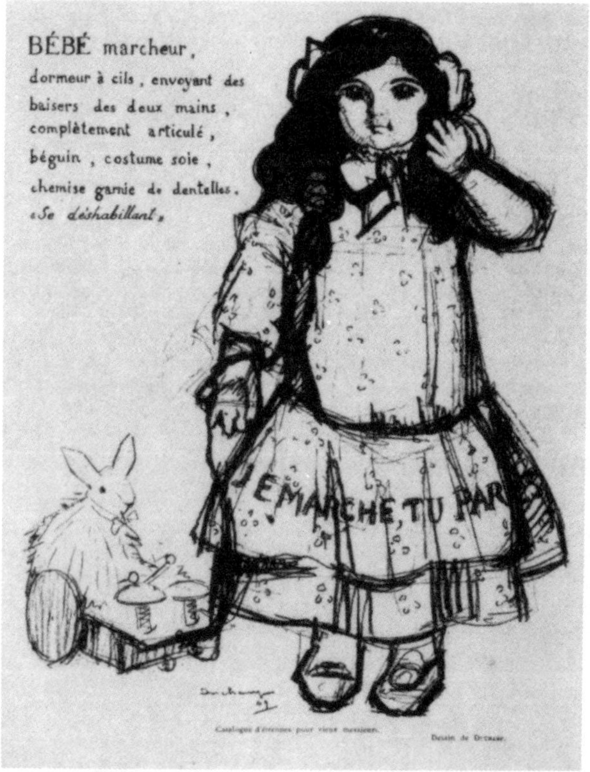

Walking Doll,
1910

Paroi parée de paresse de paroisse.

The "wall bedecked with parish idleness" reappeared in *A.H.N.* and in *V.* This bit of alliteration is every bit as significant as the well-known saying: "black ladders lack bladders."

Prendre 1 centimètre cube de fumée de tabac et en peindre les surfaces extérieure et intérieure d'une couleur hydrofuge.

[Take 1 cubic centimeter of tobacco smoke and paint its outer and inner surfaces with a waterproof color.] [David Ball]

This experiment is closer to the preparatory notes for the Large Glass than to the word games in *Rrose Sélavy*.

Aiguiser l'ouïe (forme de torture).

[Sharpened hearing (form of torture).] [E.P.]

Quand on a un corps étranger entre les jambes, il ne faut pas mettre son coude près des siennes.

[When you have a foreign body between your legs, you must not put your elbows next to hers.] [E.P.]

Reprinted in *V.*

Faut-il réagir contre la paresses des voies ferrées entre deux passages de trains?

[Should one react against the laziness of railway tracks between the passage of two trains?] [E.P.]

Si je te donne un sou, me donneras-tu une paire de ciseaux?

[If I give you a sou, will you give me a pair of scissors?] [E.P.]

The French custom is to give a sou to preserve friendship when offered a sharp or pointed object. Duchamp reverses what might be expected, saying in effect: "If I am good to you will you cut me out of your life?" This was also a disc.

Une boîte de Suédoises pleine est plus légère qu'une boîte entamée parce qu'elle ne fait pas de bruit.

[A full box of wooden matches is lighter than an opened box because it doesn't make any noise.] [E.P.]

This was reprinted in *A.H.N.* "Suédoises" can also mean Swedish women. "Allumettes" are matches and "allumeuses" are teasers. It may not be too far-fetched to believe that there is another connection here.

Bains de gros thé pour grains de beauté.

Duchamp cleverly manipulates initial consonants here, "*b*ains de *g*ros" becoming "*g*rains de *b*eauté." The rhyme itself is nonsensical. The "bains de gros thé" are baths in tea and the "grains de beauté" are beauty spots or moles. A variant reads: "Matin et soir" (morning and evening): "bains de gros thé pour grains de beauté sans trop de Bengué" [Ben–Gay]. Also a disc.

Fossettes d'aisances.

"Fossettes" are dimples and "aisance" is ease. However the Sélavy kick is poised because a "lieu d'aisance" or "cabinet d'aisance" is a public toilet. Furthermore "fossettes" contain the word "fosse" and a "fosse d'aisance" is a cesspool. So the normally and superficially appealing (dimples) is savagely degraded. This short saying appeared in *W.B., A.H.N.,* and *V.*

Nous nous cajolions (nounou; cage aux lions).

[We're a-flirting (We're rough, lurking).] [David Ball]

Once again a single pronunciation permits more than a single meaning. "Nous nous cajolions"—"we were cajoling each other" contains a second possibility: "nounou," nanny, in the lion's cage. Just as a too easy susceptibility to physical beauty in the preceding saying can land you in the cesspool, light and flattering romantic banter can end in terrible danger. This appeared as a rebus in Maurice Nadeau's *Histoire du surréalisme* (Paris: Club des Editeurs, 1958), p. 100.

M'amenez-y.

[I'm easier.] [Trevor Winkfield]

"Amenez–y" sounds like "amnésie" or amnesia. This was the title suggested for a painting by Duchamp's friend, Francis Picabia, in 1918 as well as the title for a proposed review by Céline Arnauld which never was printed. It was also printed in *V.*

Etrangler l'étranger.

[Strangle strangers.] [E.P.]

This was also printed in the *A.H.N.* and *V.* Other anagrams in the *W.B.* include "église–exil" and "ruiner–uriner." One of Duchamp's favorite writers, Léon–Paul Fargue, was a master of this sort of thing, transforming mockingly "La rosette de la Légion d'honneur" into "La roseur de la légion d'honnête."

Orchidée fixe.

[Affixed idea.] [Roger Shattuck]

An "orchidée" is an orchid, but the French word also contains "idée," idea, in it; and an "idée fixe" is an obsession. This first appeared in *W.B.*

Abcès opulent.

[Opulent abscess.] [E.P.]

The abscess is not only opulent, it is "au pus lent" or slowly pussing. In *L.*, Duchamp speaks of lancing an "abcès au pus lent." The above version appeared in *A.H.N.*

Anémic cinéma.

This, perhaps the most famous of Duchamp's anagrams, is the title of a short film which he made in Paris with Man Ray and Marc Allégret in 1925–26.

Lits et ratures.

[Litter erasure.] [E.P.]

Francis Picabia used this for the title of his sketch for the cover of André Breton's *Littérature*, nouvelle série, no. 7, 1922. It was reprinted in *V.* The "beds and erasures" deriding of "literature" is in the spirit of an avant-garde periodical which made fun of traditional concepts of writing.

Oh! do shit again! . . .
Oh! douche it again! . . .

Rrose Sélavy

391, no. 18 (July, 1924). Appears on page 121 of the Terrain Vague reedition.

Inceste ou passion de famille.

W.B., *V.* It also forms part of a disc.

Eglise, exile.

[Sacristan, ostracism.] [E.P.]

W.B.

Ruiner, uriner

[Ruined, urined] [Trevor Winkfield]

W.B.

Cuisse enregistreuse

[Ass register] [Ron Padgett]

The word normally preceding "enregistreuse" is "caisse," cash. "Cuisse" means thigh. *W.B.*

Poulet Exaucé

[Chicken Divan.] [E.P.]

W.B. "Exaucer" means to answer a prayer, but the word "sauce" is also found in "exaucer" when pronounced. The chicken might also be "dessosé" or boned.

Oseur d'Influence

A.L.N., and *London Bulletin*, no. 13 (April 15, 1939), p. 12. The "influential darer" when pronounced in French sounds much like "aux heures d'affluence" or "at rush hours."

"Sa robe est noire," dit Sarah Bernhardt.

Reprinted without quotation marks in the *V.* and *A.H.N.*

Je purule, tu purules, la chaise purule grâce à un rable de vénérien qui n'a rien de vénérable.

Everything is pustulating in this conjugation exercise because of an affliction which is more venereal than venerable. Sent as a cable on the occasion of the opening of the Exposition International du Surréalisme at the Galerie Daniel Cordier in Paris in the winter of 1959–60.

Pierre de Massot

de MA Pissotière
j'aperçois
Pierre de Massot

Duchamp's anagram for his good friend Pierre de Massot was "From my pissoir." It is inscribed on the side of a drawing of what is politely called a Vespasien and appears on a card to be sold at an auction in Massot's benefit at the Hôtel Drouot in Paris on March 17, 1961.

Czech Check

John Cage, a very close friend of the Duchamps, got Marcel to sign his membership card in a Czech Mycological association. It is reproduced on page 546 of the *Complete Works of Marcel Duchamp*.

L'aspirant habite Javel et moi j'avais l'habite en spirale.

An "aspirant" is a midshipman. He inhabits ("habite") Javel, while the author had a spiral-shaped capstan ("habite"). "La bite" is a term for penis. This was inscribed on a disc which, when set in motion, indeed produced the spiral.

Les toiles, c'est laid.
L'étoile aussi.

Rrose Sélavy

Duchamp did not remember having written this text, which was distributed at the opening of the surrealist gallery, L'Etoile scellée, in Paris in 1953. The play on words involves "les toiles" (the canvases) and "l'étoile" (star) and "c'est laid" (it's ugly) and "scellée" (sealed).

Objet Dard

['ard object] [Ron Padgett]

An "objet dard" differs from an objet d'art other than in pronunciation. "Dard" is a common word for penis and Duchamp's sculpture piece, *Objet Dard,* is indeed in a vaguely phallic shape.

Et Qui Libre?

[Equal librium] [Roger Shattuck]

"Et qui libre?," a phonetical rendering of "Equilibre" (equilibrium), was a sketch by Duchamp illustrating a 1917 poem by Francis Picabia. It is reproduced in *The Complete Works of Marcel Duchamp,* p. 533.

A Guest + a Host = a Ghost

This inscription on the inside of a candy wrapper was distributed at the Bill Copley exposition in Paris in 1953.

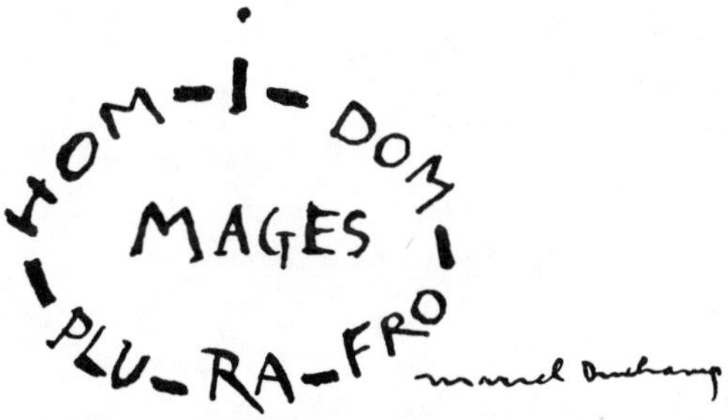

The cover for the catalog "Le Dessin dans l'art magique," Galerie Rive Droite, Paris, 1958. The French words are "images," "dommages," "fromages," "ramages," "plumages," and "hommages."

La Vie en Ose

on suppose
on oppose
on impose
on appose Man Ray
on dépose
on repose
on indispose et finallement une dose de ménopause
avec repose
scélérose
et ankylose
mais la chose qui ose

This meditation on "ose" (dare) which replaces "Rose" was written for the Man Ray show at Cordier and Ekstrom, New York, April 30–May 18, 1963.

SALISSEZ (PRONOUNCE: SALLY SAYS)

MESENS' CHAUSSETTES (PRONOUNCE: SHOW SET)

FOR JULY AND AUGUST

MARCEL

Text of a cable sent from Duchamp in New York for the opening of the E. L. T. Mesens's exhibition at Knokke Le Zoute, Belgium, in July–August, 1963.

Cops pullulate, Copley Copulates

Invitation note for Copley's show at the Alexander Iolas Gallery in New York in January, 1960.

There was a painter named Copley
Who never would miss a good lay
And to make his paintings erotic
Instead of brushes, he simply used his prick

Marcel Duchamp 1963

Appeared in *Iris Time Unlimited,* no. 6, Paris, 13 mai 1963, p. 2.

De plante de serre à fleur de pot (Le Parfait Jardinier)

Duchamp's pun is on "à fleur de peau" or skin deep. This was published as *Quatre inédits de Marcel Duchamp* (PAB: Alès, France, 1960).

Des corsets Quai d'Orsay

Ibid.

Sels de bains belle de seins

Ibid. For the 1947 International Surrealist Exposition catalog cover Duchamp created a woman's breast with the inscription "Please do touch."

Mes salutations très Mistinguett

Ibid. Here the name of a music hall star is substituted for "distinguées."

Marcel Duchamp, Criticavit

The Great Trouble with Art in This Country

The great trouble with art in this country at present, and apparently in France also, is that there is no spirit of revolt—no new ideas appearing among the younger artists. They are following along the paths beaten out by their predecessors, trying to do better what their predecessors have already done. In art there is no such thing as perfection. And a creative lull occurs always when artists of a period are satisfied to pick up a predecessor's work where he dropped it and attempt to continue what he was doing. When on the other hand you pick up something from an earlier period and adapt it to your own work an approach can be creative. The result is not new; but it is new insomuch as it is a different approach.

Art is produced by a succession of individuals expressing themselves; it is not a question of progress. Progress is merely an enormous pretension on our part. There was no progress for example in Corot over Phidias. And "abstract" or "naturalistic" is merely a fashionable form of talking—today. It is no problem: an abstract painting may not look at all "abstract" in 50 years.

During the other war life among the artists in New York was quite different—much more congenial than it has been during these last few years. Among the artists there was much more cohesion—much closer fellowship, much less opportunism. The whole spirit was much different. There was quite a bit of activity, but it was limited to a relatively small group and nothing was done very publicly. Publicity always takes something away. And the great advantage in that earlier period was that the art of the time was laboratory work; now it is diluted for public consumption.

From an interview with James Johnson Sweeney, *The Bulletin of the Museum of Modern Art,* Vol. XIII, no. 4–5, 1946, pp. 19–21.

The basis of my own work during the years just before coming to America in 1915 was a desire to break up forms—to "decompose" them much along the lines the cubists had done. But I wanted to go further—much further—in fact in quite another direction altogether. This was what resulted in *Nude Descending a Staircase,* and eventually led to my large glass, *The Bride Stripped Bare by Her Bachelors, Even.*

The idea of the *Nude* came from a drawing which I had made in 1911 to illustrate Jules Laforgue's poem *Encore à cet astre.* I had planned a series of illustrations of Laforgue's poems but I only completed three of them. Rimbaud and Lautréamont seemed too old to me at the time. I wanted something younger. Mallarmé and Laforgue were closer to my taste—Laforgue's *Hamlet,* particularly. But perhaps I was less attracted by Laforgue's poetry than by his titles. *Comice agricole,* when written by Laforgue, becomes poetry. *"Le soir, le piano"*—no one else could have written this in his time.

In the drawing *Encore à cet astre* the figure is, of course, mounting the stairs. But while working on it, the idea of the *Nude,* or the title—I do not recall which—first came to my mind. I eventually gave the sketch to F. C. Torrey of San Francisco who bought the *Nude Descending a Staircase* from the 1913 New York Armory Show.

No, I do not feel there was any connection between the *Nude Descending a Staircase* and futurism. The futurists held their exhibition at the Galerie Bernheim Jeune in January 1912. I was painting the *Nude* at the same time. The oil sketch for it, however, had already been done in 1911. It is true I knew Severini. But I was working quite by myself at the time—or rather with my brothers. And I was not a café frequenter. Chrono-photography was at the time in vogue. Studies of horses in movement and of fencers in different positions as in Muybridge's albums were well known to me. But my interest in painting the *Nude* was closer to the cubists' interest in decomposing forms than to the futurists' interest in suggesting movement, or even to Delaunay's *Simultaneist* suggestions of it. My aim was a static representation of movement—a static composition of indications of various positions taken by a form in movement—with no attempt to give cinema effects through painting.

The reduction of a head in movement to a bare line seemed to me defensible. A form passing through space would traverse a line; and as the form moved the line it traversed would be replaced by another line—and another and another. Therefore I felt justified in reducing a figure in movement to a line rather than to a skeleton. Reduce, reduce, reduce was my thought;—but at the same time my aim was turning inward, rather than toward externals. And later, following this view, I came to feel an artist might use anything—a dot, a line, the most conventional or unconventional symbol—to say what he wanted to say. The *Nude,* in this way, was a direct step to the large glass, *The Bride Stripped Bare by Her Bachelors, Even.* And in the *King and Queen* painted shortly after the *Nude* there are no human forms or indications of anatomy. But in it one can see where the forms are placed; and for all this reduction I would never call it an "abstract" painting . . .

Futurism was an impressionism of the mechanical world. It was strictly a continuation of the Impressionist Movement. I was not interested in that. I wanted to get away from the physical aspect of painting. I was much more interested in recreating ideas in painting. For me the title was very important. I was interested in making painting serve my purpose, and in getting away from the physicality of painting. For me Courbet had introduced the physical emphasis in the XIXth century. I was interested in ideas—not merely in visual products. I wanted to put painting once again at the service of the mind. And my painting was, of course, at once regarded as "intellectual," "literary" painting. It was true I was endeavouring to establish myself as far as possible from "pleasing" and "attractive" physical paintings. That extreme was seen as literary. My *King and Queen* was a chess king and queen.

In fact until the last hundred years all painting had been literary or religious: it had all been at the service of the mind. This characteristic was lost little by little during the last century. The more sensual appeal a painting provided—the more animal it became—the more highly it was regarded. It was a good thing to have had Matisse's work for the beauty it provided. Still it created a new wave of physical painting in this century or at least fostered the tradition we inherited from the XIXth century masters.

Dada was an extreme protest against the physical side of painting. It was a metaphysical attitude. It was intimately and consciously involved with "literature." It was a sort of nihilism to which I am still very sympathetic. It was a way to get out of a state of mind—to avoid being influenced by one's immediate environment, or by the past: to get away from clichés—to get free. The "blank" force of Dada was very salutary. It told you "don't forget you are not quite so blank as you think you are!" Usually a painter confesses he has his landmarks. He goes from landmark to landmark. Actually he is a slave to landmarks—even to contemporary ones.

Dada was very serviceable as a purgative. And I think I was thoroughly conscious of this at the time and of a desire to effect a purgation in myself. I recall certain conversations with Picabia along these lines. He had more intelligence than most of our contemporaries. The rest was either for or against Cézanne. There was no thought of anything beyond the physical side of painting. No notion of freedom was taught. No philosophical outlook was introduced. The cubists, of course, were inventing a lot at the time. They had enough on their hands at the time not to be worried about a philosophical outlook; and cubism gave me many ideas for decomposing forms. But I thought of art on a broader scale. There were discussions at the time of the fourth dimension and of non-Euclidean geometry. But most views of it were amateurish. Metzinger was particularly attracted. And for all our misunderstandings through these new ideas we were helped to get away from the conventional way of speaking—from our café and studio platitudes.

Brisset and Roussel were the two men in those years whom I admired for their delirium of imagination. Jean-Pierre Brisset was discovered by Jules Romains through a book he picked up from a stall on the quais. Brisset's work was a philological analysis of language—an analysis worked out by an incredible network of puns. He was a sort of a Douanier Rousseau of philology. Romains introduced him to his friends. And they, like Apollinaire and his companions, held a formal celebration to honor him in front of Rodin's *Thinker* in front of the Pantheon where he was hailed as *Prince of Thinkers.*

But Brisset was one of the real people who has lived and will be forgotten. Roussel was another great enthusiasm of mine in the early days. The reason I admired him was because he produced something I had never seen. That is the only thing that brings admiration from my innermost being—something completely independent—nothing to do with the great names or influences. Apollinaire first showed Roussel's work to me. It was poetry. Roussel thought he was a philologist, a philosopher and metaphysician. But he remains a great poet.

It was fundamentally Roussel who was responsible for my glass, *The Bride Stripped Bare by Her Bachelors, Even.* From his *Impressions d'Afrique* I got the general approach. This play of his which I saw with Apollinaire helped me greatly on one side of my expression. I saw at once I could use Roussel as an influence. I felt that as a painter it was much better to be influenced by a writer than by another painter. And Roussel showed me the way.

My ideal library would have contained all Roussel's writings—Brisset, perhaps Lautréamont and Mallarmé. Mallarmé was a great figure. This is the direction in which art should turn: to an intellectual expression, rather than to an animal expression. I am sick of the expression "bête comme un peintre"—stupid as a painter."

"Regions which are not ruled by time and space. . ."

JJS So here you are, Marcel, looking at your *Large Glass*.

MD Yes, and the more I look at it the more I like it. I like the cracks, the way they fall. You remember how it happened in 1926, in Brooklyn? They put the two panes on top of one another on a truck, flat, not knowing what they were carrying, and bounced for sixty miles into Connecticut, and that's the result! But the more I look at it the more I like the cracks: they are not like shattered glass. They have a shape. There is a symmetry in the cracking, the two crackings are symmetrically arranged and there is more, almost an intention there, an extra—a curious intention that I am not responsible for, a ready-made intention, in other words, that I respect and love.

JJS This was one of your most ambitious undertakings, wasn't it?

MD By far the most ambitious. I worked eight years on it, and it is far from finished. I do not even know if it will ever be finished; but some of these were finished.

JJS There is the *Chocolate Grinder*.

MD Yes, one of the two I made; the third one is on the *Large Glass* itself.

JJS You made several versions of the *Nude Descending a Staircase*, too, didn't you?

MD Yes, three; but this one is the one that was shown at the Armory Show in 1913.

JJS The one the newspaperman called an explosion in a shingle factory?

MD Yes. That was really a great line he put out. Now this is the *Boxing Match*. As you see the drawing is completely geometrical or mechanical because that was the period when I changed completely

Edited version of "A Conversation with Marcel Duchamp," television interview conducted by James Johnson Sweeney, *NBC*, January 1956. The interview was filmed at the Philadelphia Museum of Art.

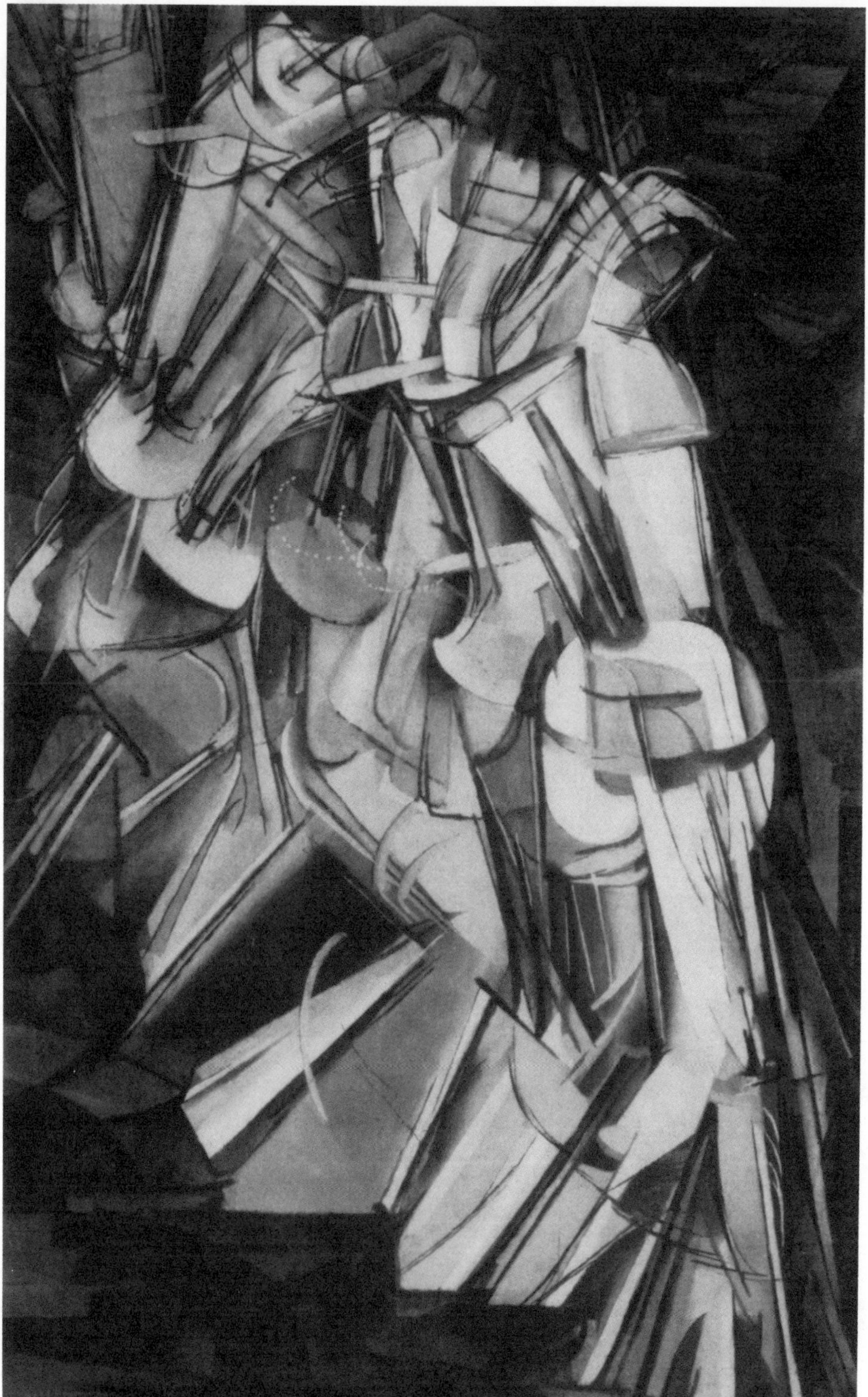

Nude Descending a Staircase, No. 2, 1912

from splashing paint on the canvas to an absolutely precise coordinate drawing, with no relation to arty handiwork.

JJS This was one of the elements of the *Glass* that wasn't incorporated?

MD That's it, yes, it was supposed to be in. It never was incorporated. It should have been somewhere here but never was finished. I felt it was not quite what I wanted.

JJS Marcel, these are not your earliest works.

MD No, no, no. The earliest is this one in the corner, the church. That was done in my village in 1902. I was fifteen then. I went on, I did more paintings then but they are not here.

JJS It is rather impressionist, isn't it? That was the vogue.

MD Yes; well, it was not just the vogue, it was the only thing we talked about. It was a little advanced at the time, but when you look at these two which are later, you can see impressionism was already a thing of the past.

JJS They are more structured.

MD They are more structured. Cézanne was the great man then. This is my two brothers playing chess in their garden and this is my father. You can see Cézanne's influence easily.

JJS Your whole family were painters; your sister and brothers.

MD My sister paints, yes, but especially by brother Jacques Villon.

JJS Did they move you towards this Cézannesque impressionism?

MD No, no; we each went his own separate way. And my father was very nice about it. In fact, it was very difficult then, as it is now, to become a painter on your own. How can you expect to live? He was a good man.

JJS He looks patient, to have set that portrait out.

MD He used to give all four of us a small allowance, just enough for us to live on. He was always very understanding and always helped us out of scrapes, for a long time even after we were adults. And he had very odd ideas, very French. He told us "All right, I'm going to give you what you want, but listen: there are six of you. Anything I give you while I'm alive I will deduct from your inheritance." So he kept a careful account of all the amounts, and when he died these amounts had been deducted from our inheritance. Not so stupid, actually, that idea: it helped us all manage.

JJS Well, there seems to be quite a step between that family portrait and the *Nude Descending a Staircase*.

MD Yes, the *Nude* was two years later . . .

JJS 1912.

MD 1912; and it was after these that I decided to get away from all the influences I had been under before. I wanted to live in the present, and the present then was cubism. You see, in 1910, 1911, and 1912 cubism was new: the approach was so different from the previous movements that I was very much attracted toward it. I became a Cubist painter and gradually came up with the *Nude.*

JJS The *Nude,* however, has movement in it, and the cubists didn't seem to be particularly interested in movement.

MD Yes. But don't forget there was also futurism at the same time. Italian futurism, though I didn't know about it. I was in Munich. I didn't even know of the futurists' existence. The famous futurist show came to Paris in January 1912, at exactly the time I was painting this *Nude.* Was that a coincidence or was it in the air? I don't know. But I did this painting with the idea of using movement as one of the elements in it. The next year, I sent the *Nude* to New York at the suggestion of two American painters, Davis and Walter Pach.

JJS That was an event in the history of American painting.

MD I know, but we only know it now, forty years later. At the time it could have been just an explosion: a successful week or two, and then nothing. But that was not enough for me. I went on with the idea that, all right, I had done what I could with cubism but now it was time to change. It was always the idea of changing, not repeating myself. I could have done ten other nudes at that time if I had wanted to. But the fact is I did not want to. But I went on immediately to another formula, the formula of the *Chocolate Grinder.* I used to walk around the streets of old Rouen. One day I saw an actual chocolate grinder working in a shop window, and it fascinated me so much that I took it as a point of departure.

JJS Well, what was different in your point of view here than in any normal still life of a chocolate grinder? Was it a mechanical interest, is that it?

MD Yes. The mechanical aspect of it influenced me then, or at least that was also the point of departure of a new form of technique. I couldn't go into the haphazard drawing or the paintings, the splashing of the paint. I wanted to go back to a completely *dry* drawing, a *dry* conception of art. I was beginning to appreciate the value of the exactness, of precision, and the importance of chance. The result was that my work was no longer popular with amateurs, even among those who liked impressionism or cubism. And the mechanical drawing for me was the best form for that dry conception of art.

JJS And that was the real beginning for the *Large Glass.* At the time you did this, did you have a precise idea of what was coming?

MD I was already beginning to make a definite plan, a blueprint for the *Large Glass.* The *Chocolate Grinder* was one point of departure, and then came the *Sliding Machine* on the side. All this was con-

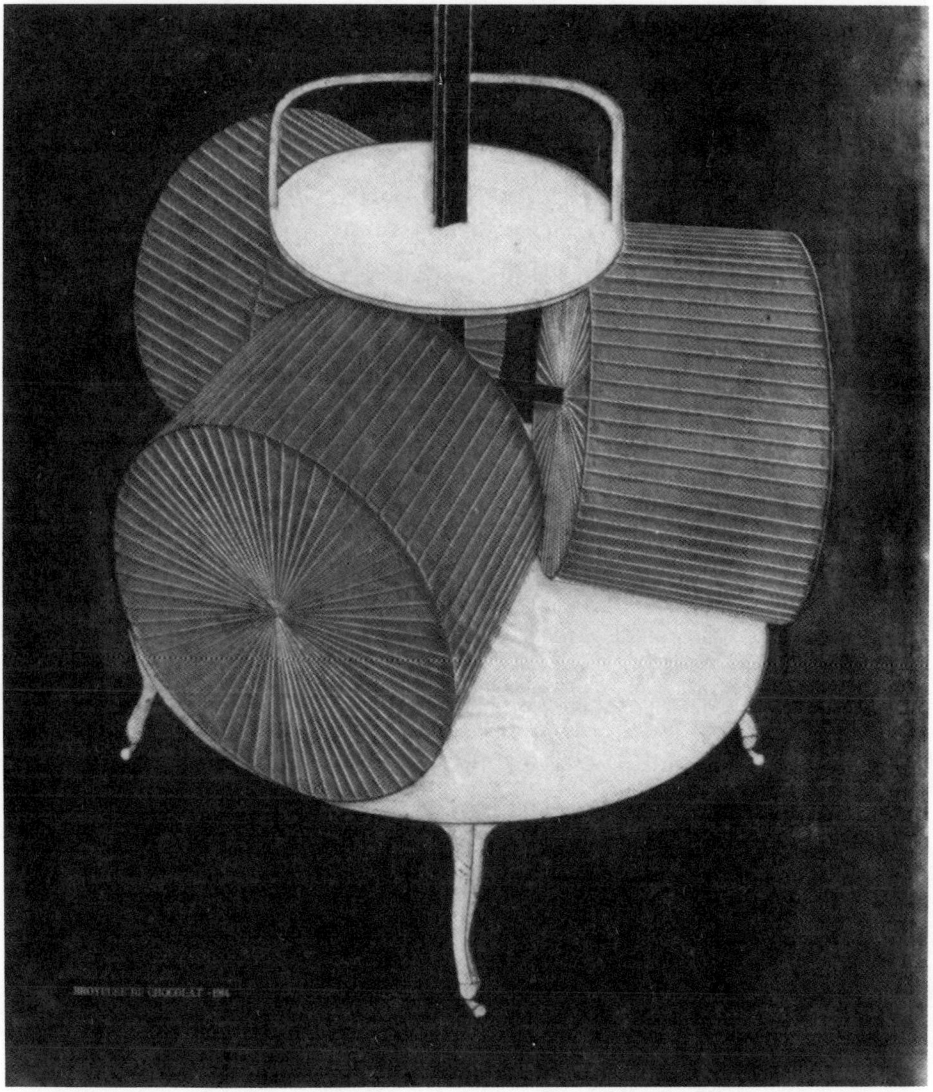

Chocolate Grinder, No. 2, 1914

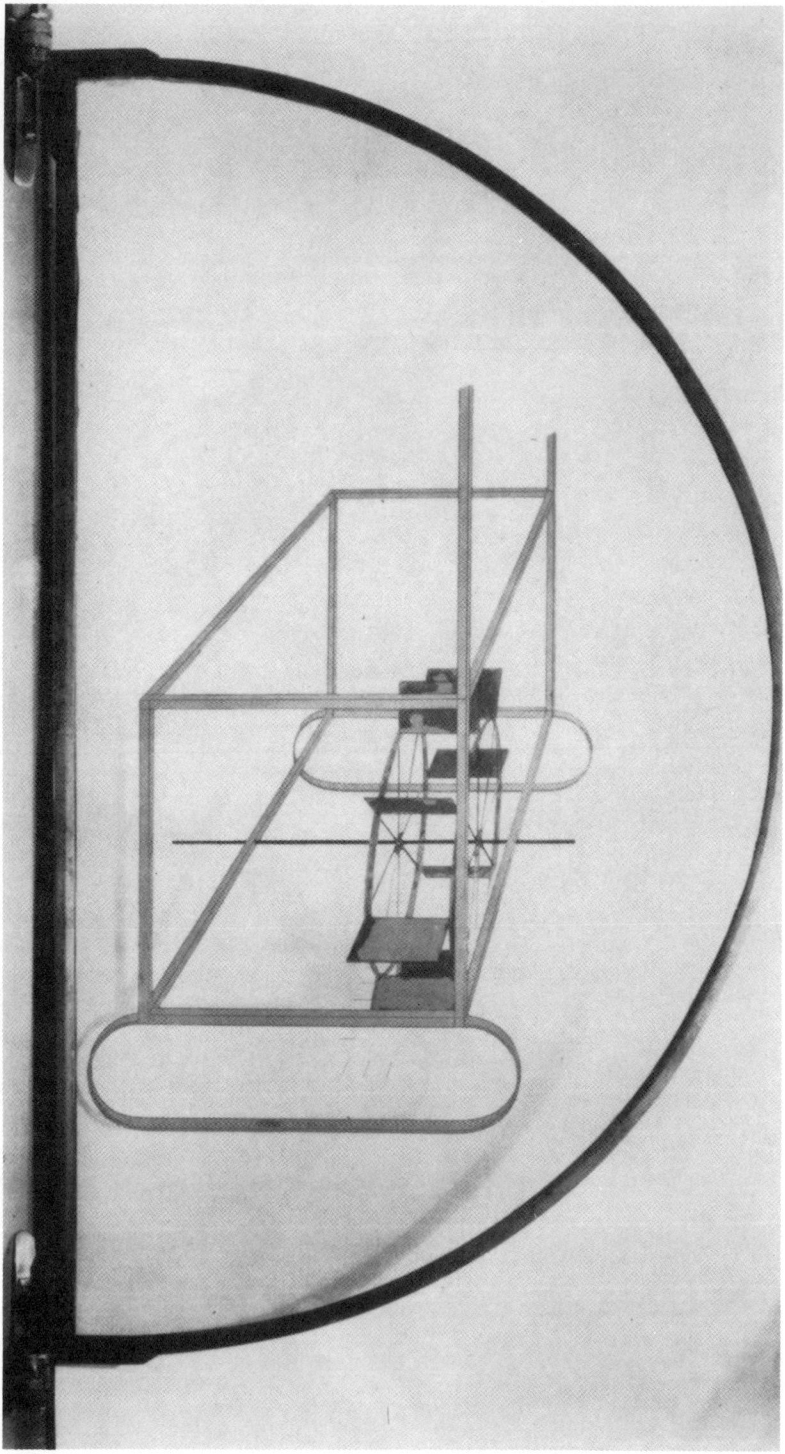

Glider Containing a Water Mill in Neighboring Metals, 1913-15

ceived, drawn, and on paper in 1913-14. It was based on a perspective view, meaning complete knowledge of the arrangement of the parts. It couldn't be haphazardly done or changed afterwards. It had to go through according to plan, so to speak.

JJS Well, I imagine you feel that the *Chocolate Grinder* heralded something in your work, something of that break you have often told me about.

MD Yes, it was really a very important moment in my life. I had to make big decisions then. The hardest was when I told myself "Marcel no more painting, go get a job." I looked for a job in order to get enough time to paint *for myself.* I got a job as a librarian in Paris in the Bibliothèque St. Geneviève. It was a wonderful job because I had so many hours to myself.

JJS You mean painting for yourself, not merely to please other people?

MD Exactly. And that led me to the conclusion that you either are a professional painter or not. There are two kinds of artists: the artist that deals with society, is integrated into society; and the other artist, the completely freelance artist, who has no obligations.

JJS You mean the man in society has to make certain compromises to please it; is that why you took the job?

MD Exactly, exactly, I didn't want to depend on my painting for a living.

JJS But, Marcel, when you speak of your disregard for the broad public and say you are painting for yourself, wouldn't you accept that as painting for the ideal public, for a public which would appreciate you if they would only make the effort?

MD Yes, indeed. It is only a way of putting myself in the right position for that ideal public. The danger is in pleasing an immediate public; the immediate public that comes around you and takes you in and accepts you and gives you success and everything. Instead of that, you should wait for fifty years or a hundred years for your true public. That is the only public that interests me.

JJS That is a rather aesthetic point of view. I don't think you ever felt that a person was justified in living in an ivory tower and disregarding the intelligent and sympathetic public.

MD No, no, no ivory tower in my idea at all.

JJS I remember a line in a piece by Henri-Pierre Roché in which he referred to you as saying that you were always careful to find a way to contradict yourself. I imagine you mean by this you were trying to avoid repeating yourself. Is this right?

MD You see the danger is to "lead yourself" into a form of *taste,* even the taste of the *Chocolate Grinder*—

JJS Taste then for you is repetition of anything that has been accepted; is that what you mean?

MD Exactly; it is a habit. Repeat the same thing long enough and it becomes taste. If you interrupt your work, I mean after you have done it, then it becomes, it stays a thing in itself; but if it is repeated a number of times it becomes taste.

JJS And good taste is repetition that is approved by society and bad taste is the same repetition which is not approved; is that what you mean?

MD Yes, good or bad is of no importance because it is always good for some people and bad for others. Quality is not important, it is always taste.

JJS Well, how did you find the way to get away from good or bad taste in your personal expression?

MD By using mechanical techniques. A mechanical drawing has no taste in it.

JJS Because it is divorced from conventional expression in painting?

MD Exactly, at least I thought so at that time, and I think the same today.

JJS Then does this divorce from all human intervention in drawing and painting have a relationship to the interest you had in Ready-mades?

MD It was naturally, in trying to draw a conclusion or consequence from the dehumanization of the work of art, that I came to the idea of the Ready-mades. That is the name, as you know, that I gave to those works which in effect are already completely made. Let me show you: this is a Ready-made bird cage with, if you see me, I am having a hard time because this is not sugar, that is marble, and

"Why Not Sneeze Rose Sélavy?", 1921

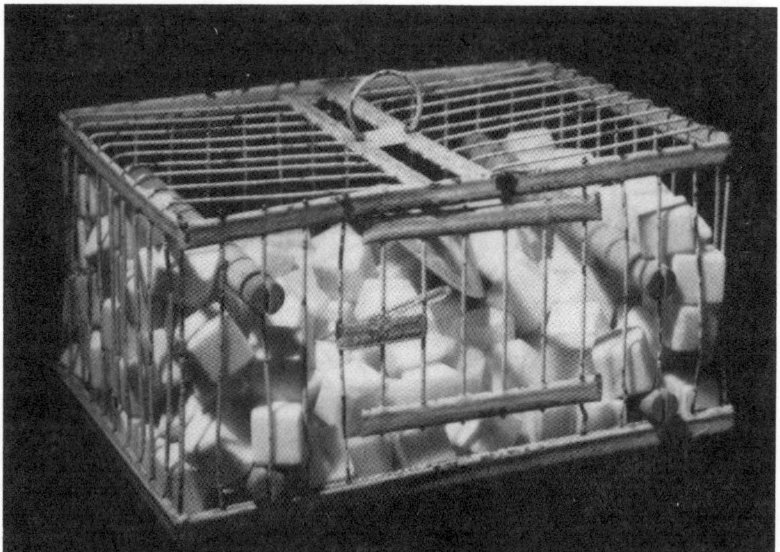

it weighs a ton, and that was one of the elements that interested me when I made it, you see. It is a Ready-made in which the sugar is changed to marble. It is sort of a mythological effect. This is a Ready-made dating back from 1916. It is a ball of twine between two plaques of copper, brass. Before I finished it Arensberg put something inside the ball of twine, and never told me what it was, and I didn't want to know. It was a sort of secret between us, and it makes a noise, so we called this a Ready-made with a hidden noise. Listen to it. I don't know; I will never know whether it is a diamond or a coin.

JJS Did you know Arensberg before you came to the United States?

MD No. I came to New York in 1915. Arensberg's place was my first port of call on this continent; it was the beginning of a long friendship. He published two little magazines with my friends, which only had one or two issues, *Rongwrong* and *The Blindman.* The magazines were, if not dadaist, at any rate inspired by the dada movement. Dada was no longer concerned with the plastic arts properly speaking, it wasn't interested in questions of technique or with the movements before it. It was more interested in literature. In fact it was negative, a total refusal.

JJS The Arensberg group was associated with several other groups, wasn't it?

MD Yes, there was Katherine Dreier for example, who was also a patron of art, and she started a museum called Société Anonyme. Its purpose was to bring paintings from abroad to get a sort of communication between the two sides of modern art, and it was quite successful then. It was from then on that America was absolutely modern art conscious, which it had never been before.

JJS I see. Well, Katherine Dreier also owned your *Large Glass* which we were looking at a little while ago.

MD Yes, but first it was in the Arensbergs' collection in 1920, at the time of its near-completion. In 1921, when they were leaving New York for California, they didn't want to take it with them because it was too fragile to transport, given its size.

JJS Marcel, from what you say the *Glass* was never really finished.

MD No. No. The last time I worked on it was in 1923.

JJS So it remains a sort of unfinished epic. And also for me it seems to indicate that you were never really dedicated to conventional painting in the ordinary sense of the word. I imagine that there is something broader in your concept of what art is than just painting.

MD Yes. I considered painting as a means of expression, not an end in itself. One means of expression among others, and not a complete end for life at all; in the same way I consider that color is only a means of expression in painting and not an end. In other words, painting should not be exclusively retinal or visual; it should have to do with the gray matter, with our urge for understanding. This is generally what I love. I didn't want to pin myself down to one little circle, and I tried at least to be as universal as I could. That is why I took up chess. Chess in itself is a hobby, is a game, everybody can play chess. But I took it very seriously and enjoyed it because I found some common points between chess and painting. Actually when you play a game of chess it is like designing something or constructing a mechanism of some kind by which you win or lose. The competitive side of it has no importance, but the thing itself is very, very plastic, and that is probably what attracted me in the game.

JJS Do you mean by that an enjoyment, a sort of fuller living? That is to say another form of expression?

MD Yes, at least it was another facet of the same kind of mental expression, intellectual expression, one small facet if you want, but it differed enough to make it distinct, and it added something to my life.

JJS Marcel, you spent quite a bit of time in the late 1930's and the early 1940's on your *Valise;* do you regard that as a distinct expression of your personality too?

MD Yes. Absolutely. It was a new form of expression for me. Instead of painting something the idea was to reproduce the paintings that I loved so much in miniature. I didn't know how to do it. I thought of a book, but I didn't like that idea. Then I thought of the idea of the box in which all my works would be mounted like in a small museum, a portable museum, so to speak, and here it is in this valise.

JJS It is a sort of ready-made catalogue, isn't it? I think almost all your work is in here.

MD Almost all of it. These are the Roto-reliefs, a series of twelve drawings based on this spiral, to be used on a phonograph, and the effect is when you turn them at a certain speed like thirty-three and a half turns a minute you get the effect of a growing form like a cone or corkscrew. But they are different drawings. This one, for example, is a glass. It doesn't look like a glass here but when it turns this comes up like in third dimension. Then we have this one here, from the dada period, the Mona Lisa with the mustache and a goatee. That was, of course, an iconoclastic gesture on my part and violently—

JJS Sacrilegious.

MD Sacrilegious, blasphemous, everything. But besides this I have other gestures of the same kind from the dada period. Like this check. I paid my dentist with this check which was an original check drawn by myself, and drawing on no bank at all. And he accepted it! So what happened? The funniest part of it is that ten or fifteen years later I saw him again, I bought the check back for my own collection, and there it is. There is also this gambling system, which I thought up to win at roulette at Monte Carlo. Of course I never broke the bank with it. But I thought I found a system. I made some shares I sold to different people to make capital to break the Monte Carlo bank.

JJS Did you win anything?

MD No, I never won anything. But at any rate as you know, I am interested in the intellectual side, although I don't like the word "intellect." For me "intellect" is too dry a word, too inexpressive. I like the word "belief." I think in general that when people say "I know," they don't know, they believe. I believe that art is the only form of activity in which man as man shows himself to be a true individual. Only in art is he capable of going beyond the animal state, because art is an outlet toward regions which are not ruled by time and space. To live is to believe; that's my belief, at any rate.

The Box in a Valise

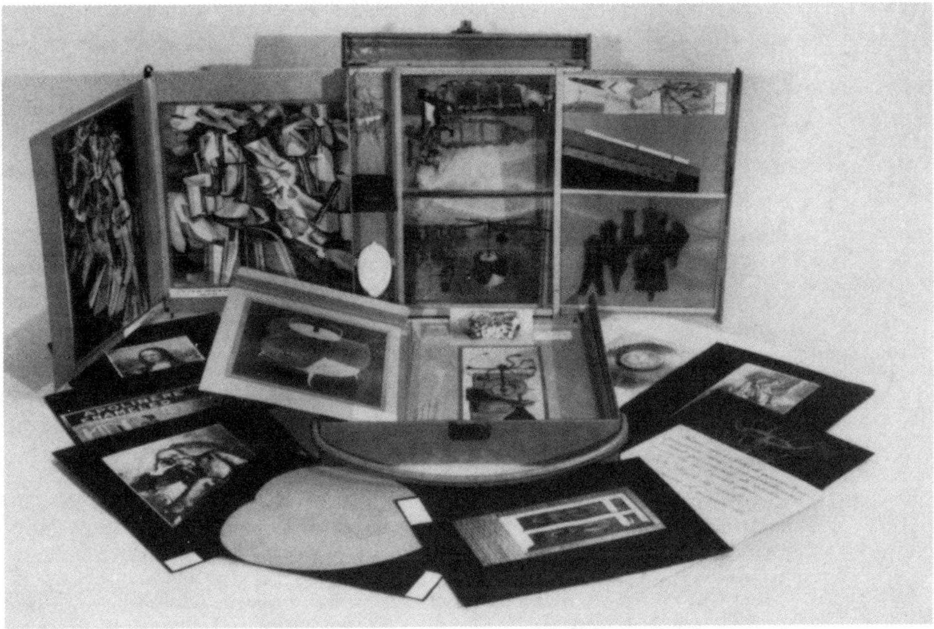

The Creative Act

Let us consider two important factors, the two poles of the creation of art: the artist on one hand, and on the other the spectator who later becomes the posterity.

To all appearances, the artist acts like a mediumistic being who, from the labyrinth beyond time and space, seeks his way out to a clearing.

If we give the attributes of a medium to the artist, we must then deny him the state of consciousness on the esthetic plane about what he is doing or why he is doing it. All his decisions in the artistic execution of the work rest with pure intuition and cannot be translated into a self-analysis, spoken or written, or even thought out.

T. S. Eliot, in his essay on "Tradition and the Individual Talent," writes: "The more perfect the artist, the more completely separate in him will be the man who suffers and the mind which creates; the more perfectly will the mind digest and transmute the passions which are its material."

Millions of artists create; only a few thousands are discussed or accepted by the spectator and many less again are consecrated by posterity.

In the last analysis, the artist may shout from all the rooftops that he is a genius; he will have to wait for the verdict of the spectator in order that his declarations take a social value and that, finally, posterity includes him in the primers of Art History.

Text of a talk given by Duchamp in Houston at the meeting of the American Federation of the Arts, April 1957. Duchamp, who labeled himself a "mere artist," participated in a roundtable with William C. Seitz of Princeton University, Rudolf Arnheim of Sarah Lawrence College, and Gregory Bateson. Reprinted from *ARTnews,* Vol. 56, no. 4 (Summer 1957). The French translation, done by Duchamp himself, appeared in *MDS.*

I know that this statement will not meet with the approval of many artists who refuse this mediumistic role and insist on the validity of their awareness in the creative act—yet, art history has consistently decided upon the virtues of a work of art through considerations completely divorced from the rationalized explanations of the artist.

If the artist, as a human being, full of the best intentions toward himself and the whole world, plays no role at all in the judgment of his own work, how can one describe the phenomenon which prompts the spectator to react critically to the work of art? In other words how does this reaction come about?

This phenomenon is comparable to a transference from the artist to the spectator in the form of an esthetic osmosis taking place through the inert matter, such as pigment, piano or marble.

But before we go further, I want to clarify our understanding of the word "art"—to be sure, without an attempt to a definition.

What I have in mind is that art may be bad, good or indifferent, but, whatever adjective is used, we must call it art, and bad art is still art in the same way as a bad emotion is still an emotion.

Therefore, when I refer to "art coefficient," it will be understood that I refer not only to great art, but I am trying to describe the subjective mechanism which produces art in a raw state—*à l'état brut*—bad, good or indifferent.

In the creative act, the artist goes from intention to realization through a chain of totally subjective reactions. His struggle toward the realization is a series of efforts, pains, satisfactions, refusals, decisions, which also cannot and must not be fully self-conscious, at least on the esthetic plane.

The result of this struggle is a difference between the intention and its realization, a difference which the artist is not aware of.

Consequently, in the chain of reactions accompanying the creative act, a link is missing. This gap which represents the inability of the artist to express fully his intention; this difference between what he intended to realize and did realize, is the personal "art coefficient" contained in the work.

In other words, the personal "art coefficient" is like an arithmetical relation between the unexpressed but intended and the unintentionally expressed.

To avoid a misunderstanding, we must remember that this "art coefficient" is a personal expression of art *"à l'état brut,"* that is, still in a raw state, which must be "refined" as pure sugar from molasses, by the spectator; the digit of this coefficient has no bearing whatsoever on his verdict. The creative act takes another aspect when the spectator experiences the phenomenon of transmutation; through the change from inert matter into a work of art, an actual transubstantiation has taken place, and the role of the spectator is to determine the weight of the work on the esthetic scale.

All in all, the creative act is not performed by the artist alone; the spectator brings the work in contact with the external world by deciphering and interpreting its inner qualifications and thus adds his contribution to the creative act. This becomes even more obvious when posterity gives its final verdict and sometimes rehabilitates forgotten artists.

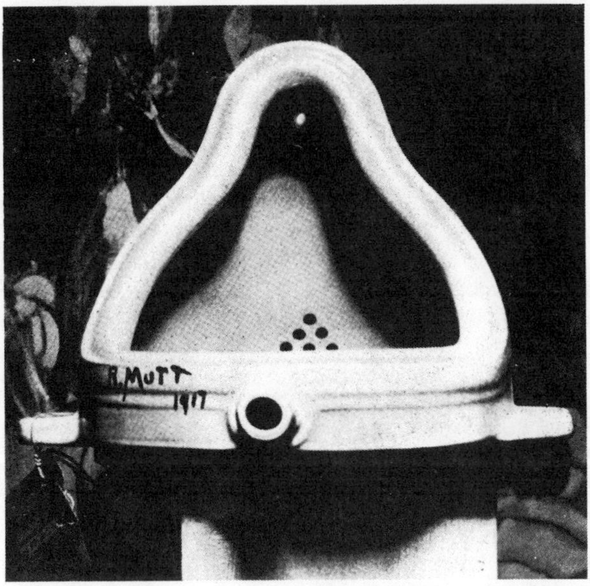

Fountain, 1917

Apropos of "Readymades"

IN 1913 I HAD THE HAPPY IDEA TO FASTEN A BICYCLE WHEEL TO A KITCHEN STOOL AND WATCH IT TURN.

A FEW MONTHS LATER I BOUGHT A CHEAP REPRODUCTION OF A WINTER EVENING LANDSCAPE, WHICH I CALLED "PHARMACY" AFTER ADDING TWO SMALL DOTS, ONE RED AND ONE YELLOW, IN THE HORIZON.

IN NEW YORK IN 1915 I BOUGHT AT A HARDWARE STORE A SNOW SHOVEL ON WHICH I WROTE "IN ADVANCE OF THE BROKEN ARM."

IT WAS AROUND THAT TIME THAT THE WORD "READYMADE" CAME TO MIND TO DESIGNATE THIS FORM OF MANIFESTATION.

A POINT WHICH I WANT VERY MUCH TO ESTABLISH IS THAT THE CHOICE OF THESE "READYMADES" WAS NEVER DICTATED BY ESTHETIC DELECTATION.

THIS CHOICE WAS BASED ON A REACTION OF VISUAL INDIFFERENCE WITH AT THE SAME TIME A TOTAL ABSENCE OF GOOD OR BAD TASTE . . . IN FACT A COMPLETE ANESTHESIA.

ONE IMPORTANT CHARACTERISTIC WAS THE SHORT SENTENCE WHICH I OCCASIONALLY INSCRIBED ON THE "READYMADE."

THAT SENTENCE INSTEAD OF DESCRIBING THE OBJECT LIKE A TITLE WAS MEANT TO CARRY THE MIND OF THE SPECTATOR TOWARDS OTHER REGIONS MORE VERBAL.

Talk delivered by Duchamp at the Museum of Modern Art, New York, Oct. 19, 1961. Published in *Art and Artists* (London), 1, no. 4. (July 1966), p. 47. The original text is in the Simon Watson Taylor collection.

SOMETIMES I WOULD ADD A GRAPHIC DETAIL OF PRESENTATION WHICH IN ORDER TO SATISFY MY CRAVING FOR ALLITERATIONS, WOULD BE CALLED "READYMADE AIDED."

AT ANOTHER TIME WANTING TO EXPOSE THE BASIC ANTINOMY BETWEEN ART AND READYMADES I IMAGINED A "RECIPROCAL READYMADE": USE A REMBRANDT AS AN IRONING BOARD!

I REALIZED VERY SOON THE DANGER OF REPEATING INDISCRIMINATELY THIS FORM OF EXPRESSION AND DECIDED TO LIMIT THE PRODUCTION OF "READYMADES" TO A SMALL NUMBER YEARLY. I WAS AWARE AT THAT TIME, THAT FOR THE SPECTATOR EVEN MORE THAN FOR THE ARTIST, ART IS A HABIT FORMING DRUG AND I WANTED TO PROTECT MY "READYMADES" AGAINST SUCH CONTAMINATION.

ANOTHER ASPECT OF THE "READYMADE" IS ITS LACK OF UNIQUENESS . . . THE REPLICA OF A "READYMADE" DELIVERING THE SAME MESSAGE; IN FACT NEARLY EVERY ONE OF THE "READYMADES" EXISTING TODAY IS NOT AN ORIGINAL IN THE CONVENTIONAL SENSE.

A FINAL REMARK TO THIS EGOMANIAC'S DISCOURSE:

SINCE THE TUBES OF PAINT USED BY THE ARTIST ARE MANUFACTURED AND READY MADE PRODUCTS WE MUST CONCLUDE THAT ALL THE PAINTINGS IN THE WORLD ARE "READYMADES AIDED" AND ALSO WORKS OF ASSEMBLAGE.

Marcel Duchamp 1961

From the Catalog

Collection of the Société Anonyme

Alexander Archipenko
Sculptor, Painter

Archipenko was among the few sculptors attracted by the Cubist creed. Even though his first sculptures were inspired by the revolutionary theories, he showed immediately his strong personality by introducing an entirely new conception of sculpture. He gave the name "Sculpto-Peintures" to reliefs generally made of plaster, carved and painted. This polychrome conception of sculpture, though not an innovation in itself, was in its results quite startling. He succeeded in expressing more than an attractive technique through his new ideas of form. Archipenko's important contribution to sculpture has been to do away with volumes. The old massive classic treatment was probably a practical consequence of the process of casting. His technique of "direct cutting" in plaster, wood and different materials made each piece an original not to be duplicated. In recent years Archipenko has turned back to a more classical technique. He will, nevertheless, always be regarded as a pioneer.

1943

Sophie Taeuber-Arp
Painter, Sculptor, Designer

If one of the characteristics of modern art since Courbet has been the cult of the subconscious hand, quite a number of artists in the last thirty years have abandoned this cult and turned toward a consciously accurate technique, leaving nothing to the hazards of brushwork. Sophie Taeuber-Arp was among the first artists to have felt the danger of indulging in "automatic" painting. She made it her task to execute a drawing as "planned" beforehand. And, most important, she reintroduced the geometric arabesque as one of the major artistic concepts. Curiously enough, as "abstract" as she was, she often liked to use a title which evoked a human analogy in the painting ("six espaces aux teintes ensoleillées"). Moreover, the titles as well as the paintings themselves were adorned with a definite sense of humour so often lacking in abstract art. Sophie Taeuber-Arp, in her attitude of detachment about herself as an artist, reminds one of the anonymous artisan of the Middle-Ages.

1949

Jean (Hans) Arp
Sculptor, Painter, Writer

Based on the metaphysical implications of the Dadaist dogma, Arp's *Reliefs* between 1916 and 1922 are among the most convincing illustrations of that anti-rationalistic era. The important element introduced then by Arp was "humor" in its subtlest form; the kind of whimsical conceptions that gave to the Dada Movement such an exuberant liveliness as opposed to the purely intellectual tendencies of Cubism and Expressionism. Arp showed the importance of a smile to combat the sophistic theories of the moment. His poems of the same period stripped the word of its rational connotation to attain the most unexpected meaning through alliteration or plain nonsense. His contribution to Surrealism, his *Concrétions,* show his masterly technique in the use of different materials, and in many instances are like a three-dimensional pun—what the female body "might have been." For Arp, art is Arp.

1949

Umberto Boccioni, 1882-1916
Painter, Sculptor, Writer

Unlike other art movements, Futurism had a dynamic literary leader in Marinetti—but the prince of Futurism was Boccioni, who conceived the most convincing manifestos at a time when the world was thirsty for new art expressions. Boccioni's paintings and sculptures demonstrated the theory and completed point by point the explanations which words are unable to give. Of all the Futurists, Boccioni was the most gifted, and his premature death was certainly a reason for the breaking up of the movement in its further development. But since movements in art remain only as vague labels representing a period, the artist continues to live through his work. Thus Boccioni will be remembered, not so much as a Futurist but as an important artist.

1943

Georges Braque
Painter, Sculptor, Illustrator

The "heroic" period of painting around 1910 was marked by a confusion which only recently has been cleared by art historians, when the greater talents revealed themselves with time. Among the numerous artists trying to free themselves from Impressionism and the short-lived revolt of Fauvism was Braque who is recognized as one of the outstanding inventors of the Cubist formula. As early as 1908 he showed at the Paris *Indépendants* his famous view of a Mediterranean town which is considered the arrow pointing toward the new road. For ten years Braque devoted himself, as a chemist might, to creating delicate oil color combinations. His discoveries in color and form were directed by an inner sense of geometry, not by the intellectual application of scientific theories. The end of World War I freed him from the disciplinarian technique to which he had submitted himself. Yet one can feel the structural conception underlying the realism of his recent paintings.

1943

Alexander Calder
Sculptor, Painter, Illustrator

Among the "innovations" in art after the first World War Calder's approach to sculpture was so removed from the accepted formulas that he had to invent a new name for his forms in motion. He called them *mobiles*. In their treatment of gravity, disturbed by gentle movements, they give the feeling that "they carry pleasures peculiar to themselves, which are quite unlike the pleasures of scratching," to quote Plato in his *Philebus*. A light breeze, an electric motor, or both in the form of an electric fan, start in motion weights, counter-weights, levers which design in mid-air their unpredictable arabesques and introduce an element of lasting surprise. The symphony is complete when color and sound join in and call on all our senses to follow the unwritten score. Pure *joie de vivre*. The art of Calder is the sublimation of a tree in the wind.

1949

John Covert
Painter

Among the young American painters who, in 1915, joined forces with the pioneers of the new art movements, John Covert was an outstanding figure from the beginning. Instead of following and adopting one of the new expressions, he found his personal form in a combination of painting and sculpture, reliefs made of superimposed planes. If this technique, as such, showed Covert's imagination, far more important was the direction given to the material by his idea: the unrolling of interwoven surfaces. The same process was used later in several institutes of mathematics to illustrate the non-Euclidean geometries as well as in Pevsner's latest sculpture. For a number of years Covert went on affirming his first intentions and giving an American interpretation of these new esthetic needs at the time of the first World War.

1945

Joseph Alexandre Czaky
Painter, Sculptor

Czaky belongs to a group of sculptors, who, before 1914, gave a new direction to their work. The theory of Cubism was then the springboard to unexplored regions, and Czaky, although influenced by Cubism, introduced his own views on the treatment of space. At first his work appeared more theoretical and intellectual than later when he found his more personal development in an atmospheric structure.

1943

Giorgio de Chirico
Painter, Writer, Illustrator

Witnessing the rise of new esthetics, in contact with the different expressions of the "heroic" period in the early part of the twentieth century, de Chirico found himself in 1912 confronted with the problem of following one of the roads already opened or of opening a new road. He avoided Fauvism as well as Cubism and introduced what could be called "metaphysical painting." Instead of exploiting the coming medium of abstraction, he organized on his canvases the meeting of elements which could only meet in a "metaphysical world." These elements, painted in the minutest technique, were "exposed" on a horizontal plane in orthodox perspective. This technique, in opposition to the Cubist or purely abstract formula in full bloom at the moment, protected de Chirico's position and allowed him to lay down the foundation of what was to become Surrealism ten years later. About 1926 de Chirico abandoned his "metaphysical" conception and turned to a less disciplined brush-stroke. His admirers could not follow him and decided that de Chirico of the second manner had lost the flame of the first. But posterity may have a word to say.

1943

André Derain
Painter, Graphic Artist

At the turn of the century, when Impressionism and Pointillism were a "recognized revolution," the younger generation felt the urge for further experimentation in the realm of color. Among the Fauves, Derain stands out as a pioneer of this experiment, based on optical contrasts of vivid colors applied to a systematic distortion of the natural form. While at the same time the "Intimists," Bonnard, Vuillard and others, were applying Impressionist technique to indoor scenes, Derain and the Fauves rehabilitated black as a color and used the heavy lined form in reaction to the delicate and nebulous painting of Monet and Cézanne. The three important "Fauves," Matisse, Braque and Derain, had too great personalities to keep to a strict common formula. And as early as 1907 Derain had already switched away from Fauvism proper to a more somber technique, in many ways a forerunner of the Cubist palette. Braque turned to Cubism and Matisse became Matisse. Derain is consistently adverse to "theories." He has always been a true believer in the artistic message unadulterated by methodical explanations and to this day belongs to the small group of artists who "live" their art.

1949

Katherine S. Dreier
Painter, Lecturer, Writer

Katherine S. Dreier belongs to the fortunate generation of painters who, in their prime, witnessed the blossoming of complete freedom in art. She started as a pupil of Shirlaw, and went abroad to study with Colin in Paris. Later she studied in Munich and Florence with Gustav Britsch who through his teaching developed strict discipline and a keen observation governing the laws of art. Well acquainted with the treasures of the European museums, she was ready to welcome the new ideas when, in 1913, she cooperated with the Armory Exhibition which linked America and Europe for a new stride into artistic freedom. Katherine Dreier felt a kinship for what was to be called abstract art and experienced the full change in her understanding of form and color, applying her own measure to a series of canvases in a delicate balancing of abstract forms and mellow colors. Free-hand geometric patterns set in backgrounds of color perspective and interwoven in the general framing of the abstract theme are the chief characteristics of her personal contribution to painting, best shown in her "psychological portraits" as well as in her "cosmological" interpretations. Understanding the new aim of the artist, Katherine Dreier as early as 1920 established a Museum of Modern Art, the "Société Anonyme." In the true sense of the word the "Société Anonyme" is today the only sanctuary of esoteric character, contrasting sharply with the commercial trend of our times.

1946

Raymond Duchamp-Villon, 1876-1918
Sculptor

Raymond Duchamp-Villon had already received recognition as a sculptor when the new art theories tempted him and made him the first exponent of Cubist sculpture. His well known *Horse* will always be remembered as one of the landmarks of the Cubist Movement. His premature death makes one feel, very acutely, the significance of the far too few pieces he left behind. His *Baudelaire* and *Seated Woman* are two fine examples of his simplification which at the time the work was done, about 1908, even exceeded Rodin's synthesis of the *Walking Man*, and are still in advance of much of the sculpture of today.

1943

Louis Eilshemius, 1864-1941
Painter, Writer, Poet, Musician

In Eilshemius we face a tragedy which, although comparable to that of many artists, nevertheless takes an acute form for us, helpless witnesses to his long struggle. Eilshemius' tragedy was not a daily struggle to live, for the material side of his life was, like Cézanne's, modestly but well provided for. Eilshemius, born in the United States, never was able to convince his fellow citizens that his paintings were the expression of a subtle America, since through his training, partly abroad and partly here, he developed a conception entirely devoid of the teachings of any of the art schools of the moment. He was a true individualist, as artists of our times should be, who never joined any group. This attitude is only one reason for his late recognition. He was a poet and painted like one, but his lyricism was not related to his time and expressed no definite period. He painted like a "Primitive"—but was not a primitive—and this is the origin of his tragedy. His landscapes were not landscapes of a definite country; his nudes were floating figures with no studied anatomy. His allegories were not based on accepted legends. One can hardly find words to define him. Eilshemius' paintings speak for themselves.

1943

Max Ernst
Painter, Sculptor, Author

The Dada Movement was an anti-movement which corresponded to a need born of the first World War. Although neither literary nor pictorial in essence, Dada found its exponents in painters and writers scattered all over the world. Max Ernst's activities in Cologne in 1917 made him the foremost representative of the Dada painters. Between 1918 and 1921 his paintings, drawings and collages depicting the world of the subconscious were already a foretaste of Surrealism. Among his technical discoveries the use of the old Chinese "frottage" or rubbing technique shows "automatic" textures of wood and different materials. When the Surrealist Movement took shape in 1924, Max Ernst was the only painter in the group of Dadas who joined the writers in the Surrealist venture. In fact his previous achievements had certainly influenced, to a great extent, the literary Surrealist exploration of the subconscious. Extremely prolific, Max Ernst has had a long Surrealist career and given through his work a complete *exposé* of the different epochs of Surrealism.

1945

Albert Gleizes
Painter, Writer

On the strength of the first tangible results which Cubism had already obtained, in 1912 Gleizes and Metzinger wrote a book, *Du Cubisme,* in which they clarified the mental chemistry of Cubism. Through the analysis and conclusion Gleizes showed the connection between the theoretical mind and the brush, winning the reading public to the new cause. In his personal approach to Cubism, he dissected several large compositions of a descriptive character. This was in opposition to the almost microscopic research of Braque. Gleizes was among the first to see the application of the new methods to the "Unanimist" scenes. The "Unanimists" were members of a literary group in Paris, about 1905, who concerned themselves with the conflicts between organized bodies of society one against another, or organized bodies of society one against the individual. Gleizes showed great personality in his form of painting, and later on when the technique of Cubism became more a dogma than a necessity Gleizes turned to his writing again, this time with a humanitarian touch. It was natural, therefore, that in later years, he should have left the Cubist world, as all Cubists have done, and have continued to develop his own ideas of visualization. Albert Gleizes is deeply concerned with the social problems of our day especially those affecting the workman. His recent paintings serve a definite religious purpose and have become the stained-glass windows of his new creed.

1943

Juan Gris
Painter

Like many painters of his generation Juan Gris started life as an able cartoonist and illustrator in Paris. But the daily contact with a Spanish colony of painters caused him to join the Cubists when they were nothing but a name given to a few by a few. Gris immediately imposed his conception of Cubism on his own work. This was rather an explanation of forms than a complication of forms. He applied his own rules to dissect the motif with consistency. You can feel in his first canvases the self-imposed discipline of simplification, instead of adding through complexity. In contrast to the other Cubists who constructed artificial worlds around the central motif, Gris built his personal approach from the inner structure of the motif. He pursued this line of expression to the end and methodically polished one of the purest facets of Cubism.

1943

Wassily Kandinsky
Painter, Writer

Kandinsky was a witness to many "isms" of his day. He belonged to the generation of those who wanted to make clear that painting could be born again in spite of the great domination of Impressionism.

As a first reaction Expressionism found in Kandinsky and Franz Marc its best exponents. His early writings present his theories at the time he created his first abstract paintings when the word "abstract" was not yet invented. Kandinsky's period of "Expressionism" is not his period of "Abstractionism." In the beginning there was always a "motif" of which hardly a naturalistic detail remained. Later Kandinsky came to a purer expression doing away with the skilful qualities of his hand, which he submitted to greater discipline. In tracing his lines with ruler and compass, Kandinsky opened to the spectator a new way of looking at painting. It was no more the lines of the subconscious, but a deliberate condemnation of the emotional; a clear transfer of thought on canvas. This has been the real contribution of Kandinsky towards a conception of esthetics not related to the preceding or following "isms."

1943

Paul Klee, 1879-1940
Painter, Graphic Artist, Writer

A deep conception of the use of watercolor, a personal method in oil painting applied to apparently decorative forms, have made Klee stand out in contemporary painting as unrelated to anyone else. On the other hand his experiments over the last thirty years have been used by other artists as a basis for new developments in the different fields of art. The first reaction before a painting by Paul Klee is a pleasant realization of what we all might have done when drawing in childhood. Most of his compositions show this delightful side of unsophisticated, naïve expression. But this is only the first contact with his work and a very appealing one. When we look closer we immediately discover how incomplete the first impression was and if Klee often uses a "childish" technique, it is applied to a very mature form of thinking which an analysis of his work discovers. His extreme fecundity never shows signs of repetition as is generally the case. He has so much to say that a Klee is never like another Klee.

1949

Fernand Léger
Painter

Léger, for example, never painted cubes. His first attempts at a new expression in art were more in the vein of dynamic forms. He was inspired by the mechanical achievements of the modern world and translated them into concise fragmentation. His color scheme was expressed in primary colors which added force to the subject matter. For the same purpose Léger used the cylinder shape in the drawing of his figures, trees, etc. His paintings of 1912 were called "cylindrist" and had only a remote relation to Cubism. In 1918 Léger reached the fullness of his expression—volumes and strong hues of primary blue, red, and yellow depict large scenes of contemporary life. He is among the rare painters of our time who have treated the technique of mural painting with modern comprehension. Léger's recent large compositions are imposing in their directness.

1943

Jacques Lipchitz
Sculptor

The main roots of Cubism are to be found in Cézanne's last paintings and in negro sculpture. This explains why the Cubist sculptors had to work "backward" so to speak, when they tried to apply the principles of Cubism to their work. Lipchitz, the youngest of the Cubist sculptors, shows evidence of the negro influence in his first experiments. Interpenetration of planes marks his second period. In his search for a colder and dryer use of sharp planes he discarded exotic sculpture. All the time, true to the cubist tradition, he kept in close contact with nature and never turned to complete abstraction. The titles of his sculptures helped the "reading" of the complicated lines. After the war of 1914-18 Lipchitz gradually developed a more personal formula from which the Cubist synthesis is excluded. Doing away with "compactness," he introduces air again in sculpture. The pieces from that period are in a more poetic vein and deal more with thoughts than with representation. In recent years he has been interested in open-air sculpture, obtaining remarkable results in the study of relationship between sculpture and a fixed out-of-door perspective.

1945

Man Ray
Painter, Photographer, Writer

Before World War I Man Ray already belonged to the group of painters whose works made history in the development of revolutionary ideas in art. His paintings of 1913–1914 show the awakening of a great personality in his own interpretation of Cubism and abstract painting. He arrived in Paris in 1921, already known as a Dadaist, and joined the ranks of this active group with Breton, Aragon, Eluard, Tzara, and Max Ernst, the founders of Surrealism three years later. The change of milieu gave a new impetus to Man Ray's activities. He took up photography and it was his achievement to treat the camera as he treated the paint brush, a mere instrument at the service of the mind. It was also in Paris at the Institut Poincaré that he was attracted by the "mathematical objects always beautiful in their very nature," and he has painted many canvases bringing this inherent beauty in contact with organic themes. Today, back in Hollywood where he writes, lectures, paints, Man Ray has his place among the "old masters of Modern Art." Incidentally, the name "Société Anonyme" was suggested by Man Ray, who has been an active member from the start.

1949

Louis Marcoussis
Painter, Graphic Artist

Louis Markous, after spending only a few months at the Académie Julian in 1903, realized the shortcomings of academic training and started on his own, painting and trying to earn a living by drawing for the illustrated magazines, as Jacques Villon, Juan Gris and many others did at that time. He lived in Montmartre, then the village of all artists and between 1908 and 1910 the headquarters of the Cubist Revolution. Apollinaire, the apostle, was the central figure and grouped the scattered adepts. Around 1911 Louis Markous, changing his views on painting, joined the Cubists and became Marcoussis. Of the two Cubist factions (Picasso, Braque on one side; Gleizes, Metzinger, Léger on the other) Marcoussis felt more affinity with the former and remained faithful to its discipline long after many Cubists had taken great liberties with their own dogmas and in many cases had abandoned Cubism altogether. A very important contribution of Marcoussis was his application of Cubism to engraving, and his portrait of Apollinaire is among the best etchings produced at that time. In book illustration, Marcoussis was also an innovator and showed the same qualities as in his easel painting: the evocation of space beyond the three dimensions.

1949

Henri Matisse
Painter, Sculptor, Graphic Artist

As early as 1904 Henri Matisse began his search for new fields of expression using thin, flat, colored surfaces, framed in a drawing of heavy lines—to oppose Pointillism, the last stronghold of Impressionism. The movement which was to be called Fauvism was sponsored by a number of young painters who felt the necessity of avoiding the impasse to which Impressionism and Pointillism had brought them. But Matisse, like all pioneers, was more than a theoretician of the moment. His first important reaction was in the treatment of form, starting from natural representation. He purposely ignored all conventions of anatomy and perspective in order to introduce whatever drawing he felt adequate to give maximum values to the flat hues of colors inserted within the intentional outlines. Coming just after the recognition of Van Gogh, Cézanne and Seurat, Matisse's idea was a deliberate attempt to open new roads in the physics of painting. Around 1907 he showed several large compositions which contained all the elements of his masterly conception. Perspective had been discarded and replaced by the relationship of strong forms which produced a three-dimensional effect of its own. Figures and trees were indicated in heavy lines, building the arabesque adjusted to the flat areas of colour. The ensemble created a new scenery in which the objective composition appeared only as a remote guide. Ever since these early achievements, Matisse has added to his physical treatment of painting a very subtle chemistry of brushwork which amplifies the completeness of his latest work.

1943

Matta
Painter

A few years before World War II Matta started his career as an architect but very soon turned completely to painting and to the Surrealist theories which, although then twenty years old, had been kept alive by the constant flow of young new talents. Matta was among the last newcomers. He did not undergo the routine schooling but at once imposed his personal vision. His first and important contribution to Surrealist painting was the discovery of regions of space hitherto unexplored in the realm of art. Matta followed the modern physicists in the search for his new space which, although depicted on canvas, was not to be mistaken for another three-dimensional illusion. His first "period" was characterized by the slow rendering of an exploration, the fight with all the obstacles of oil painting, a medium lending itself to centuries-old interpretations. Later he succeeded in introducing in "his space" descriptive and figurative elements which added to the completion of his important achievement. Still a young man, Matta is the most profound painter of his generation.

1946

Jean Metzinger
Painter, Writer

In 1911 two distinct groups of painters were giving form to the new theory of Cubism which was then brooding in an incubating period. Picasso and Braque on one side; Metzinger, Gleizes and Léger on the other. Metzinger was then the most imaginative theoretician of Cubism and must be held responsible in a large measure for the critical and ever-increasing interest which the general public took in this new form of expression. Through his articles and his book, *Du Cubisme,* written in collaboration with Gleizes, he managed to give a substantial *exposé* of the main intentions of the new painters and helped to clarify the really obscure results thus far achieved. His paintings of the first period were marked by a rich technical discipline, coupled with a very deep insight, leaning towards the intellectual. Such activities made Metzinger one of the outstanding pioneers of Cubism. Later his vigor lessened and he did not repeat his early achievements.

1943

Joan Miró
Painter

Miró came of age as an artist just at the time World War I ended. With the end of the war came the end of all the new pre-war art conceptions. A young painter could not start as a Cubist or a Futurist, and Dada was the only manifestation at the moment.

Miró began by painting farm scenes from the countryside of Barcelona, his native land. Although realistic in appearance, these first pictures were marked with a definite sense of unreal intensity.

A few years later he came to Paris and found himself among the Dadaists who were, at that time, transmuting into Surrealism. In spite of this contact Miró kept aloof from any direct influence and showed a series of canvases in which form submitted to strong coloring expressed a new two-dimensional cosmogony, in no way related to abstraction. He also made some constructions directly related to Surrealism but his real self was best exteriorized in the play of colored elements one upon another.

1946

Emile Nicolle 1830-1894
Painter, Engraver

Born in Rouen, France, where, after attending the Lycée, he studied art with Bérat. Until 1874 he held the office of "courtier maritime" in Rouen when he resigned to devote the rest of his life to painting and engraving. From 1864 he exhibited at the *Salon* in Paris. He was mainly a landscape painter and was especially fond of painting the underbrush of the woods in the manner of Harpignies. His farm studies in Normandy as well as his seascapes and his cliffs of St. Valéry show some affinity with the school of Boudin. He was also a passionate etcher.

Black and white etchings of the churches, old streets and houses in Rouen were treated with great mastery and, although one might recognize some relationship to Meryon's street scenes of old Paris, Emile Nicolle introduced to engraving the broad spirit of a painter. His famous large etching, *Notre Dame de Paris*, can compare with any masterpiece of that period. As children we were surrounded by hundreds of his paintings on the walls of our home, and this detail may well have been an additional incentive to the atavistic and avocational careers of Jacques Villon, Raymond Duchamp-Villon, Suzanne and Marcel Duchamp, his grandchildren. Some of his paintings and etchings are at the Museum in Rouen. The Chalcographic Department of the Louvre has all his copper plates. The Print Room in the Bibliothèque Nationale in Paris has one series of etchings from his album, Vieux Rouen.

1949

Antoine Pevsner
Sculptor, Painter

Pevsner started as a painter in Russia long before the Revolution; his wax paintings of 1913 show his awakening interest in the technique of transparency and already announce his later experiments with translucent materials. But *trompe l'œil* painting was too limited a medium for Pevsner who, quite naturally, turned to sculpture.

Sculpture of construction, or Constructivism, is an esthetic attitude toward life which the two brothers, Gabo and Pevsner, conceived and expressed in their 1920 Manifesto.

Pevsner's demands on art could not be satisfied by volume sculpture, but led him to create a new "setting," a sort of "chamber architecture" to express his space-time reality. In his recent works on the analysis of the "surface," Pevsner uses bronze instead of transparent materials. The surface, expressed only by its generating elements, fine lines close together, becomes a "denatured" surface, another important discovery of Constructivism. The surface is suggested by the lines but not actually seen or visible as real surface.

1949

Francis Picabia
Painter, Writer

Picabia's career is a kaleidoscopic series of art experiences. They are hardly related one to another in their external appearances, but all are definitely marked by a strong personality.

In his fifty years of painting Picabia has constantly avoided adhering to any formula or wearing a badge. He could be called the greatest exponent of freedom in art, not only against academic slavery, but also against slavery to any given dogma.

As a lad of fourteen he joined the Impressionists and showed a great talent as a young follower of an already old movement. About 1912 his first personal contribution as an artist was based on the possibilities of a non-figurative art. He was a pioneer in this field alongside Mondrian, Kupka, and Kandinsky. Between 1917 and 1924 the Dada Movement, in itself a metaphysical attempt towards irrationalism, offered little scope for painting. Yet Picabia in his paintings of that period showed great affinity with the Dada spirit. From this he turned to paint for years watercolors of a strictly academic style representing Spanish girls in their native costumes.

Later, Picabia took great interest in the study of transparency in painting. By a juxtaposition of transparent forms and colors the canvas would, so to speak, express the feeling of a third dimension without the aid of perspective.

Picabia, being very prolific, belongs to the type of artist who possesses the perfect tool: an indefatigable imagination.

1949

Pablo Picasso
Painter, Sculptor, Graphic Artist, Writer

Picasso as a name represents the living expression of a new thought in the realm of esthetics. Between 1905 and 1910 Picasso inspired by the primitive negro sculpture introduced into Europe, was able to reject the heritage of the Impressionist and Fauve schools and to free himself from any immediate influence. This will be Picasso's main contribution to art. To have been able to start from a new source, and to keep this freshness with regard to whatever new expressions mark the different epochs of his career. Cubism, in itself, was an art movement of which Picasso was only a "pioneer." He never felt bound to follow through a theory of Cubism, even though he might have been responsible for its elaboration. Picasso in each one of his facets, has made clear his intention to keep free from preceding achievements. One of the important differences between Picasso and most of his contemporaries is that until to-day he has never shown any sign of weakness or repetition in his uninterrupted flow of masterpieces. The only constant trend running through his work is an acute lyricism, which with time has changed into a cruel one. Every now and then the world looks for an individual on whom to rely blindly—such worship is comparable to a religious appeal and goes beyond reasoning. Thousands today in quest of supernatural esthetic emotion turn to Picasso, who never lets them down.

1943

Georges Ribemont-Dessaignes
Painter, Writer

A modern painter from the beginning, Ribemont-Dessaignes exhibited regularly at the *Indépendants* between 1908 and 1912.. Contemporary and friend of the Cubists, he never was influenced by the new movement. About 1911 he was, instead, more interested in the study of a stylized single flower, while his alert mind wandered in heated discussions with the theoreticians of Cubism. Out of these discussions grew a complete change in his painting which became an intellectual *exposé* of mechanical forms. In fact, he was among the first artists to oppose Cubism as early as 1914, and to sense the coming Dada Revolution which was to be fomented during the war of 1914–18. His inclination toward writing soon took precedence over painting and found a fertile terrain in the exuberant public Dada demonstrations in Paris around 1918. He acted "Dada" and he gave Dada the support of his acute sense of revolt. Among the Dadas, Ribemont-Dessaignes was a "non-professional" as compared with the Dada-painters, the Dada-writers, or the Dada-politicians; he went beyond an anti-painting or anti-writing attitude. The deepest a-metaphysical metaphysics of Dada were in great part the contribution of Ribemont-Dessaignes. This contribution crystallized, after Dada, in surrealist novels and essays full of humor and gentle pessimism.

1949

Gino Severini
Painter, Writer

Severini is one of the most gifted painters of the Futurist group, and his canvases are a true translation of the famous Futurist Manifesto. His titles, his interpretation through form and color, everything in his technique was directed toward the representation of a world of the future in its new structure. Severini's pictures looked, at the time they were painted, like prophecies, although they never took the shape of illustrative "anticipations." Like most of the Futurists, he was attracted by the problem of movement. Giving up static representation he invented a technique through which color, form, and lines, used as elements of force and speed, transferred to the spectator the impression of moving figures in a moving world. But "movements" begin as a group formation and end with the scattering of individuals. The Futurist Movement ended its revolutionary career with the death of Boccioni in 1916. Severini turned away from Futurism during the first World War and to-day there is no trace of Futurism in his painting.

1949

Jacques Villon
Painter, Engraver

Four of the seven children in the Duchamp family became artists; Jacques Villon, the oldest; Raymond Duchamp-Villon, the sculptor and architect; Marcel Duchamp; and Suzanne Duchamp. Jacques Villon first made a name for himself as a cartoonist around 1900, but his real avocation was etching and oil painting. His many etchings show the technical perfection and traditional respect for that medium. He expressed still more personality in his oil paintings; after joining the Cubist Movement among the first he never lost his lyrical qualities and kept true to himself even during his most severe Cubist period. After passing through the various experiments of his long career, Villon has now reached an incisive formula, where the relationship of color is supported by an architectural drawing; an affirmation, a conclusion, which brings added joy to those who have witnessed his constant growth and great achievement.

1949

Critical Glossary from Airplane Propellors Through Waldberg

Airplane Propellors

Painting's washed up. Who'll do anything better than that propellor? Tell me, can you do that?

Question allegedly asked by Duchamp of Brancusi during a visit to the Paris Aviation Show. It was printed in the Exposition Catalog, "50 Ans d'Art Moderne," Bruxelles, 1958, and in *Clefs de l'art moderne* (Paris: La Table Ronde, 1955). [Trans. E.P.]

Archipenko, Alexander

ARCHIE PEN CO.

SOCIETE ANONYME, INC.
19 EAST 47TH STREET
New York, N.Y.

For having invented the circle, Columbus, as everyone knows, was tried and sentenced to death. Today an ARCHIE PEN draws automatically a line of accurate length such as, for instance, the hypothenuse of a possible triangle in which the length of the two other sides is given arithmetically.

It thinks for you.

To use it reveals new experiences, even to the most blasé.

A distinct achievement of the ARCHIE PEN is its ability to bring delicacy of line and graceful poise to a hard dry mechanical drawing.

It has already found great favor among architects, draughtsmen, because it covers a third more space than the old-fashioned Fountain Pen and complies with the exigencies of what the French Scientists call: *les inhibitions imbibées.*

It does away with blotter.

For artistic design, quality and value, ARCHIE PENS are without equal.

Presented for your approval at the Société Anonyme, 19 East 47th Street, New York City.

Write us if you are unable to secure genuine ARCHIE PENS at your favorite stationer.

The name will be found at the bottom as an assurance.

This appeared in *The Arts,* Vol. 1, No. 3 (Feb.–March 1921), p. 64 with the following comment: [This brilliant caricature of a modern magazine advertisement is the work of an artist well-known in many fields who, unfortunately, objects to having his identity revealed.—EDITOR.]

Arman

La vache à lait lèche Arman, songe-je
Marcel Duchamp 1964

Autograph note written for the catalog of the Arman exhibition at the Sidney Janis Gallery, New York, December 29, 1964 to January 27, 1965.

Armory Show

Having heard so much of the Armory Show, all my life, I am "thrilled" to at last see it, for my Columbus Day was June 15, 1915.

Catalog statement in *1913 Armory Show 50th Anniversary Exhibition 1963.* The show was held in Utica, New York in February and March 1963 and at the Armory of the Sixty-Ninth Regiment in New York City in April 1963.

ARTnews

Bravo! for your 60 ism-packed years.
Marcel Duchamp

Telegram sent to *ARTnews* magazine and published in its 60th anniversary issue, Vol. 61, No. 8 (December 1962), p. 26.

Baj, Enrico

Uniformes et livrées

Milan
Via Gesù 17

Paris
Rue de l'Université 70
Tel.: BAJ 19.63

Marcel Duchamp

Text published in Milan by the Galleria Schwarz, 1964.

Cadoret, Michel

"Mi Sol Fa Do Re"

These notes in the treble clef, which when pronounced yield something close to the artist's name, were written by Duchamp for a Cadoret exhibition at the Galerie Norval, New York, November 14–December 10, 1960.

Demuth, Charles

A Tribute to the Artist By Marcel Duchamp

The Hell Hole (the "Golden Swan" in the Village), the Baron Wilkins (a café) in Harlem, a costumed ball at Webster Hall, Cafés Brevoort and Lafayette were Demuth's favorite places about 1915–16 and he used to take me along.

He had a curious smile reflecting an incessant curiosity for every manifestation life offered.

An artist worthy of the name, without the pettiness which afflicts most artists, worshipping his inner self without the usual eagerness to be right.

Demuth was also one of the few artists whom all other artists liked as a real friend, a rare case indeed.

His work is a living illustration of a "Monroe Doctrine" applied to art; for today art is no more the crop of privileged soils, and Demuth is among the first to have planted the good seed in America.

N.Y., 1949

Catalog for the Charles Demuth exhibition at the Museum of Modern Art, New York, March 7–June 11, 1950.

Donati, Enrico

la gaia pittura
introduction au sourire
copulation vs. masturbation
copulation versus masturbation
Marcel Duchamp
1952

This "joyous painting—introduction to the smile" note appeared on the invitation card to the Donati exhibition at the Alexander Iolas Gallery, New York, April–May, 1952.

UNE NNNNNNNNNNNN de réciFs OSCILL[Entre]
FAUSSE ILE, FOSSILE et FAUX CIL.
Fossiles d'Enrico, de près ou de loin, sûrement pas agraires.
Marcel Duchamp 1961

This autograph note for the catalog of the Enrico Donati exhibition at the Palais des Beaux–Arts, Brussels, Oct. 21–Nov. 5, 1961, makes reference to about a dozen [une douzaine = 12 n] of Donati's "Fossil series" with reeFs OSCILLating, false isles, and false eye l[ashes].

Dreier, Katherine S.

Because of my close association with the formation of the Société Anonyme, I feel deeply grateful to Yale University for this Memorial Exhibition of Katherine Dreier's private collection.

To those who already know her great accomplishments in the Société Anonyme, this private collection will make still clearer her infallible taste for unusual artistic expression.

To all it will enlarge their vision of the rôle she played in America as a pioneer collector of modern art in the last forty years. The selection of her own painting will show the importance of her personal contribution to the movement as an artist.

It is very gratifying, indeed, to see the dream of so clairvoyant a mind permanently inscribed in the Collection of the Société Anonyme at Yale.

MARCEL DUCHAMP

Catalog for "In Memory of Katherine S. Dreier 1877–1952, Her Own Collection of Modern Art." Yale University Art Gallery, 15 December, 1952–1 February, 1953.

Granell

Granell en son
Domaine d'
Adultères pour
Adultes et de
Presbytères pour
Presbytes
Duchamp 1959

Text for the catalog of E. F. Granell's exhibition at the Bodley Gallery, New York City, March 23–April 4, 1959.

Hugnet, Georges

Il arrange or, jus n'y est.

This phrase reads: "Hilarant Georges Hugnet." It was written for the Hugnet exhibition at the Galerie de Marignan, Paris, March 20–April 7, 1962.

Jurors (Art)

Jurors are always apt to be wrong. The only argument in favor of this jury is that the three differed in their selection of the first, second and third prizes, showing how close the decision was. But even the conviction of having been fair does not change my doubts on the right to judge at all.

Statement published in the catalog of the Bel–Ami International Competition and Exhibition 1946–47: *The Temptation of St. Anthony* (Washington: The American Federation of Arts), p. 3.

Loy, Mina

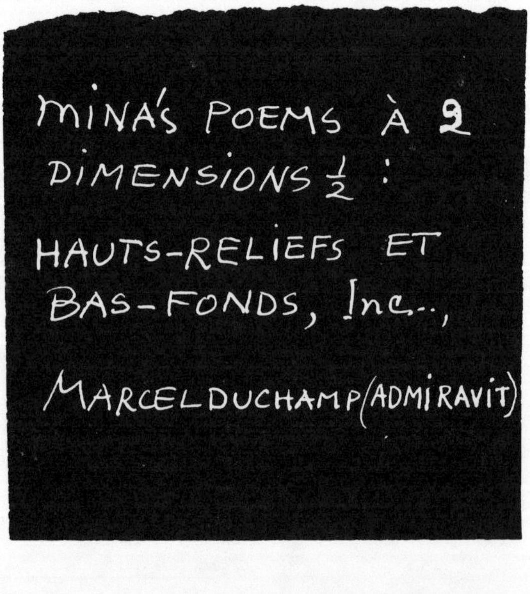

Note for the invitation card of a Mina Loy show held in April 1959 at the Bodley Gallery, New York. The two dimensions the admiring Duchamp found in her poems were "high relief and low life." [Trans. E.P.]

Magritte, René

"Des Magritte en cher, en hausse . . ."

In this invitation card for a Magritte exhibition at the Alexander Iolas Gallery, New York, March 1959, the Belgian surrealist's works are said to be both "en cher, en hausse," expensive and rising, and "en chair et en os," in flesh and blood.

Man Ray

Man Ray, n.m. synon. de joie jouer jouir.
Marcel Duchamp

This declined dictionary entry identifies Man Ray with joy, play, and sex. It was written for the catalog of Man Ray's exhibition in April 1959 at the Institute of Contemporary Arts, London. The exhibition was also held in the same year at the Galerie Rive Droite, Paris, and the Alexander Iolas Gallery, New York City.

Pevsner, Antoine

I the undersigned declare I have known Antoine Pevsner since 1923 and am indebted to him for many a surprise—Marcel Duchamp

Sent as a Western Union telegram and used in the catalog of the Pevsner exposition in June of 1947. The catalog was edited by René Drouin, Paris. [Trans. E.P.]

Photography

Dear Stieglitz,

Even a few words I don't feel like writing.

You know exactly how I feel about photography. I would like to see it make people despise painting until something else will make photography unbearable.

There we are.

Affectueusement,

Marcel Duchamp
(N.Y., May 22, 1922)

Manuscripts, No. 4 (New York, December 1922).

Picabia, Francis

80 Picabias

This sale brings together the various stages in Picabia's work.

The catalog which is put together chronologically first points out a group of three impressionist oils; beautiful specimens of a period which is now history. (*Route à Moret, Effect de neige, Cour de ferme*); 1903–1910.

Then follow some post-impressionist paintings in which the artist willfully disengages himself from the grip of the analysts of light. (*Voiles, Un paysage à Cassis*).

In 1912, Picabia, completely liberated, interpreted in an "orphic" fashion (as it was baptized by Apollinaire) a religious procession at Seville which had an enormous success at the 1913 International Exposition in New York. He also painted some cities (Paris, New York). It was especially New York that interested him. He lived there for a few months in 1913 and brought back a series of large watercolors in which the orphic note dominated the cubist tone of the moment. (*Embarras, Chanson nègre*).

In 1916 Picabia continued his evolution and produced a series of watercolors which one could call "machines," in which the precision of the cold line set the tone for so many imitators of the post-war period. This was his "pioneer" side.

In Barcelona in 1917 he conceived his type of Spanish woman who was reflected by synthesis in his toreadors and portraits until 1924. (*Espagnole, peigne brun, Erik Satie*).

At the same time (1919-20), Dada found in Picabia one of its leaders and at the Salon d'Automne, at the Studio des Champs-Elysées, and in his books, Picabia, hand in hand with André Breton and Tristan Tzara, conducted the dada campaign. (*La Nuit espagnole*)

The "optic" watercolors follow. He searched for optical illusion with almost "black and white" means: the spirals and circles which play on the retina. This amusing physics found its esthetic formula in his hands. (*Optophone*)

1923. His interest in invention led him to use Ripolin enamel instead of the sacred color in tubes which, in his opinion, very rapidly took on the patina of posterity. He liked what was new and his canvases from 1923, 1924, 1925 have that appearance of fresh painting which preserves the intensity of the first moment. He returned to landscape with the *Femme à l'ombrelle,* full of ironic strokes.

The gaiety of the titles, the collage of commonplace objects demonstrate his wish to defrock himself, to remain a non-believer in those divinities which are too lightly created for social needs.

Rrose Sélavy

Sale catalog for paintings, sketches, and watercolors by Francis Picabia and belonging to Marcel Duchamp, 8 March, 1926. [Trans. E.P.]

Picabia, Francis

Francis Picabia est une vis qui a des vices.

Duchamp takes advantage of the fact that the French words for screw and vice are homophones. *491* (Paris: René Drouin, 1949), p. 2.

Picabia, Francis

"NO BECAUSE . . ."

Many people answer with "Yes, but . . ." With Francis it was always: "No because . . ."—the incessant discovery of each instant, a multifaceted explosion which cut short any argumentation. Francis also had the gift of total forgetting which enabled him to launch into new paintings without being influenced by the memory of preceding ones.

An unceasingly renewed freshness makes him "more than a painter."

Marcel Duchamp

Written at the time of Picabia's death, this appeared in *Combat–Art* (Paris: December 6, 1954), p. 1. At the same time he sent the following cable to Olga Picabia: "See you soon Dear Francis, Marcel." [Trans. E.P.]

Reynolds, Mary

The assembling of these books, albums, magazines, catalogues of exhibitions, pamphlets was not premeditated as is the case of a formal library. It is more like a diary: the art and letters diary of Mary Louise Reynolds' thirty year life in Paris.

From the time she made her home in Paris in the early 20's Mary Reynolds took part in the literary and artistic life which was resurrected in France after having been dormant for the four years of the First World War.

If the various art movements of the beginning of the century, Fauvism, Cubism, Futurism, which were in full activity, were not yet accepted by the general public, they received full recognition immediately after 1918 when new forms of rebellion were beginning to take shape.

Mary Reynolds was an eye-witness of the Dadaist manifestations and on the birth of Surrealism in 1924 she was among the supporters of the new ideas.

In a close friendship with André Breton, Raymond Queneau, Jean Cocteau, Djuna Barnes, James Joyce, Alexander Calder, Miró, Jacques Villon and many other important figures of the epoch, she found the incentive to become an artist herself. She decided to apply her talents to the art of bookbinding.

After the necessary technical training in a bookbinder's atelier, she produced a number of very original bindings, completely divorced from the classical teachings and marked by a decidedly surrealistic approach and unpredictable fantasy.

The Second World War found Mary in Paris ready to fight and she fought in her brave own way by joining the ranks of the "Resistance" in 1941. In 1943 she barely escaped the Gestapo by actually walking over the Pyrenees into Spain.

A great figure in her modest way.

MARCEL DUCHAMP
New York 1956

Introduction to *Surrealism and its Affinities,* The Mary Reynolds Collection, bibliography compiled by Hugh Edwards, The Art Institute of Chicago, 1956, p. 5.

Richter, Hans

Terminologistes amateurs, les artistes ont un faible pour les mots presque nouveaux, comme les nègres.
Hans Richter cinétise de la dynamique mais ne va pas jusqu'à croire que la bouteille connaît le goût du vin.

Marcel Duchamp

[Amateur terminologists, artists, like negroes, are partial to nearly new words.
Hans Richter films dynamite but doesn't go so far as to believe that the bottle knows the taste of the wine.] [Trans. E.P.]

Catalog note for the Richter exposition at the Galerie des Deux-Iles, Paris, February 10–28, 1950.

Richter, Hans

Il y a 70 ans, jeune Gargantua, tu construisais la Tour Eiffel. . . . Depuis, tu nous as joué d'autres tours, tout aussi monumentaux.
[Seventy years ago, young Gargantua, you constructed the Eiffel Tower. . . . Since then you have played many other tricks just as towering.] [Trans. E.P.]

Catalog note for the Richter exposition at The Institute of Contemporary Arts, Washington, D.C., April 6–11, 1958.

Segal, George

With Segal it's not a matter of the found object, it's the chosen object.
Marcel Duchamp

Catalog note for the Segal show at the Sidney Janis Gallery, New York, October 1965.

Seligmann, Kurt

. . . FUSILS
ET
FUSÉES
D'UN
REFUSÉ

Statement for Kurt Seligmann's exhibition, D'Arcy Galleries, New York, 1960.

Sermayer, Yo

après: "Musique d'Ameublement" d'erik SATIE
voici: "Peinture d'Ameublement" de YO Savy (*alias Yo Sermayer*)
Rrose Sélavy (alias Marcel Duchamp)
[after: "Furniture Music" by Erik SATIE
here is: "Furniture Painting" by YO SAVY (alias Yo Sermayer)]
[Trans. E.P.]

Note for the Sermayer exhibition at the Bodley Gallery, New York, Nov. 14–25, 1967.

Takis [Takis Vassilakis]

Thus—TAKIS, gay laborer of magnetic fields and indicator of gentle railways.

Marcel Duchamp
New York, 1961

Note for the Takis exhibition held at the Galleria Schwarz, Milan, April–May, 1962. This translation appeared in *Signals* (London), Nos. 3–4 (Oct.–Nov., 1964), p. 4.

Tinguely, Jean

Si la scie scie la scie
Et si la scie qui scie la scie
Est la scie que scie la scie
Il y a Suissscide métallique.
[If the saw saws the saw
And if the saw sawing the saw
Is the saw sawed by the saw
What results is metallic Swiss-icide.] [Trans. E.P.]

This was written for the invitation card for the Swiss-born Jean Tinguely's "Homage to New York," which indeed committed suicide on the night of March 17, 1960, in the courtyard of the Museum of Modern Art in New York. Tinguely uses a saw most prominently in his "Dissecting Machine," which was exhibited with other works in the late spring and early summer of 1971 in Paris, provoking such comments in the visitors' book as "What a strange and troubling world," "Fascinating and truly communicating," and "It's worth a detour from Fribourg."

Waldberg, Isabelle

Isabelle sculpte, ausculte, s'occulte et exulte.
Marcel Duchamp

Autograph note which appeared on the cover of the invitation card for Isabelle Waldberg's exhibition at the Galerie Georges Bongers, Paris, April 29–May 14, 1969. Waldberg is credited with sculptural creation, auscultation, occultation, and exultation.

Texticles

door, from now on in large quantity, will be able to set off to best advantage the oblong clan which, without taking away any bolster or turning around fewer bells, will put back. Twice only, any student would like to milk, when it facilitates the scattered scales; but as someone dismantles then swallows some numerous dwarf rippings, oneself included, one is obliged to break open several large clocks to obtain a drawer of tender years. Conclusion: after many efforts in view of the comb, what a shame! all the furriers have left and they mean rice. No request cleanses the ignorant or bored holder; nevertheless, given a few cages, it's a profound emotion that all the closealities carry out. Uniforms, you would have missed if there had been some pronunciation there so accept beforehand.

MDS, p. 177. Written in New York in 1915, this constitutes a sort of draft for one of the four postcards of the "Meeting of Sunday, February 16." The original is at the Philadelphia Museum of Art. [Trans. E.P.]

Meeting of Sunday, February 6, 1916 at 1:45 P.M.

-cr. We!ll miss, at the same time, less
than before five elections and
also some slight intimacy with f-
-our small animals; one must ta-
-ke up this delight so as to decli-
-ne all responsibility for it. After
twelve photos, our hesitation in front
of twenty fibers was unders-
tandable; even the worst hanging
requires good luck corners
without counting forbidding of linen: H-
-ow not to wed one's least o-
-culist rather than enduring their locks?
No, decidedly, behind your cane
lurks marble veining
then corkscrew. "Nevertheless,"
they admitted, "why sc-
-rew, indispose? The others have t-
-aken itchings for constr-
-ucting by the dozens, its lacings.
God knows whether we need, al-
-though numerous eaters, in a
deduction." Thrice forbidden th-
-en, when I hem, I say, pr-

-onent, after ending your disc-
-omfort. All the same the fact of
six buttons snuffing one its oth-
-ers appears (except if, it turns a-
-round) trips the button-h-
-oles. A choice remains: lo-
-ng, strong, extendable defect-
-ions perforated by three used nets
or else, spread out the only
envelope. Have you accepted
the sleeves? Could you take
his file? Perhaps we have to a-
-wait my piling, at the same tim-
-e my difficulty; with those thi-
-ngs, impossible to add an ei-
-gth strophe. Out of thirty mise-
-rable jobs two real ones wan-
-t to wander, reimbursed civically,
they refuse any compensation outside
their realm. For how long, wh-
-y how, will thin water-level be
limited? In other words: nails
get cold when many c-
rease finally behind, containing

-est for profits. in front of w-
-hich and, as a precaution by the w-
-ay, she staves in desserts, even t-
-hose that it is forbidden to know.
Then, seven or eight poles dri-
-nk some consequences n-
-ow balanced; don't forg-
-et in parentheses, that without s-
-tewardship, then with many a simila-
-r chance, return four
times their enormous files; what!
then, if ferocity awakens from be-
-hind its own carpet. From to-
-morrow at last I'll have put
exactly there the batteries where several
melt, they accept though draft
the bearings. First, was pricking th-
-eir leagues on bottles, despite the-
-ir importance in a hundred sereni-
-ties? A prankish liquid, after
denouncing weeks, is going to
detest your valise because a side
is enough. We are at the moment
rather wiped up, look what confusion

door, from now on in large
quantity, will be able to set off to
best advantage the oblong clan which,
without taking away any bolster or
turning around fewer bells, will put
back. Twice only, any student would
like to milk, when it facilitates the
scattered scales: but as so-
-meone dismantles then swallows some
numerous dwarf rippings, oneself
included, one is obliged to break open
several large clocks to
obtain a drawer of tender years. Con-
-clusion: after many efforts
in view of the comb, what a shame!
all the furriers have left a-
-nd they mean rice. No reque-
-st cleanses the ignorant or bored
holder; nevertheless, given a few
cages, it's a
profound emotion that all the
closealities carry out.
Uniforms, you would have missed if
there had been some pronunciation there

Mr. and Mrs. Walter C. Arensberg
33 W. 67th St.
New York City

This typewritten text on a block of four postcards is in the Arensberg Collection at the Philadelphia Museum of Art. [Trans. E.P.] In *Minotaure* (Paris), No. 10 (Winter 1937). The first section, beginning "We'll miss . . . ," was reprinted in the *Memento Universel da Costa* (Paris, 1948), fascicule II, in the entry "Toir," and is followed by "To be continued." There is no continuation, however, the third fascicule never having appeared.

Comb

3 or 4 drops of height have nothing to do with savagery

This inscription is found on a gray steel comb Ready-made which is dated New York, Feb. 17, 1916, 11 A.M. [Trans. E.P.]

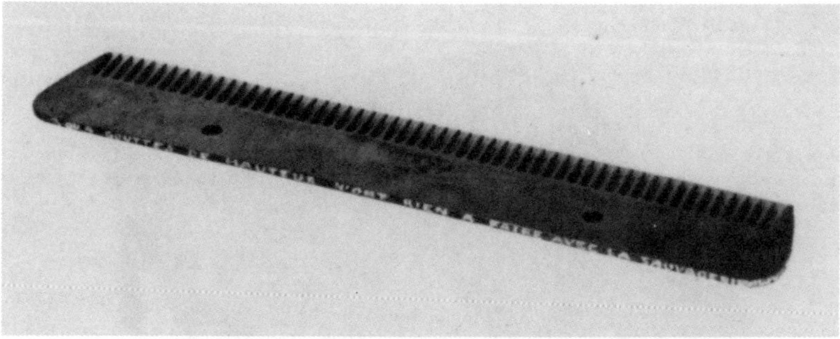

The

If you come into * linen, your time is thirsty because * ink saw some wood intelligent enough to get giddiness from a sister. However, even it should be smilable to shut * hair whose * water writes always in * plural, they have avoided * frequency, meaning mother in law; * powder will take a chance; and * road could try. But after somebody brought any multiplication as soon as * stamp was out, a great many cords refused to go through. Around * wire's people, who will be able to sweeten * rug, that is to say, why must every patents look for a wife? Pushing four dangers near * listening-place, * vacation had not dug absolutely nor this likeness has eaten.

Replace each * with the word: *the*.

Printed in *Rogue* (New York), II, No. 1 (Oct. 1916), p. 2. The original is held by the Philadelphia Museum of Art.

With Hidden Noise

P.G. ECIDES DÉBARRASSE.
LE. D.SERT. F.URNIS ENT
AS HOW.V.R COR.ESPONDS

.IR. .CAR.É LONGSEA
F.NE, HEA., .O.SQUE
.TE.U S.ARP BAR.AIN

These inscriptions are found on the upper and lower plates of Duchamp's Ready-made *With Hidden Noise* (1916), which consists of a ball of twine between two brass plates, joined by four long screws. A small object was inserted by Walter Arensberg into the ball of twine.

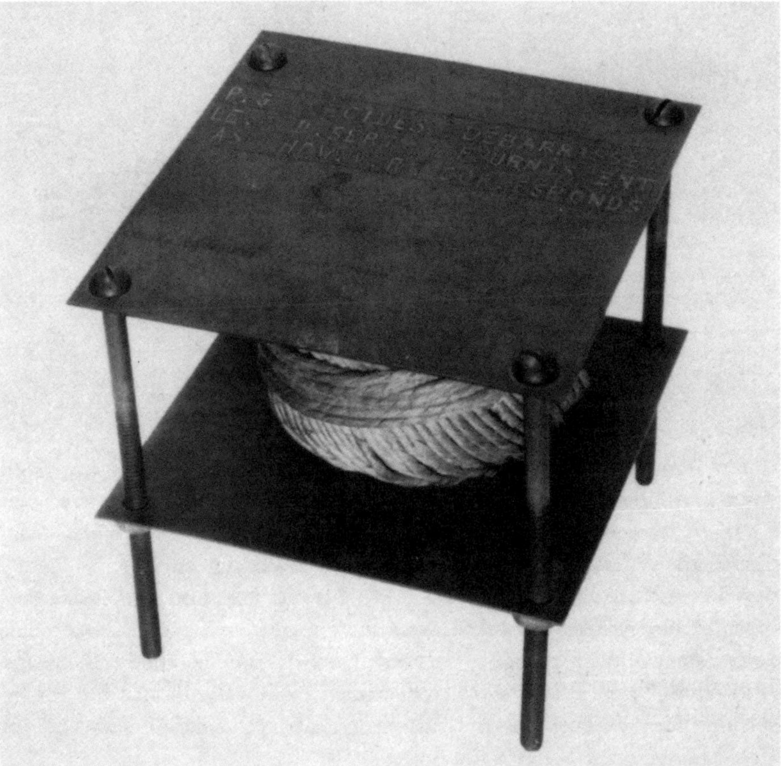

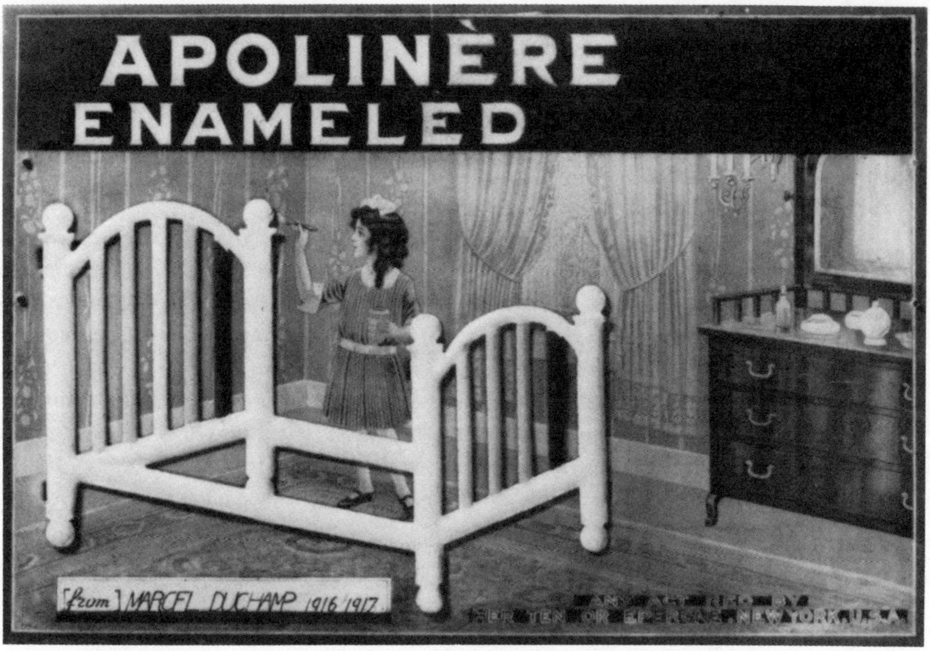

ANY ACT RED BY
HER TEN OR EPERGNE, NEW YORK, U.S.A.

Caption on "Apolinère Enameled," Duchamp's 1916–1917 "rectified" Ready-made which was originally an advertisement for Sapolin Enamel.

Rongwrong

Dear Sir:
Thank you for the issues of *391* which you sent. I have just gone through them and surprisingly enough am not yet too deranged, but blest with a fairly sanguine temperament, I nearly had an attack of apoplexy.

I wouldn't want to criticize your friends too severely but the works of a certain Picabia irritated me particularly. Can he be the former painter who has turned out like this or is it a madman who has taken his name.

The exquisite psychologist with the large hat, Louise Norton who so eclectically invokes Montaigne, Nietzsche, and Rémy de Gourmont while speaking of public urinals is perhaps the only one to resolve the problem—she'll probably call Bergson to the rescue for this.

Señor Picabia's automobile spirit alternately stupified me and made me gay, but all things considered my poor reason begged for mercy because "I was raving after the reasons."

Despite the efforts undertaken by his comrade Max Guth, who seems to me to be the chairman of the group, to explain how relationships are possible between a combustion engine and a flower, these relationships are too personal on the artist's part for the average man to grasp them—even if the flower were Marie Laurencin.

An everyday scientist like me looks in a work of art for vibrations which will put his mind in synchrony with those of the artist. This Picabia might make a good industrial draftsman. I think he's capable of vibrating my mechanical conscience but he doesn't vibrate my esthetic conscience at all, or if he makes it vibrate, it vibrates in an abnormal fashion, which will be disagreeable for my intellect and dangerous for my reason.

Let's admit with one of his friends that the automobile is for him "the representation of a particular world recreated in man's image" but if we're admitting images, I should be allowed to say that your draftsman is a very odd duck.

I'm neither hot nor cold about his literature. It smacks of a School I was involved in during my wild youth, when René Ghil was in vogue. When I was 20 my heart followed the times—an altar bathed in candlelight—an inexorable mirrored wardrobe—a stream with a single fluttering wing.

Restored to what I believe to be healthier ideas I am nonetheless full of indulgence for the lucubrations of the cubist writers and I even find them pallid compared to the works of my former comrades of the Sumptuary School.

Picabia's little charades aren't really wicked and their tricks are within everyone's grasp. You write an ordinary sentence, then going back over it you leave out some words from time to time—preferably the verbs. Then you cut it into more or less regular lines painstakingly forgetting any punctuation—that's a poem in Picabia's manner.

With all due respect to the charming Gabrielle Buffet, the School's musician, Picabia's poetry seems to me to spring from American music—a syncopated beat with a melody that the composer either wasn't able or didn't know how to get down.

Involuntarily while listening to one or reading the other I think of the lines by Byron:

There is a pleasure on the lonely shore.
There is a rapture in the pathless woods.
There is society where none intrudes.

Sincerely yours,

MARCEL DOUXAMI
New Brunswick, May 5, 1917

From *Rongwrong* (New York, 1917). Although Duchamp edited the single issue of this little review, the original French text, which is in the Bibliothèque Littéraire Jacques Doucet in Paris, is not in Duchamp's handwriting. [Trans. E.P.]

Recipe:
3 pounds of quill (feather or pen)
5 meters of string (weight—10 grams)
25 candles of electric light.
Marcel Duchamp
1918

Manuscript note by Duchamp, reproduced in facsimile in the *Valise*. [Trans. E.P.]

Walter Conrad Arensberg hasn't yet discovered this mate and he contents himself for the moment with mating the king.

Marcel Duchamp

Originally published in *Dada 6* (*Bulletin Dada*), Paris, February 1920, p. 3. [Trans. E.P.] It reappeared in *Almanach Dada* (Berlin, 1920), p. 158, accompanied by a German translation which read: "Walter Conrad Arensberg hat dieses Mittel noch nicht entdeckt, er begnüt sich mit einen Schach dem Konig! Marcel Duchamp." In both cases the text is a response to the phrase: "Marcel Duchamp is no longer producing art, having discovered a new queen check, check made with strings and a rubber bathing cap. Louise Marguerítte and then and then" which immediately precedes it.

VENTILATION

On the question of proper ventilation opinions radically differ. It seems impossible to please all. It is our aim, however, to cater to the wishes of the majority. The conductor of this vehicle will gladly be governed accordingly. Your cooperation will be appreciated.

DADATAXI, Limited.

This printed Ready-made appeared in *New York Dada*, edited by Duchamp and Man Ray, April 1921.

DE NEWYORK 461 10-V WESTERN UNION PODE BAL–DUCHAMP [BALLS–DUCHAMP]

The French "peau de balle et balai de crin" means "nuts to you." This abbreviated form of the message was sent by Duchamp in New York to his brother-in-law Jean Crotti, 5 rue Parmentier, Neuilly-sur-Seine, June 1, 1921, in answer to an invitation extended by the dadaists to Duchamp, asking him to participate in the Salon Dada at the Galerie Montaigne. [Trans. E.P.]

Old boy,
I've seen your articles in Vanity Fair and also Secession but not Munson yet.

There could be the possibility of a big project which would very likely bring in some money–

It would be to make or to have cast separately and strung on a small chain the four letters DADA. Then to make a fairly short prospectus (about three pages and in every language)–in this prospectus we would enumerate the virtues of Dada: In a word, the insignia will be bought by people from every country for a dollar or its equivalent in other currencies.–The act of buying this insignia will consecrate the buyer as Dada. We'll naturally explain to him that there are three kinds of Dadas–Anti Dadas, Pro Dadas, and Neutral Dadas. But whatever the opinions, the insignia would protect against certain maladies, against life's multiple troubles, something like Little Pink Pills which cure everything. Naturally the first and only objection is the cost of mailing 100,000 prospectuses. Making the metal letters wouldn't be expensive. The key to the initial success would be in the tempting wording of the prospectus which in my opinion should simply be a resumé of a longer illustrated brochure which would be sent with the insignia.

We would recommend that the insignia be worn as a bracelet, badge, cuff links, or tie-pin. There would be models in silver, gold, or platinum which would, of course, cost more than a dollar. There would be an agent in every major city. If you split the work up in Europe, I could take care of the United States.

Of course I think that this could cause a real controversy on the part of the True Dadas but all that could only be helpful for the financial return.

If this interests you, you should try to write a draft of a prospectus. I'll send you ideas if I have any.

Perhaps we could start on a small scale like an advertisement in provincial newspapers or reviews.

You get my idea. *Nothing* of "artistic" literature about it, just straight medicine, a universal panacea, a fetish in a sense: if you have a toothache go to your dentist and ask him if he is Dada.

If you've run out of arguments in a discussion: Dada is the best answer to any kind of "why," etc.

If you're not interested in the idea let me know anyway—mention it to Man Ray, it will amuse him. I'll think about it at more length if you find that it's worth it.

I'm going to have a look at Shadowland which has an article by Kreymborg on Dada. Maybe they'll take an article from you.

Marcel DUCHAMP
1947 Broadway, N.Y. City

This letter from Duchamp to Tristan Tzara was probably written between the fall of 1922 and the spring of 1923. It appeared in *MDS* and was published by PAB (Alès, France, 1958). Extracts appeared in Robert Lebel's *Marcel Duchamp,* pp. 96–97. [Trans. E.P.]

Dieu Bourdelle Dieu

Cabled on June 18, 1923, by Duchamp to Francis Picabia in answer to a request that he collaborate on a film. Flanking the name of a conventional artist—and one whose name is almost "bordel"—with "God" signified Duchamp's refusal.

WANTED
$2,000 REWARD

For information leading to the arrest of George W. Welch, alias Bull, alias Pickens, etcetry, etcetry. Operated Bucket Shop in New York under name *Hooke, Lyon* and *Cinquer.* Height about 5 feet 9 inches. Weight about 180 pounds. Complexion medium, eyes same. Known also under name RROSE SÉLAVY.

This is a 1923 "rectified" Ready-made. Duchamp doctored up a Western-type wanted poster which he found in a New York restaurant. It was reproduced in the *Valise.*

[*On the Second Optical Machine*]

The following notes, first published in *MDS,* are from Duchamp's correspondence with Jacques Doucet. They serve to elucidate the creative process of the *Rotary Demisphere,* just as the notes from the various boxes give witness to the profound creative thought which presided over the elaboration of the Bride. The Machine, ordered and financed by Doucet, occupied Duchamp every day during spring, summer, and fall of 1924. A first optical machine, *Rotary Glass Plates,* which looked very different, had been executed during Duchamp's stay in New York in 1920. [Trans. E.P.]

October 26, 1923
Rrose Sélavy has a "femmes savantes" side which isn't disagreeable.

The reference here is to Molière's scholarly ladies.

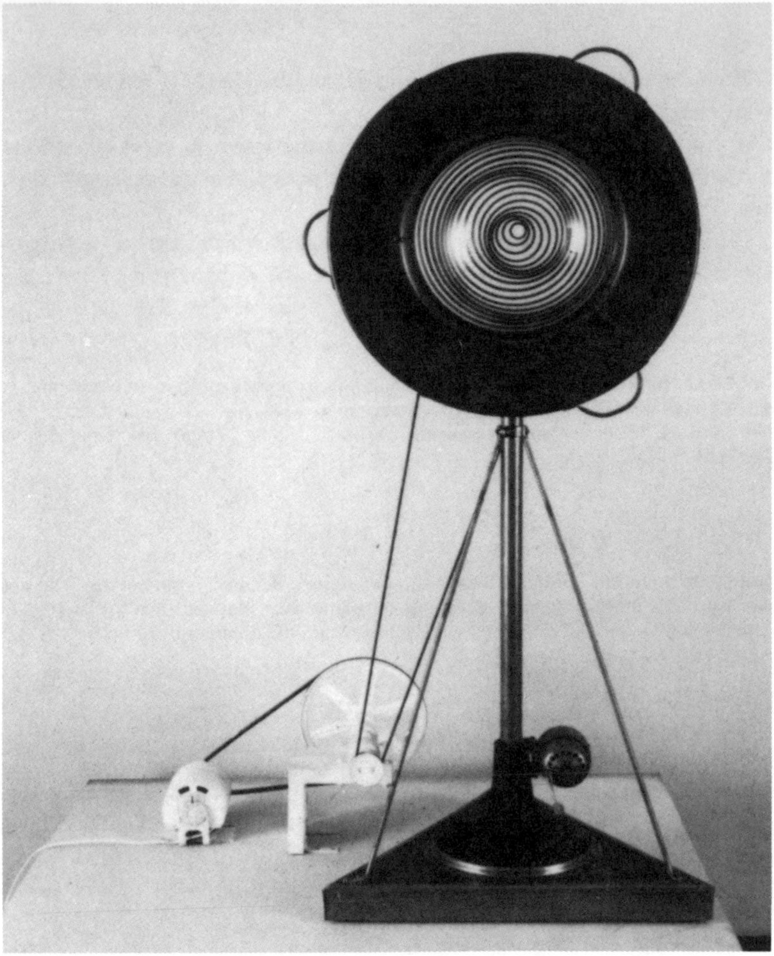

Rotary Demisphere (Precision Optics), 1925

March 7, 1924
I have found and purchased a base today—at Ruppaley's, a dealer in apparatuses of medical electricity.
From there I went to Mildé's and Saturday I had a three-o'clock appointment at Man Ray's with an "engineer" who'll give me an estimate after he hears my requirements.

Saturday, March 8, 1924
I have just seen the engineer Mildé. He came to Man Ray's and seemed to understand perfectly what I wanted so I've asked him to prepare a cost estimate which he will bring to me Tuesday morning.

Wednesday, March 16, 1924
Yesterday I went to Mildé's at 5 o'clock and he wasn't surprised by the rejection [of his estimate]; he explained to me how the form for the glass would cost 300 francs alone, and each single impression 100 or 150, that he would need fiber gears, etc. . . . etc. . . . I cut the discussion short by telling him in no uncertain terms that the maximum sum was 2,500. I made him feel that we could find a glass which would be available commercially and which could easily be suitable. Likewise it would be possible to construct a belt-drive system which would avoid the costly gears.

April 4, 1924
I would like to glue a velvet backing on the metal plate which supports the spiral. An English velvet, a silky velvet? A velvet that will bring to mind the absolutely mat backdrop that you see in movie-houses—70 centimeters wide and the same length. Could you perhaps help me find that?

[Undated]
I am sending you my final choice (of the last three). I prefer the blacker of the two. The coarser would give off a gray color compared to the other which gives off a reddish black. When everything is finished I'll have backdrops in painted aluminum made which we'll be able to put on and take off the velvet, each creating a different backdrop.

Wednesday, July 3, 1924
I'd gladly lend a hand to the mounting of the globe. Man Ray made an excellent photograph of it which will appear in *391* if you don't have any objections.

Val de la Haye—Friday, August 8, 1924
I've moved the work of mounting ahead a great deal. Yesterday morning I was able to obtain two copper and steel plates—the most important task. I took it all to the fitter and after discussing the price I can tell you that the entire thing won't go over 1,000 francs.

August 15, 1924
Our mechanic will be working at this time and I hope that in spite of all the details the object will run by the end of September at the latest.

Sept. 15, 1924
I came back Sunday with pitiful results. I tried to speed our mechanic up and I almost (!) finished mounting the striped globe on the first plate. He's busy (!) with the motor. He's had a wooden triangle made to give more stability to the whole thing. All in all, I'm sure we'll get there but it will require your patience and mine.

Rouen, Sept. 22, 1924
Your letters seem to have had a magic effect. The mechanic achieved in one day what it seemed would take him a week. Now we're at a point where we can expect a rotation experiment next week. We're not in agreement on the question of velvet. That's the only way to get a surface that's absolutely mat and absolutely black at the same time. But we can make some tests.

October 3, 1924
I've received your note and the sample which seems perfect to me. The circle is 0 meters 60 in diameter and as a consequence we'll have to cut back a bit on the rear side. I'm busy now with the glass globe which I'm having mounted on the copper circle.

P.S. I very much like your idea of different lightings and also the backdrops which we'll add.

Wednesday [no date]
I'm getting the velvet which I hope will be perfect. I'll just prepare it because come what may, I'll have to wait until the rest is finished before putting this coat on it.

October 21, 1924
Today I took the outer copper plate to an engraver who is to inscribe a saying in a circle. That as well as a copper hammering job which I'll do myself will give the object, even when it's still, a curious appearance. Because, as you've pointed out so well, it could become tedious seeing it turn too often. The engraver quoted me an approximate price of 300 francs. The work will be done in 5 or 6 days.

I find the lettering and copper hammering indispensible especially in order to avoid the kitchen utensil effect which red copper always has. I still haven't put the velvet in place and am waiting until everything on the construction side is finished.

Friday [undated]
I've finally seen something turn. Tomorrow I'll see the motor in place: and if you're free Monday afternoon around 3 P.M., I'd like to see you at Man Ray's and take you to meet the mechanic. You'll see the instrument there in its unfinished state.

Friday, October 31, 1924
Beyond what you saw turning at Man Ray's there is a disk in red copper which holds up the glass globe: (section and profile of the glass globe and copper disk).
On the copper disk, at the edge and all around, I had a saying engraved by an engraver—geographer—who did a remarkable job for me. I saw

him today and I enclose his bill for 300 francs. Next week everything will be finished.

The "saying" is "Rrose Sélavy et moi esquivons les ecchymoses des Esquimaux aux mots exquis."

October 19, 1925 (?)
A friend has asked me to exhibit the globe which you have, telling me that you've agreed to lend it to him.
To tell you the truth, I'd rather not. And I'll only do it if you insist.
All expositions of painting or sculpture make me ill. And I'd rather not involve myself in them.
I would also regret it if anyone saw in this globe anything other than "optics."

[*The Monte Carlo Bond*]

"Marcel Duchamp has formed a stock company of which he is the Administrator, etc. Shares are being sold at 500 francs. The money will be used to play a system in Monte Carlo. Stockholders to receive 20 percent interest, etc. Some of the shares have arrived in this country and are very amusing in make-up. They carry a roulette wheel with a devil-like photograph of Marcel pasted upon it, they are signed twice by hand—Rrose Sélavy (a name by which Marcel is almost as well-known as by his regular name) appears as president of the company. If anyone is in the business of buying art curiosities as an investment, here is a chance to invest in a perfect masterpiece. Marcel's signature alone is worth much more than the 500 francs asked for the share. Marcel has given up painting entirely and has devoted most of his time to chess in the last few years. He will go to Monte Carlo early in January to begin the operation of his new company."

The Little Review (Vol. X, No. 2) (New York, Fall–Winter, 1924–25), p. 18.

Extracts from the Company Statutes

Clause No. 1. The aims of the company are:
1. Exploitation of roulette in Monte Carlo under the following conditions.
2. Exploitation of Trente-et-Quarante and other mines on the Côte d'Azur, as may be decided by the Board of Directors.
Clause No. 2. The annual income is derived from a cumulative system which is experimentally based on one hundred thousand rolls of the ball; the system is the exclusive property of the Board of Directors.

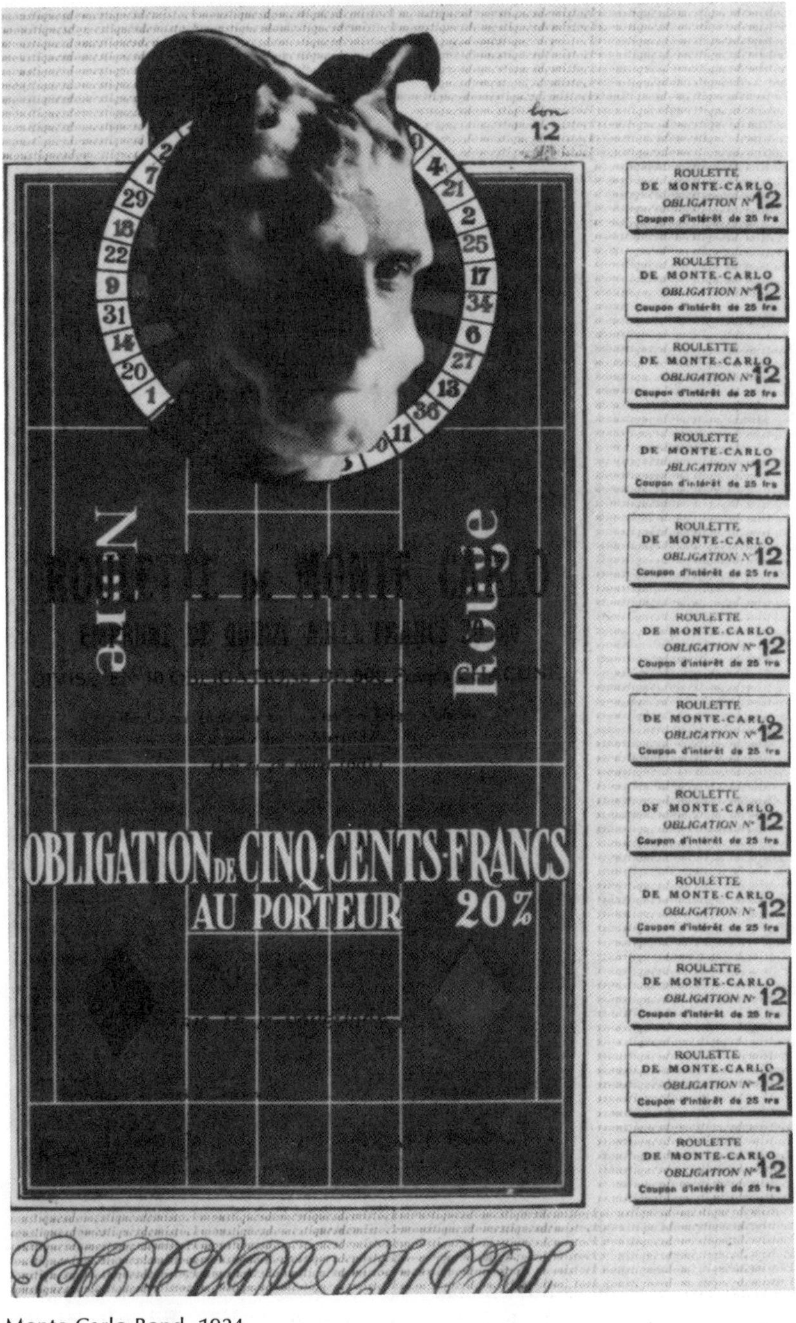

Monte Carlo Bond, 1924

The application of this system to simple chance is such that a dividend of 20% is allowed.

Clause No. 3. The Company shall be entitled, should the shareholders so declare, to buy back all or part of the shares issued, not later than one month after the date of the decision.

Clause No. 4. Payment of dividends shall take place on March 1 each year or on a twice yearly basis, in accordance with the wishes of the shareholders.

These statutes appear on the back of the *Monte Carlo Bond*.

Café de Paris
Monte Carlo — Thursday [undated] 1924
Téléphone: 2-50

For five days with very little capital I have tried out my system. Every day I have won steadily—small sums—in an hour or two.
I'm still polishing the system and hope to return to Paris with it completely perfected.
It's delicious monotony without the least emotion. The problem consists in finding the red and black figure to set against the roulette.
The Martingale is without importance. They are all either completely good or completely bad.
But with the right number even a bad Martingale can work and I think I've found the right number.
You see I haven't quit being a painter, now I'm sketching on chance.

Letter to Francis Picabia. Published in *MDS, p. 192.* [Trans. E.P.]

Monaco, Tuesday [no date] 1924
I'm beginning to play and the slowness of progress is more or less a test of patience. I'm staying about even or else am marking time in a disturbing way for the aforementioned patience. But still, doing that or something else. . . .
I'm neither ruined nor a millionaire and will never be either one or the other.

Letter to Jacques Doucet. *MDS*, p. 193. [Trans. E.P.]

Paris, 16 January 1925
I've just mailed the bond which we spoke about yesterday. It is self-explanatory, I have studied the system a great deal, basing myself on my bad experience of last year. Don't be too sceptical, since this time I think I have eliminated the word chance. I would like to force the

roulette to become a game of chess. A claim and its consequences: but I would like so much to pay my dividends.

Letter to Jacques Doucet. *Ibid.* [Trans. E.P.]

December 2, 1925
Finally I enclose the 50 francs which I owe you for six months of the Monte Carlo bond.

Letter to Jacques Doucet. *Ibid.* [Trans. E.P.]

Men Before the Mirror

Many a time the mirror imprisons them and holds them firmly. Fascinated they stand in front. They are absorbed, separated from reality and alone with their dearest vice, vanity. However readily they spread out all other vices for all, they keep this one secret and disown it even before their most intimate friends.

There they stand and stare at the landscape which is themselves, the mountains of their noses, the defiles and folds of their shoulders, hands, and skin, to which the years have already so accustomed them that they no longer know how they evolved; and the multiple primeval forests of their hair. They meditate, they are content, they try to take themselves in as a whole. Women have taught them that power does not succeed. Women have told them what is attractive in them, they have forgotten; but now they put themselves together like a mosaic out of what pleased women in them. For they themselves do not know what is attractive about them. Only handsome men are sure of themselves but handsome men are not fitted for love: they wonder even at the last moment whether it suits them. Fitted for love are the great ugly things that carry their faces with pride before them like a mask. The great taciturns, who behind their silence hide much or nothing.

Slim hands with long fingers or short, that grasp forth. The nape of a neck that rises steeply to lose itself in the forest's edge of the hair, the tender curve of the skin behind an ear, the mysterious mussel of the navel, the flat pebbles of the knee-caps, the joints of their ankles, which a hand envelops to hold them back from a leap—and beyond the farther and still unknown regions of the body, much older than it, much more worn, open to all happenings: this face, always this face which they know so well. For they have a body only at night and most only in the arms of a woman. But with them goes always, ever present their face. The mirror looks at them. They collect themselves. Carefully, as if tying a cravat, they compose their features. Insolent, serious and conscious of their looks they turn around to face the world.

Rrose Sélavy

Man Ray, *Photographies 1920–1934* (Paris: Cahiers d'Art, 1934), p. 67. *MDS,* p. 195. The German translation of this text (*Mann vor dem spiegel*) appears on the following page. The text is apocryphal, and constitutes a kind of literary Ready-made. Written by a German friend of Man Ray's, L.D., in her mother tongue, translated into English, it was then signed by Marcel Duchamp (Rrose Sélavy).

Henri-Pierre Roché
MARCELDUCHAMPSOPTICALDISCS

Marcelduchampsaystomelikehowaboutit
we'llmakeadealbothofus
you'llputupthemoneyandi'll
furnishtheopticaldiscstherotoreliefs
likeicallthemwe'llexhibitthematthe
inventors'fairandwe'llsplitthetakeif
thereisanyokitellhimwe'llmake
adirectpitchtothepeopleandwe'llsee

whenthedaycomesigotothefair
andiseemarcelathislittlestand
surroundedbyhisopticaldiscswhichwereturning
horizontallyandverticallyitwasasigh
thelookedlikeasmilingandob
jectivesalesgirlandistoppedaways
awaytowatchhimtherewasthefis
hwhichwasturningthechampagneglasswhich
wasturningthecirclesturningallofittur
ningandfinallyigotsicktomystomach
watchingthemturnhewasn'tsick
becausehewasn'twatchingthem

onhisleftttherewasaguywhowasse
llingamachineforcrushinghousehold
garbageitwasreallyeasyyourolleditup
withyourfingersinalittlecylindery
outurnedwithavicelikeawinepress
oritmadelittlecombustible
coneslikehesaidbutyouweren'tsupposedtoputin
rottencabbageordogcrap

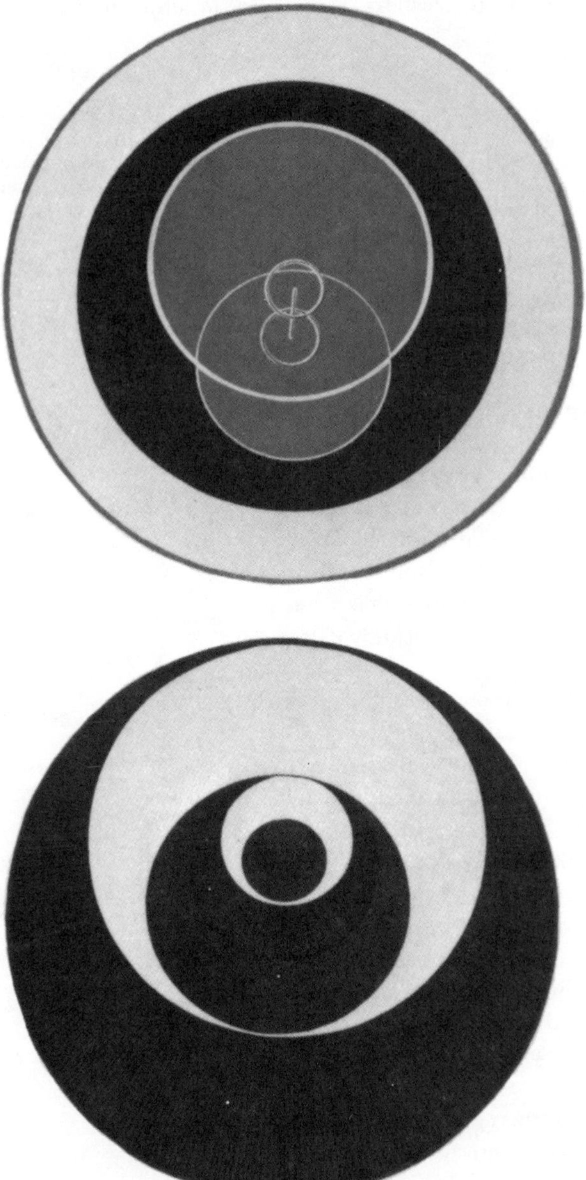

Two Rotoreliefs

onhisrightababewasselling
instantaneouspotatopeelers
theywereturninglikepencilsharpeners
onapotatostuckonaforkzap
alldone

inthemiddletherewasmarcelinfront
ofallthatwasthepublicwhichwalkedbyonly
thepublicdidn'tnoticemarcelor
hisdiscsthepublicrushedstraightfrom
thegarbagecrushertothe
potatopeelerwithoutstopping
itwasareversemiracle

iwasworriedaboutmyinvestment
butevenmoreformarcel
buthewassmilingafterahalfhour
hecalledmeoverandidAfter
saidthere'snodoubtit'snodoubtwe're
ahundredpercentwrong
atleastthat'sclear

thosediscsarenowindemand
bycollectorsnotbythepeople
butallthesamethepeople
canseethemonSundaysiftheygotothemuseum.

Article by Henri-Pierre Roché quoting Duchamp's proposal of a business association for the production of the *Rotoreliefs,* in *Phases* (Paris), No. 1, January 1954, and *MDS* (illus. at p. 161). [Trans. E.P.]

A transformer designed to utilize the slight, wasted energies such as:
the excess of pressure on an electric switch.
the exhalation of tobacco smoke
the growth of a head of hair, of other body hair and of the nails.
the fall of urine and excrement.
movements of fear, astonishment, boredom, anger.
laughter.
dropping of tears.
demonstrative gestures of hands, feet, nervous tics.
forbidding glances.
falling over with surprise.
stretching, yawning, sneezing.

ordinary spitting and of blood.
vomiting.
ejaculation.
unruly hair, cowlicks.
the sound of nose-blowing, snoring.
fainting.
whistling, singing.
sighs, etc. . . .

Anthologie de l'humour noir, under "Duchamp." [Trans. E.P.]

SURcenSURE [*RErePROACH*]

LET'S BE SERIOUS
I should first like to say that
. . . .
. . . .
. . . . that it is number one in the world, and notably superior . . . .
We approve in advance . . . .
. . . . which he orders . .
. . . .
we are convinced that . . . .
. . . . inspired by the highest reason
Thus we will willingly keep of it . . . .
. . . .
. . . . unfortunately . . . .
. . . .
. . . .
who is thus completely innocent . . . .
. . . .
. . . .
. . . . brings us at the same time both joy and despair
. . . .
. . . .
. . . .
. . . .
obliged to spread each day on the physiognomy . . . .
. . . .
. . . .
. . . . It was a feat of strength
. . . .
comrades of Phynance, as King Turd would say . . . .
. . . .
. . . .
. . . .
. . . .
. . . .
. . . .

But watch out!

. . . .
. . . .

L'Usage de la parole, No. 1 (Paris, December 1939), p. 16. Reprinted in *Salamander* No. 1 (Malmo, 1955). Translated into Swedish by E. Lindegreen and I. Laaban. [Trans. E.P.]

Luggage Physics

Determine the difference between the volumes of air displaced by a clean shirt (ironed and folded) and the same shirt when dirty.

Coincidental fitting of objects or parts of objects; the hierarchy of this kind of fitting is directly proportional to the "disparate."

London Bulletin, No. 13, April 15, 1939; *MDS,* p. 197. [Trans. E.P.]

After having completed this card which is strictly limited to correspondence of a personal nature, delete unnecessary indications.—Write nothing outside of the lines.

NOTICE.—Any card whose text is not exclusively of a personal nature will not be forwarded and will probably be destroyed.

________ ……Paris…… the 17 January 1941……

……Mary and I in good health scarcely tired.

…… ~~slightly, severely ill, wounded.~~

…… ~~killed~~ …… ~~prisoner.~~

…… ~~deceased~~ have received ~~without~~ news.

~~of~~ from you thanks ~~The family~~ …… ~~is well.~~

…… ~~needs provisi~~ons …… ~~money~~.

~~news, luggage~~ …… ~~has returned to~~ ……

……I am working at my box which ~~will enter~~

is finished

~~the school of~~ …… ~~has passed~~

……If you go to New York ~~the~~ find me

an artistic (sic) mission so……

that I can spend some time there……

Fondest thoughts. Kisses and all from

two of us to you two

Signature. M Duchamp

View, No. 7–8, Oct.–Nov., 1941; *MDS,* p. 198. Card—the only correspondence allowed by the occupation authorities in 1941—sent by Duchamp in Paris to André Breton in New York. [Trans. E.P.]

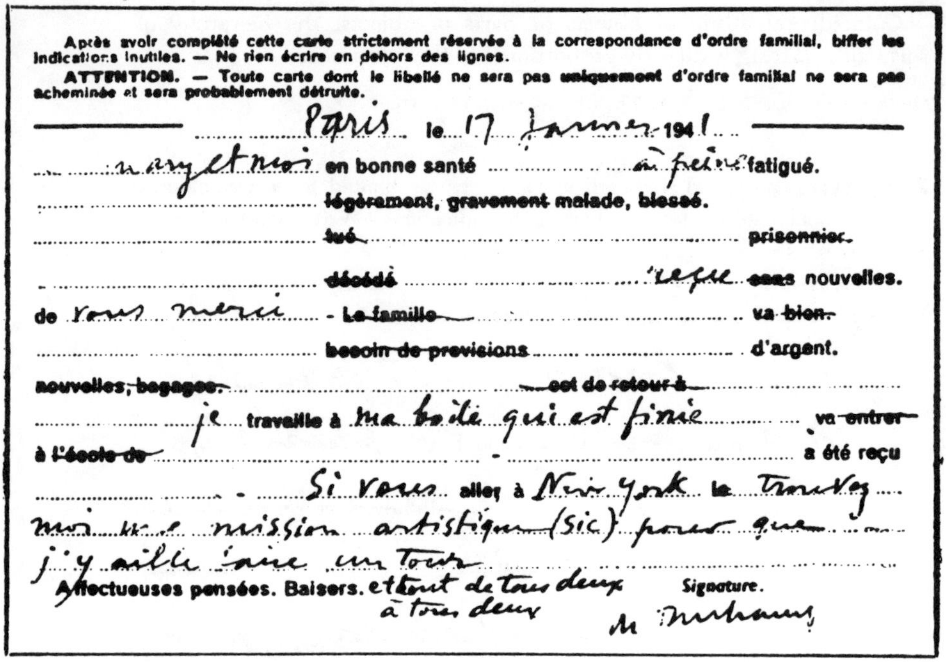
Après avoir complété cette carte strictement réservée à la correspondance d'ordre familial, biffer les indications inutiles. — Ne rien écrire en dehors des lignes.

ATTENTION. — Toute carte dont le libellé ne sera pas uniquement d'ordre familial ne sera pas acheminée et sera probablement détruite.

Paris le 17 Janvier 1941

Mary et moi en bonne santé à peine fatigué.

légèrement, gravement malade, blessé.

tué prisonnier.

décédé reçu sans nouvelles.

de vous merci - La famille va bien.

besoin de provisions d'argent.

nouvelles, bagages. est de retour à

je travaille à ma boîte qui est finie va entrer

à l'école de a été reçu

Si vous allez à New York trouvez moi une mission artistique (sic) pour que j'y aille faire un tour

Affectueuses pensées. Baisers. et tout de tous deux à tous deux

Signature. M Duchamp

WHEN
THE TOBACCO SMOKE
ALSO SMELLS
OF THE MOUTH
WHICH EXHALES IT
THE TWO ODORS
ARE MARRIED BY
INFRA-SLIM

Marcel Duchamp

View, 5, no. 1 (March 1945). Reproduced in facsimile in *The Complete Works of Marcel Duchamp* and analyzed on pp. 519–20. In "Marcel Duchamp, mine de rien," *Preuves* (Paris), XVIII, No. 204 (Feb. 1968), pp. 43–47, Denis de Rougemont quotes Duchamp as saying that he "chose on purpose the word slim which is a word with human, affective connotations, and is not an exact laboratory measure. The sound or the music which corduroy trousers, like these, make when one moves, is pertinent to infra–slim. The hollow in the paper between the front and back of a thin sheet of paper. . . . To be studied! . . . it is a category which has occupied me a great deal over the last ten years. I believe that by means of the infra–slim one can pass from the second to the third dimension."

SENSES:

One can look at seeing. Can one hear hearing, feel breathing, etc. . . . ? (M.D.)

In the *Memento Universel Da Costa* (Paris: Jean Aubier, ed., 1948), p. 15. This note is a variation of a note from the *1914 Box*.

NOUS, MARCEL DUCHAMP,

déclarons à toutes fins utiles que le porteur du présent

CERTIFICAT INALIENABLE ET INTRANSMISSIBLE

est lecteur agréé et agrégé du recueil de poèmes de

ARTURO SCHWARZ

intitulé

IL REALE ASSOLUTO

Le porteur de ce *Certificat Inaliénable et Intransmissible* est seul détenteur du *Droit de Libre Lecture* du dit receuil et a versé pour jouir de ce privilège la somne de mille lires italiennes.

Fait en cent exemplaires numérotés et signés en notre résidence habituelle à New York le 29 février de l'année bissextile 1964

This "non-transferable and inalienable certificate" identifies the bearer as an endorsed and examined reader of a collection of poems by Arturo Schwarz. It also confers the privilege of reading these poems freely—for a sum of 1,000 lire. Finally it should be pointed out that this Duchampian decree was signed on February 29 of leap year 1964. It appears in Arturo Schwarz, *il reale assoluto* (Milan: Schwarz, 1964).

Bibliographical Notice

The single most inclusive listing of works on and by Marcel Duchamp is found in Arturo Schwarz's *The Complete Works of Marcel Duchamp* (New York: Abrams, n.d.), although the Selected Bibliography prepared by Bernard Karpel for Pierre Cabanne's *Dialogues with Marcel Duchamp* (New York: The Viking Press, 1971) is also very helpful. Key texts published in English on Duchamp include Robert Lebel's *Marcel Duchamp* (New York: The Grove Press, 1959); Calvin Tomkins' *The Bride and the Bachelors* (New York: The Viking Press, 1965); the catalog prepared by the Arts Council of Great Britain, *The Almost Complete Works of Marcel Duchamp at the Tate Gallery* (London, 1966); the study of Duchamp's last work by Anne d'Harnoncourt and Walter Hopps, *Etant Donnés: 1° la chute d'eau 2° le gaz d'éclairage: Reflections on a New Work by Marcel Duchamp* (Philadelphia Museum of Art, 1969); Octavio Paz's *Marcel Duchamp or the Castle of Purity* (New York: Cape Goliard Press, 1970); John Golding's *Marcel Duchamp: The Bride Stripped Bare by her Bachelors, Even* (New York: The Viking Press, 1973); and finally the important catalog prepared by the Museum of Modern Art in New York and the Philadelphia Museum of Art for the 1973-74 Duchamp retrospective, edited by Anne d'Harnoncourt and Kynaston McShine.